Maverick Zone

By JOHN MYERS MYERS

Novels: THE HARP AND THE BLADE
OUT ON ANY LIMB
THE WILD YAZOO
DEAD WARRIOR

Romance: SILVERLOCK

Americana: THE ALAMO
THE LAST CHANCE
DOC HOLLIDAY
I, JACK SWILLING

Poetry: MAVERICK ZONE

MAVERICK ZONE

Red Conner's
Night in
Ellsworth

The Sack of
Calabasas

The Devil
Paid in
Angel's Camp

By JOHN MYERS MYERS

HASTINGS HOUSE PUBLISHERS

NEW YORK 22

Copyright © 1958, 1961 by John Myers Myers

Published simultaneously in Canada
by S. J. Reginald Saunders, Publishers, Toronto 2B.

Library of Congress Catalog Card Number: 61-14216

Printed in the United States of America

To WILLIAM VOGT

These Flasks of Heliconian Jameson

Contents

Contents

Forenote

THE SEED MATTER of the three pieces of Columbiana which make up the body of this book is a mixture of history and legendary lore. The same method of molding American traditional matter into verse narratives has not been adhered to in all alike, however.

In "THE DEVIL PAID IN ANGEL'S CAMP" the taking-off point is the avowed circumstance that pall bearers abandoned a corpse in order to help corner and hang a man who began fleeing his murder of another just as the biersmen were passing a saloon where death broke up a card game. The body of the story, complete with most episodes and all details of local color, emerged from the chronicles, reminiscences and journals of a wide range of Forty-niners. Some specific features of Angel's Camp are cited, but the true scene is composite Eldorado, in town and out. Aside from the arbitrarily used trio of demises, history contributed the remarkable tavern keeper, Ross Coon, and that pan-Western figure, Peg-leg Smith, whose far wanderings took him to Cibola at sundown.

In "RED CONNER'S NIGHT IN ELLSWORTH" Seth
Mabry's historical beef drive to Idaho in the year of
Ellsworth's railhead floreat provided the logic of a
brief visit to that town, in place of the prolonged
sprees which would have been in order, had the camp
capped a trail drive in place of merely serving as a
punctuation mark. Another shaping circumstance was
the traditional wager which resulted in a two-gun
Godiva act afoot on the part of Ellsworth's leading
red-light belle, who actually was known as Prairie
Rose, and by no other recorded name. Other histor-
ical characters are the scholarly bad hat, Johnnie
Ringo, the four marshals with the distinguishing nick-
names here given, and Ben (Thompson). The latter
was a chosen comrade of Happy Jack Morco, who did
traditionally go east to reach the Western frontier of
that era. As for the scene, Ellsworth then rejoiced in
two Main Streets, as well as the hardcase suburb of
Nauchville.

"THE SACK OF CALABASAS" is based on the actual
circumstance of a town that owed its origin and col-
lapse to the mistaken belief that the Southern Pacific
would follow the Santa Cruz Valley into Mexico. The
core of the tale was extracted from a collection of
prose sketches titled *Calabazas* (sic, although the spell-
ing which appears in most other Arizona records has
been followed here). Written by one John Cabell
Brown, who followed the course of the tent metropolis
from his post as a border customs collector, it outlined
the deeds of the arch con man, Abimelech Jones, and
provided such details as the Golden Fleece Saloon and
the canvas hotel maintained by the close son of the
Celestial Empire.

Admittedly these three are not poetical pieces of
the exact phylum to which such justly honored works
as *Gawaine and the Green Knight, The Faerie Queene*
and *The Eve of St. Agnes* belong; but their subjects

were of the Old World, and anyone who leads from the strength natural to him as a native of the New will search in vain for any similar matter. Let those grieve for that lack who see in poetry but a narrow accommodation for things already done in place of the all-embracing cosmos that it is. There are other splendors than those which drape castle walls, and the trust is that some of them will be marked as gracing these ivyless American structures.

J. M. M.

RED CONNER'S
NIGHT IN ELLSWORTH

I

The Paper Siren Call

A twister whipped a scrap of paper south
with other sweepings of the Kansas plains
and swirled it over tussocks sick with drouth
away from Ellsworth, journeys' end for trains,
where rambling beef and buyers fared to meeting
and Texas drovers flung abroad their gains
with all a shore-leave sailor's desperate force,
to freshen barren lives. Its pauses fleeting,

the whirlwind dodged and dove along its course
to where a warden watched some longhorns graze.
It rushed upon the herder on a horse
to break around him as he sat at gaze,
half dozing in the dawn and all unwitting,
and roughly slapped him from his sodden daze
with sand that swooped about with frantic speed
to fill his ears and leave him blind and spitting.

Yet when, with sleeve and neckerchief, he'd freed
his eyes of grit, he found the twister's gift:
the bit of paper, black with sign to read,
in transit from a knee. So he made shift

to pounce, and clutch a half a handbill, cluttered
with letters which a press had set adrift
in blurs of ink. But still he strained them out,
and as he formed the words, the rider muttered

the sounds aloud, as though confounding doubt.
He'd been to school, but here were mooted things
McGuffey hadn't moralized about:
"See Prairie Rose, the queen for cattle kings,
a leggy Venus, only better looking;
and Venus never squiggles when she sings
nor struts at the Alhambra every night—
with Rose around, Vee couldn't get a booking

in our shebang. She kicks way out of sight,
this golden charmer with the silver voice,
who's here and no place else for your delight
with tricks to make stone Indians rejoice,
though preachers needn't look but only listen;
the country's free, so that's a dealer's choice—"
The rest was torn away to put a close
to words which seemed alike to glow and glisten,

but there had been enough of dazzling prose
to make the reader blink at what he'd learned.
He read anew the runes of Prairie Rose
and scanned the north with scowls which told he yearned
to know the treats with which he'd now been taunted,
while all the cheated lust within him burned.
For here he was, Red Conner, six foot-one,
a man with virile skittles to be vaunted,

he felt; for all his twenty years had done
was fledge a mother hen with cows for chicks:
a mule begot to drudge, removed from fun
as far as fellow neuters in the fix
of duds without the charge to jump the traces.
And meanwhile girls with unimagined tricks,

enchanting granite Indians, were gold
and silver-voiced and flashed their dashing paces

in halls where men who lived as such were bold
to flush their eyes with beauty as it pranced.
Yet, blinder-harnessed, he could but behold
the cows that glumly munched as they advanced,
while days were ground to pieces with their chewing
and only gnats or dung flies ever danced.
And, too, he was condemned to rot in wait,
the sounding board for nitwit bovine mooing,

while opportunity passed out of date
for ogling golden girls, who well might wed
and drop from sight like sparks or haul silk freight
to Timbuctoo or burrow with the dead.
He cuddled with expanding grievance, moping
while white dawn chased the grey and bowed to red;
then came the blue and Sunfish, his relief,
a runt upon a frisky pony, loping

away from camp and food. "The garbage thief
which sneaks from buzzards so he needn't cook
has found," he said, "some whatsit, beans in chief,
that ptomained me from only half a look;
but eat, if you've a grudge against your liver.
No trouble, Red?" "Not by the boss's book."
The broadside found a berth in Conner's shirt.
"They imitated snags in Timber River."

Indignantly he pointed with his quirt.
"No cyclones, wolf packs, lightning or Pawnees;
no luck at all, and not a dogie hurt
or killed or stole or drifted down the breeze
to lose himself. We've still got every bawling,
bone-ugly beef with all its flies and fleas—
the whole, mean, double-cudded, idiot string.
Oh, Jesus, beans again!" But hunger's calling

was loud, if menus lacked a change to ring.
He swung about and trotted to the camp:
a dung fire near a muddy prairie spring.
There moodily he started in to champ
the food he tacked in place as soon as swallowed
with coffee hot enough to light a lamp.
He ate untasting as he strove to trace
the treacheries of fortune which had hollowed

the pitfall where he lay, as far from grace
as Satan's drop from Heaven. War had wrecked
all early likelihoods and in their place
put Reconstruction, which had raged unchecked
till he'd been swept from Alabama, living
on luck and air but dogged to direct
his motion westward, guided in his aim
by afrit voices out of Texas, giving

a cow herd's work a cavalier's acclaim.
But now, a novice of the railhead drives,
he'd ascertained how barren was the fame
of those who passed their mateless centaur lives
on Chisholm's trail for meat that marched to slaughter.
The other lobster watchmen cleaned their knives
and left him; but the broadside Red had found
had caught him so between the wind and water

he hadn't budged when riders hit the ground
to tap the coffee pot. "Why, hell," complained
the first, when he had clinked his spoon around,
"they'll get so redskin drunk they can't be brained,
not having none, but they'll find whores to marry
or try the pound on." As he spoke he pained.
"It ain't the like of drives we had before,
when Hays was all the further that we'd carry,

or Abilene; for, Seth, we got the chore
of pushing balky beef to Idaho!

We'll need to have good medicine, what's more,
to beat the clouds, which spout like whales to snow
and reach one pass, they tell me." Cool and stable,
Jim Brill was foreman, made by nature so,
a driving, keen, sardonic man for whom
the zest for work and sense of being able

were king and ace of life this side the tomb.
His native eagerness to put things through
left tolerance for play but midget room;
unchecked, he might have twisted down the screw
too tight for bearing by less dedicated
and root-hog-minded members of the crew.
But Major Mabry, owner of the steers,
though prizing Brill and industry, was gaited

to walk in other worlds. The frosting years
of war, and losing war, which blighted some
had ripened him. Where cattle made frontiers
or trails and rails converged to draw men from
the empty, vast, coyote-haunted ranges
whose silences they challenged with the drum
of racing bronco feet, Seth Mabry's lean
but grosbeak face was known. In all exchanges

with humans, beasts or fortune, fair or mean,
he held, or so men said of him, his own
with sureness which, withal, was never seen
to crowd the decencies. And he was known
alike for canny dealing and for daring
to drive his stock to such an untried zone
as was his project now. "A night awing,"
he told the other, offhand in his bearing,

"is what they need, I'd say, to keep the string
from tightening on the banjo till it snaps.
It's June bug time, and since the turn of spring
they've followed wall-eyed longhorns, scratching chaps

on sun-fried chapparal. A *stretch* of boozing
would make some hard to push again perhaps,
but single goes at poker, rye or tarts
cannot so spavin them that we'll be losing

our chance to lead the snow in lofty parts."
His voice took on the edge of will. "And, Jim,
we need some grizzly blood to boost our hearts
from drudging grooves and keep our brains in trim.
I'm game as most to down my dram of duty
but, taken neat, it's tolerable grim
and turns a man to something like an owl
that mixes catching mice with moral beauty

and flocks with other double-meaning fowl,
all hooting, 'God is cash.' To keep in sense
a man must keep in moons at which to howl,
so we'll now make that move of self defense."
Seth Mabry's word, however lightly spoken,
was doomsday law for Brill. He lost his tense,
bone-digging air. "If that's the way she stands,"
he said, together with a grin in token

that he was lief to buckle to commands,
"why I could use a night of cutthroat draw
as well as you or any of the hands;
and I *would* sort of like to serve my craw
a store-bought supper, floated some in liquor."
"Good man." The Major peered as if he saw
beyond the arching earth and viewed a den
for cards and drink. "To box the compass quicker,

we'll start around this morning, sending men
to raid like Stuart, in and back to base;
all over, birdsong early. H-m. At ten
we'll launch a relay, and I'll lead my ace,"
he drained his cup, "as Mr. Hoyle advises.
Select two gents and sasshay up the trace,

the van of us, and get the velvet stripped
from off your horns before tomorrow rises;

then while we all get curry combed and clipped,
why you'll stand watch. Take Colorado Byrd
or anyone who won't get whiskey whipped,
like Crowne or Treviston or—" "Me!" The word
was barked by Conner, on his feet and striding
to join the pair. As though he hadn't heard,
the rancher told his foreman, "Pound the trail
to Pawnee Spring, and there you'll find us biding.

You got a question, Red?" "I want to nail
a spot amongst the first to hit for town."
"I reckon I would let you know by mail
if you was wanted; back it up, sit down
and clean your plate to help you do some growing,"
the foreman said. His rider matched his frown.
"I'm sliding," he said thickly. "Cut me loose,
if that don't gee, but here's a thing for knowing:

I don't say grace for any jay's abuse.
Explore my hide and you won't find your brand
or any man's." "Oh, hell, who'd brand a goose?"
Brill asked, but here the Major took a hand,
his words unchallenging and tuned politely
to that of friendship keen to understand.
"What's hatching, Red? Of course, you're on your own,
but when you signed, if I'm reviewing rightly,

you said you'd stick the finish. What's your bone;
you tired of us?" "I'm tired of beans and sage
and riding slow and saddle-nights alone
and dust for air; and tired of drawing wage
I never get to spend. I'm tired of waiting
for cows," his tone went up the scale of rage,
"to scratch the brush for one lone clump of grass
and mosey, slow as played-out oxen, freighting,

to find the next. I want some time to pass
as more than just a cattle tick!" The rush
of verbiage ended like a burst of gas
that's burned to vanished vapor. In the hush
the rancher eyed his fuming man and wondered
just how to quench this smoldering in the brush
without a word to turn the moment bad.
He'd have to fire his rider if he blundered

and now his need was every hand he had.
Aware some wind had raised this summer storm,
he paused to ponder what would drive a lad
of ready smiling, taken by the norm,
to temperamental fits. Except for glaring
and looking boiled, the rufous weft when warm,
he seemed as ordered as a dog with fleas.
The only strangeness promising a bearing

was printed matter, riffled by the breeze
the dust made visible. "What all you got?"
the Major queried then with sleepy ease,
for pearls nor print were native to the spot
and comment natural. He touched the pocket
from which it peeped, and Red, remaining hot,
though now for warmer reasons, drew it out
as gently as a man who springs a locket

to show a lover's face. Informed about
the joys of watching Prairie Rose cavort,
the rancher spoke a phrase of courteous doubt.
"You know the lady?" "No, sir—" Red's retort
hung fire at that. He looked about him, reaching
for words which failed to come to his support
and tried it twice before he made a sound:
in part a rebel growl, in part beseeching

for aid in viewing beauty in the round.
"I want to see her." That was all he said,

but now the Major saw him well and found
the open wounds of youth from which he bled
in surging through the savage gauntlet passion
decrees for men with spring—to finish sped,
declined from shape or tempered. While he ran
through memories which it was not his fashion

to share, the rancher brooded, then began
his vocal rubrics. "I don't pension love,
nor do I hand to you or any man
the right to fly his private likes above
the work we've teamed to do. You hear me talking?
But this halfway I'll go; I'll let you shove
with Jim, and I will heel you with a split
of wage to date, to sponsor dance hall gawking;

but if you'd like the rest, you'd better flit
for camp on schedule, if you have to take
the jail you're in for overcoat." "That's it!"
When Conner'd bound the bargain with a shake,
he amplified the terms. "Forget to worry
on my account; I'll time the clock and make
the deadline follow me. I've never been
a trouble-butt; my practice is to scurry

away from it so fast I scorch my skin."
The Major groaned. "But while you're doing that,
dismount, if there's a dive that you want in;
and wing the sheriffs; don't kill any flat
or burn the town, for even quiet pleasure.
The Jayhawks are a different breed of cat
from us and don't admire us Texas men
the way we do, and have a different measure

for everything, in fact. And then again
they run two ways at once; the store man's mind
is kissing kin to that of some old hen
who wants some chicks but ain't at all resigned

to let some nasty rooster do *his* laying.
They like our rhino, near as I can find,
but not the notion we enjoy it, too.
So after we have spent the summer paying

a blockade price for goods, to see them through
the winter, why they spend that loafing time
in calculating what we'd crave to do
so they can law it out." "But, Major, I'm
the kind no sheriff ever finds in season
when hunting scalps. I'll shy away from crime—
as always, sir—like fish away from mink
and tread the narrow. They can't call it treason

to watch a dance and maybe catch a drink
and, oh yes, buy a shirt; I need a shirt."
"I shouldn't reckon that would rate the clink,"
the rancher murmured. "Still it mightn't hurt
to relay what a friend I met returning
from Ellsworth counseled. Keep vedette alert
for Jacks, he said—two pair of hearts, but black—
who prosper by a weasel scheme of earning,

as they're a cripple-hunting jackal pack
that sucked sidewinder venom at the breast:
Brocky and High-low, Long and Happy Jack,
the local marshals, paid by the arrest
and fattening on drunks like bears on dogies.
But that's forgetting what I should have guessed,
that you're a mint of meekly stolid clay
like every red poll. Join the other fogies

by all means, then. At ten you'll draw your pay."

2

The Cow-built Mecca

In June of Eighteen hundred seventy-three
the town of Ellsworth jumped with vital fire,
for nothing stoppered opportunity
or cramped the reaching hand that might aspire
to dam-divert the Eastern money flowing
for Western spending, to the heart's desire
of dollar fondlers. Boston Joe was such,
a predator of prairie commerce, blowing

from camp to camp, alert to claim and clutch
the boomer's sweepstake. Where the mushroom towns
emerged along the rails which stretched to touch
the distant Rockies, handy knock-me-downs—
among them his—were reared about the station
to catch the cash of trail-sick riders, clowns
enough to pay a city sharper's price.
He fleeced them while embezzling indignation

at every joyance helpless to entice
a nickel from his tight and righteous hold,
which also clamped its God-and-Mammon vise
about a niece not fashioned in his mold

nor reconciled. Although she dourly snuggled
with peonage, she kept his books and sold
the startling range of goods in Boston's Joe's;
his conscience and her wages deftly juggled,

Melinda was his slave. Each day she rose
to glean her barren living at the store;
the nights she spent in scheming how to close
this canto of her fate. Three years before,
a widow at nineteen, she'd fled the terror
of emptiness, to hawk for life once more
where hope, she'd heard, resided: in the West.
She'd sought her uncle then but found her error

as soon as mourning left her. What was blessed
by other spirits on the beef frontier
her own was fiercely prompted to detest:
the fenceless plains, the men of boisterous cheer,
the space, inviting loose, ungoverned action,
the sense of being boldly pioneer
and all the tumult of the westward thrust.
But most she hated, by no minor fraction,

the civic flimsies wallowing in the dust;
beginning first, for her, with Abilene.
She'd swallowed three of them from crud to crust,
but now, though working doggedly to screen
revolt from Boston Joe's acute suspicion,
she hoped—with help—to bolt the Kansas scene.
But as she hid her dream by dint of will,
another aired his dearth of inhibition

as Conner splashed across the Smoky Hill.
Devout to Prairie Rose, though pledged to tryst
with dawdling pagans, Sleepy Crowne and Brill,
at sun-up by the ford, he'd long dismissed
the pair of Philistines from ken and speeded
to reach the moment when he'd take in fist

the glories of the town. Arrived, he first
arranged to stall a paint no longer needed

by one who meant to keep himself immersed
in urban joys till night had spun its skein;
then came the tour he'd, site unseen, rehearsed.
He found two streets in Ellsworth, Main and Main,
which paralleled the sets of tracks dividing
the north one from the south. So of the twain
a side of each alone was lined with shacks,
their windows facing loading chute or siding

with empty cattle coaches on its tracks.
Aligned in raffish ranks, the buildings stood:
the second story fronts that led no backs,
the bricks of rusty metal tacked to wood
and kindred plumes of graceless frontier feather
bespeaking hopeful shots at cityhood.
A wooden sidewalk hitched along the street
between the shops and racks, where nags at tether

endured their fate, in dust which hid their feet,
beneath the fury of a falling sun;
and shade itself sucked in and held the heat
instead of fending it. The town was one
improbable to fill all hearts with rapture,
but Red had not seen Rome. He lashed his gun,
while whistling, to his thigh for greater ease
in taking in the town he'd come to capture,

though not by force of arms. The sultry breeze
which glided past his face, to spice his tour,
was rich with sounds suggesting ecstasies
unknown to him and scents which made him sure
he'd come among a people skilled to cater
to hedonists. To lasso and secure
his demon of content, he found a bar
and snapped a drink which found no insulator

of food below. It landed with a jar
but fitted there like honey in the comb;
alone but wondrous as the evening star,
it welcomed him and made him feel at home.
Anew upon the dust encrusted planking,
he was a man of mission, on the roam
to find himself a lively shirt and bath—
prerequisites in chief of gracious swanking—

but paused to read a sign which flanked his path,
for all were marvels there that met his eye;
and while so doing heard, "Why, Pete McGrath!"
The speaker, dainty at it, lifted high
her pink, impeding skirt and neared him, mincing
in little shoes. But then she shrieked. "Oh, my!"
She put a hand upon her plump young bust.
"My eyes," she blinked them at him, "need a rinsing,

for you're not Pete at all!" In happy trust
that he'd enjoy the joke, she sweetly laughed
and moved to join him, reaching to adjust
a straying lock which, through a sleight of craft
had slipped its mooring. "Do you think me awful?"
she wondered, standing where the breeze could waft
her perfume Redward. "No," he said, "not me."
He stared as hard as decency found lawful

but hardly saw her. Stark efficiency
in spotting gulls was Nancy Dover's forte,
and snagging them before they'd launched their spree
so they'd remember later and report.
As sexless as a bee, as set for battle,
when need arose, she had a worker's sort
of native competence and endless greed
for garnering. Her stock was artless prattle

which suited looks where youth could never read
her leech affinity for fluid cash

and stop-at-nothing will for it, the creed
of backwoods broker forebears. In a flash
she changed from smiling, looking up demurely
but searchingly. "Oh, anyone, you'd think,
could tell that you're not Pete. He's not as strong
or tall or—let's see—not so handsome, surely;

I bet you're angry." "No,'m; there you're wrong."
He bared his head and filled his eyes some more.
Petite and fair, she kept her ringlets long,
to play among the ruffles that she wore
as flower sepals. Moved by whiskey daring,
he grinned engagingly and sought to score
by merely blurting what he felt was true.
"You're just as pretty as the frills you're wearing,

and no one could think hard of them or you,
no Texas man, at least." She raised her hands.
"Are *you* from Texas? Pete McGrath is, too."
She seeemed to marvel over distant lands
beyond her hope to know. "It must be splendid
to ride and rope and know it by the brands
which is the longhorn cow and which the bull."
"That ain't the way we—" Red began; and ended.

"Well, that's what Pete said." "He was pulling wool,"·
he said, his horde of freckles crimson framed
and mumbling with a mouth that sounded full.
"You see— Well, anyhow the steers ain't tamed
and don't know who owns which and don't care, either;
and so we've got to mark 'em." "I'm ashamed
at being chicken brained." A child betrayed
was in the eyes he conned. "Oh, you ain't, neither,"

he comforted. "How could you guess he'd made
a yarn of snake fur?" Looking still aggrieved,
she measured him. "I wouldn't be afraid
to take *your* say. I hate to be deceived

by men who'd beat an auctioneer for lying
so they can laugh at girls that have believed;
but *you* I'd trust. Will you be long in town?"
Remembering Prairie Rose in time and trying

to hide the fact, he covered with a frown.
"The boss likes punier larks than what I'd plan,
so time in town's like powder burning down—
it's got no brakes." "The Happy Cattleman
is where I'll be tonight," she then confided,
"if mama doesn't need me. Ask for Nan.
We hold a sort of party every night,
with strangers welcome. I'll be glad, provided

I find my friend." "Why, thanks, Miss Nan, you might,"
he answered, striding forward in a glow
of self assurance, sweetened with delight
at how he'd handled matters. Heel and toe,
he swaggered up the walk until confronted
with letters urging, "Buy from Boston Joe!
The Best in Everything for Man or Beast
at Cyclone Cellar Prices. Styles You've Hunted

to Find Are Waiting, Tailored in the East
Especially for Texans." When he'd spelled
this welcome out, his confidence increased,
he bulled a door which jangled, being belled,
and tweaked his nerves. He stood a moment, blinking
at Bagdad wonders which the counters held
before he scouted deeper in the shop,
with care to keep his Spanish spurs from clinking.

But next he made a second startled stop
beside a woman, caged behind some wire,
who briefly met his stare. She had a mop
of auburn hair and eyes that were afire,
if yet not warm, and lips too full, if rigid,
to match the primness of her black attire.

She glanced at Red as though he were not seen,
but he was out of range of quaint and frigid

spitballs of etiquette. He watched her lean
above accounts and cleared his throat. "Hi, miss;
I'd like a shirt—a blue or maybe green—
with buttons shiny as your eyes." At this
she snapped erect, and though they did shine brightly,
her eyes were those of snakes which rear to hiss.
He'd found his Sunday grin to spread for her
but lost it at her tone, disgusted slightly,

as though she shooed away a prowling cur
who'd fawned upon her. "Herd your cows outside
or tap the owner there, if you prefer,
and tell him that you think *he's* button-eyed.
Moo! Can't you see I'm busy here?" Recoiling
from that assault, he jumped as some one cried
in echo, "She is busy; can't you see?"
At this, reaction set the pepper boiling

in Conner's spleen. A woman might be free
to harry him, but follow-up was male
and boomed with basso masculinity:
an older man but broad of beam and hale.
So Red, although his tongue was checked and routed
by beauty steeped in acid didn't fail
to rally. "Mister, there's a trade rat sign
which marks this hole, and as I hardly doubted

a fool for sure would fail to know his line,
I ankled in to buy. But if what's here
is just a private cache, I've cash of mine
I'll tote away." The threat made grace appear
where wrath had rather been anticipated,
for "cash" was music of the loveliest sphere
to Boston Joe. "What's on your mind—a gun,
a pair of pants, a saddle, silver plated;

a deck of cards, a neckerchief that's spun
of Chinese silk; a slicker, socks, a quirt,
a Waltham watch, a coffee pot, and one
the ocean couldn't rust—" "I'd like a shirt,
the fancy kind," said Red, forgetting anger
in eagerness for finery to flirt.
"But show me ones that sport a button flock
that's shiny." "Here's a dandy line from Bangor,

I frankly say I only keep in stock
for choosy customers with eyes for style."
The tradesman led the way and yanked a block
of rainbow tinted textiles from a pile
which glowed upon the counter. Beacon-flashing,
the colors threw their power a country mile,
and buttons gleamed amidst them. "Aren't they trick?
There's none but what would show a man as dashing—

a tall one anyhow, who plans to kick
his heels a little," Boston Joe went on.
"Why yes, I thought I'd find some salt to lick
and gander at a show before I'm gone;
and so I need to slick my feathers pretty.
You see," said Red, "I'm only here till dawn
and so—" He lowered tone. "I bet you've been
to every dandy dance hall in the city;

where's the Alhambra at? I might drop in
a minute there." He breathed the magic name
with reverence which flatly failed to win
a like response. "Alhambra" didn't frame
for Boston Joe a bright, ecstatic vision
of Prairie Rose adance. It stood for sin
and joy besides, the latter even worse;
thus much in general, but with precision

it meant Jehovah's image in reverse:
a partial owner known as Happy Jack,

a man the merchant never failed to curse
when bowed in silent prayer. Behind his back,
the lowering huckster bitterly suspected,
the monster moved in amorous attack
with dire intent to woo, remove and wed
the niece, that valued chattel, twice detected

in whispers with him recently, instead
of bending to the work she did so well.
"Alhambra" made the merchant glare at Red
as though he'd sprung from Cotton Mather's Hell.
"I don't know what the sewer's like! I never,"
he roared, "was so enmeshed in Satan's spell
I'd gad to bawdy Nauchville, with its schools
for teaching men to soil their souls forever;

a sty where money's thrown to pigs by fools
who buy perdition rather than the things
I offer here. So ask your fellow tools
of devildom about the evil springs
they suckle. *I* don't founder where demented
and bestial sons of Belial start the flings
which end in endless flames. I don't besmirch
my spirit so. I labor here, contented

with earning bread and—" "Mount upon your perch,
if preaching's what you're marketing, old coon!"
The gun was drawn and cocked. "If this is church,
I want you hiking nearer to the moon
the way a parson should that fights the Devil."
He slapped the counter. "Climb, and make it soon!
Unless you take the stump to save my soul,
you'll lose some godly hide, for on the level

the jiffy next will bore a bullet hole
below the spot your straw foot's standing at."
But with the words a shamed expression stole
to flush his face. "Oh, Lord! I can't do that;

I plumb forgot the lady." Humbly meeting
Melinda's stare, he swiftly tipped his hat.
"Don't worry, miss; I didn't think. I'll leave."
"And break your vow to shoot?" she asked. "It's cheating

to pledge the people what you won't achieve,
but politics." She bent and ceased to scold,
while Boston Joe endeavored to retrieve
his passing sale. "I've buttons, solid gold,
on silken— Wait, sir!" Conner, though, was walking
and let the door give answer, doublefold:
its slamming followed by the mocking clang
the sentry bell gave. Stamping wood in stalking

along the walk, he raged at Joe's harangue.
The eager friendliness which he had felt
when he had raced to romp among a gang
of semi-foreign townsmen had been dealt
a blow that killed it cold and set him burning
with heats alike of Southerner and Celt.
In spite of warning spelled for him with care,
what Mabry knew he only now was learning:

they didn't like a Texan, done or rare.
He hitched his belt and cocked his hat aslant,
a wolf that bristled in another's lair,
and hummed an old Confederate battle chant.
Yet still his goal was trade and never trouble,
if he could buy and dodge religious rant;
but first a cordial invitation lured:
"The Smoke House—Whiskey Priced to Give You
     Double

the Load. Come in and Get Your Bacon Cured."

3

Two in a Dovecote

Between the shallows of the Smoky Hill
and Ellsworth, where the relatively prim
could snipe at care until they made their kill,
suburban Nauchville hunkered in a grim
but yet flamboyant, noisy, reeking huddle
of lairs where women flocked to glut the whim
of transient lust; and where the sharpers lay
in wait for youngsters, liquored to a fuddle,

to buck pay-eating tigers. Here, the day
that Conner came to Ellsworth, Prairie Rose
awoke to slowly lift the lids of grey,
rapacious eyes, and—finger tips to toes—
she stretched her naked, smoothly sinuous body,
rolled over, yawning, sneezed and wiped a nose
of classic beauty on the darkling sheet
before she stilled, a gem amidst the shoddy,

and greeted Heaven and earth. "God rot this heat!"
Her next was dulcet. "Pour me out a snort
and kite me my kimono, won't you, sweet?"
The man appealed to caught the bottle short

and tilted it. "You'd think you was a possum
the way you sleep all day," he growled. "Here, sport;
try this for size." "It's only afternoon."
She pitched the whiskey in the lovely blossom

that was her mouth. "I hate to start too soon,
and you can't find the drunks to double-cross
this early on the clock, you fake baboon."
She gazed about. "You know, we ought to toss
some stuff outside or find another digging."
"There's junk been here so long it's sprouting moss,"
he shrugged, "so what's the use of noise about
the shanty's looks today? O. K., we're pigging;

but we both know you'll never sweep her out,
eh, kid?" Ignoring that, she rose to stand
before the mirror, there to peer and pout
at what it showed. "I shouldn't have got canned
last night," she said. "I look like fish left over."
Yet on the evidence it seemed the hand
of nature here had operated well.
Her skin was flushed with pink like budding clover

and from above perfection's features fell
in opulence the skein of golden hair
which handbills noted; pell it flowed, and mell
about a figure with a sumptuous flair
for drawing men to gaze and grow impassioned.
So after leveling a hostile stare,
she smiled at length upon the mirror-view,
conceding it could not be better fashioned,

and glad thereat. For here she saw and knew
the only friend that she had ever known
since fleeing north New York and East Peru,
her age fourteen, and going it alone.
A crib girl till she'd gotten past the breakers,
she'd early seen that talent was a zone

where fees and freedom which were never found
in common whoredom waited for the takers.

Wherefore she'd slipped her owners, westward bound
with Zaza, Gypsy Queen of Circus Acts,
becoming then a princess, duly crowned
at first for juggling knives and kindred knacks
but later as a trick-shot artist, snapping
at everything from cards to carpet tacks
with either hand. But having heard by then
that cattlemen had bullion ripe for tapping

by charms upon parade, she'd skipped again
and learned to sing and dance. Or so she claimed;
it didn't matter much; she drew the men,
so brothels bid for her. And now, grown famed
as Prairie Rose, the symbol of her choosing,
on westward like the sun she flared and flamed—
though night was when she surged in full career—
and conquered hearts, herself with none for losing,

in booming beef towns, new ones every year,
where cowmen came to gaze on beauty bared
with less than Euclid's calm. Now she was here,
the toast of Nauchville, in the shack she shared
with Happy Jack, her bull moose of the season,
for whom her fox fire passion coldly flared
and usefully, for if inamorate,
she gave no more to pleasure than to reason.

Some champion always guards a queen's estate,
and vice's chieftains pillaged any dove
without a guarding hawk; wherefore a mate
was practicality endorsing love.
More sure than paying off, her mack was cheaper,
for two-in-one of values, as above
his services in fending off the gnats
that else would swarm, he'd proved a rugged keeper

of pillow trysts—or grand nocturnal spats.
She prized dramatics furiously wrought
by half a stallion's temper, half a cat's,
and men who fought their bondage, being caught,
in riotous contempt of calm devotion,
like Happy Jack. In seeming deep in thought,
he now rechecked the loading of his gun
and honed his Bowie with a steady motion

that angered her, because she deemed it done
to keep from talking while he smoked his limp,
untailored cigarette. But he was fun:
John Morco, quondam San Francisco crimp
and cracksman, known as Happy Jack for grinning
unceasingly—a motley featured imp
since some one never mentioned took a whack
at stretching up his mouth from trim beginning

to near an eye. He never had gone back
to find if stillness meant he'd made her die
that foggy morning in the dock-side shack
he'd left to make long easting on the fly.
And though he took the opposite direction
from Greeley's choice, he yet had sped to try
the nascent inland West and found it right.
Of all America it was the section

where never past could follow, to alight
between a man and opportunity
to pilfer at his will. Or pick a fight
whose end was finis for the enemy—
and scoot away to other universes,
if wisdom pointed, unconcerned and free.
The bans with which a settled order blasts
the overt criminal, the while it nurses

the usurer and other subtler casts
of licensed thieves, were here of withered force.

The West was colonized by buried pasts
and moving was the order, not remorse;
so every one, on reaching new environs,
was pristine. Thus unchained to any course,
in Ellsworth protean Jack upheld the law
as marshal. For his skill with shooting irons

combined with sand enough within his craw
to deal with armed imbibers unafraid,
were all the references those men of straw,
the city fathers, asked. Police work paid
an agent, not contented with disorder,
who hunted drunks and swore they'd disobeyed
a ukase armed with fines. He notched a cut
for every mulcted, jail-rolled prison boarder

he buffaloed. This fattening of the nut
he made on dance hall shares had launched a dream
of ranking as a nabob—needing but
a coup he planned, to fructify a scheme
for flying eagle high. Bemused, he belted
his gun and knife on now. "So long." A gleam
of battle promptly shone in Rose's eye;
but, facing his, her glance as quickly melted.

"I couldn't stand to have you leave me." "Why?"
he wondered. "If you stay, I'll tell you." "Nix.
An alderman's expecting me." "And I
expect you, too." "Expect me at Van Wyck's
for dog hair and a steak." His wink denoting
eternal love and firmness in a mix,
he sidled. "Keep your nose clean, baby, while
I'm pitching hay." She dropped her look of doting

and swapped it for a Gila monster smile.
"*My* nose clean? Fly a tinder kite in Hell,"
she ordered. "Don't you think I pipe your style?
You're chicken chasing! I can always tell—

and don't forget it, slit-face—when you're lying;
and I know burning breeches by the smell.
Just tell that itch goodbye or you'll be buying

a coffin load of grief." "I never bowl
in any alley, kid, but yours," he swore;
"but just the same I've business dice to roll,
as you have, eh? And like I said before
I've got to see—" "What alderman?" she queried.
"The one," he yawned, "that keeps a dry goods store:
Joe Whozis." "You forget his handle—rich!
I'd whiff a lie like that if it was buried.

If you forget the store, I'll tell you which,
and I can help you out, if you forget
the fluff who works for Joe." "That Boston bitch!"
He scowled astonishment. "We've barely met;
she's clerking there, is all." "It could be, mister,"
she doubted. "No one's caught you with her yet
outside her uncle's booth, but still I know
from gossip slung me by a nosy sister

who found you playing stud a week ago,
you tail behind her bustle like a bull
that waits a heifer's time. You take it slow.
When I'm in any damn man's life, it's full!"
He manifested hurt. "Since you're suspicious,
I'll let you in on what I aim to pull.
She's part of it, but still I wouldn't smutch
a ten foot pole with her." "Don't get ambitious."

She wore a weary sneer. "I know this much:
unless you're shorting me, you're short of one."
"Well, anyhow," he said, "she's in the clutch
of Uncle Joe—shut up a minute, Hon,
and let me get you lined up on the story.
She wants to scat, but Joe has got the gun;

the Bible wrangler never pays the chick
but only board and keep and love and glory

for slaving there. She can't escape and kick
for dear old Cod-and-Beanville, where she's from,
and make a decent living, see, or pick
a legal rooster up. Her first went bum
and underground. It's why she faded, thinking
the West, you know, was holy kingdom come.
But now she wants to lam." "What's that to you,
if widows like the West or find it stinking?

And anyhow," quoth Rose, "it can't be true;
what's wrong with Ellsworth?" "She's lost-dogie here."
His hands were eloquent. "She can't make-do.
She savvies cities, sure, but no frontier
is ripe for wrens without the speed to hustle
if short of cash." "She hasn't got the gear,"
said Rose, and watched him as she threw that ball.
"No catch and hold for men, I guess." A muscle

in Jack's face twitched. "She's spotted me a haul
of uncle's dough," he then went swiftly on,
"and I can lift it, if I make a call
come midnight. Joe will find his cabbage gone
and likewise her. He'll bawl she took the boodle
and caught the train that whistles east at dawn;
what's more he'll find that what he screamed, she did.
Now fit the pretty picture in your noodle:

the blame'll travel eastward with the kid
to hell and gone, but my collection's half
the loot for knowing how to move the lid
of what he calls a safe. And that's a laugh;
for me it might as well be apple peeling,
and I can skin it easy as a calf
can tap a teat." "But, Jesus, won't they nab
the slut?" she asked. "Oh, Joe himself's been stealing."

"From who?" "From *her*. He'll try to have 'em grab
the twist while she's in Kansas—which they can't
unless the engine poops; but there'd be gab
from Codville lawyers, yelling he's been scant
on shelling out, if there was extraditing.
And aldermen that's Christers never pant
to have their cheating aired. Well, that's the deal,
and now I'm off to clinch it. Skip the biting

your lips at me—remember they're *my* meal,
and maybe by tomorrow I can buy
the diamond bigger than a wagon wheel
I think you'll think is cute." He cocked an eye.
"I'll join you at Van Wyck's for loading later;
at seven, say." "I'll last till then, or try."
Alone with doubt, she didn't cease to prink
but did it slowly as an illustrator

of hypnotism's power, resolved to wink
no evidence away. "I could be wrong,"
she told the mirror, "but some stories stink
because the liars lay it on so strong:
he thinks she's hogslop, and he's only robbing
to buy me ice. Perhaps. He'll be along
this evening, and I'll watch. The wolf'll drool,
if he's arranged to set her bed springs bobbing.

But he ain't all that's ever been to school
or taught it, and whoever plays that kind
of pool with me will eat the golden rule.
The skunk don't scare me none, and if I find
he's mooching hunks from any other chippie
until I'm through with him—" A noise behind
was so familiar that she didn't start
but rather stilled till, stealthily and slippy,

she drew a forty-five with craftsman art
from where it hung beside the looking glass,

which framed a monstrous rat and let her chart
its course in quest of orts. She watched it pass
a rocking chair before she whirled, discharging
a shot that knocked it kicking. Showing class
becoming to a girl who once aspired—
before horizons found a new enlarging

in skills less militant and more admired—
to head a trick-shot troupe, she loosed a flip
which sped the pistol, pointed as when fired,
to homing in her ready larboard grip.
Without an instant's pause, she pulled the trigger
and cut the tail off, shooting from the hip.
"I still am not too bad," she said. "That's nice,
in case of, well—" She shrugged and gave a snigger

which didn't reach her eyes, and nodded twice
while rubbing powder on her cheeks and chin.
"He could be mean and never won that slice
which took his mouth and ran it up his skin
for saying prayers and licking sugar candy.
I always thought a woman fixed his grin;
but if he's tough with me, he's through with time."
Meanwhile, a silken shirted, bay rummed dandy,

and licensed with a badge to war on crime,
her consort rode to Ellsworth in a mood
of sultry mirth, assured and feeling prime
anent his world. The longer that he chewed
the project over, dearer to his fancy
its graces grew. For, practically viewed,
the fact Melinda would abscond in haste
would render robbing, usually chancy,

a process where his risk would be erased
conjointly with enactment of the theft.
And her anxiety to vanish placed
his choice accomplice where she'd be bereft

of hope to duck a surcharge for his thieving,
as she would find—and pay—before she left.
And he could snap this lagniappe, steeering clear
of consequence, because the prize was leaving

and couldn't haunt his hair. She'd disappear,
and off would go his guilt. He loved the plan,
not least because he'd use Melinda's fear
of being held in town to flout the ban
on quenching yens his roving eye had heated
of sharp, untrusting Rose. She snubbed a man
too short to give exploring lust a play,
but this time she could never prove he'd cheated

by forcing more than safes to wreak his way.

4

A Wandering Scholar

The Smoke House was a dive of sun warped pine
where quids and gone cigars bestarred the floor
about a bar that forty drouths could line,
though at this hour less than half a score
were so engaged; while one, behind a table,
assessed the cuts of comers through the door.
But though he posted unobtrusive guard,
he fed his spirit on the mighty fable

of Ilium not yet fallen, from a scarred
and thumb-loved volume. Reveling in the Greek
sonorities, he rumbled with the bard
across the plains of Troy, alive with creak
of chariot wheels and charging horses bounding
amidst the hurtling spears that sped to seek
the chinks in burnished armor. None the less,
he put his eye upon a whistler pounding

the target tacks, in breezy carelessness
if wall lines paralleled the bill he nailed.
"Reward!" it snarled. "Who's getting prizes, Jess?"
the barkeep called. "A guy that bronco-bailed

a year ago from Kansas after robbing
a bank or so. Somebody thinks he's trailed
to here again to grab another load."
"He'd ought to be rewarded." Busy swabbing

mahogany, the grizzled tapster glowed
and spoke for heroes. "Jess, he's got the will
to go ahead; he sticks and can't be slowed,
like Honest Abe." His finger shot the bill.
"Has help-himself a name, or would they rather
we didn't puff his pride about his skill
and spoil the boy?" The other turned to read.
"He's fond of names, Detroit. He's got a slather:

Kid Hamlet, Johnnie Ringo, Adam Bede,
S. Valentine and Captain Singleton.
It don't say which his family thought he'd need,
but Valentine would look to be the one
he uses, reaming banks." With roaming finger
the speaker followed words. "He packs a gun;
I bet he's got a face, too. Yep, I'm right:
'has handsome, regular features.' Got no stinger

or horns, I guess it means. Six foot in height
and, say, no wonder he can crack a bank!
He's been to college. 'Cultured. Shoot on sight
or else arrest,' it says." The barkeep's lank
and solemn face grew sadder. "What they paying
for college scalps these days?" "Well, Damon Plank,
the banker that this jigger give the frisk
will pony up, according to his saying,

a thousand berries." "So you run the risk
of getting shot," the tapster brooded, "plus
the risk of trusting bankers." With a whisk
he mopped a leaving drinker's liquid muss
and spread the rag to dry. "It's too much gambling.
The house is buying, Jess." "Well, I won't fuss,"

the other vowed. He downed the proffered treat,
collected bills and hammer and went ambling

beyond the seated reader toward the street.
In time the reading stopped, the book was closed
on Hector as he stormed the Grecian fleet;
and Ringo scanned the bill which Jess had posed
before he slipped his *Iliad* in a pocket
abaft a forty-five of two that nosed
along his thighs. He strode to foot the rail.
"If you've another peg, why here's a socket,"

he said, "and, as an afterthought, the kale
to make the two as one." But as he drank
Red Conner, like a man who drives a nail
expressed a coin which landed with a clank
beneath his fingers. "Wring a stinging lizard,"
he ordered. "Give the varmint's tail a crank
and pour me out the poison while it's hot.
I need it for a poultice for my gizzard."

Yet when he'd caught and tossed the proffered shot,
the Golden Age did not prevail within.
"I'd better have another, like as not,
to give the critter company in my skin.
It's acting lonesome," Conner said, so winning
from Ringo, standing by, a kinsman's grin.
"A lonely drink is like a lover's shroud,
a flush that can't be filled or seraphs sinning—

too sad to think about, and not allowed
in ordered dukedoms. Coddle it with friends;
and I'll provide one, if you're not too proud
to share a bandit's bullion." "Boodle spends
as good as any," Red reminded, laughing.
"And, buying drink, it spurns ignoble ends,
so virtue wins," said Ringo. "That was fine
of virtue," Conner said, when finished quaffing;

"and now let's use this counterfeit of mine,
if I can pass it off. Two dying men,"
he called, and gave the barfly's countersign
of tallying fingers. All his anger then
had left a heart that rolled a carpet gaily
to toll new friendship in. "Let's try again;
we'll do it better, now that we've rehearsed,"
he urged. "Besides, my weasand still is scaly

from dust and cussing cows. Say, brother thirst,
you got a handle that the law ain't heard?"
"Why no, but—" Ringo paused. "For rogues the worst
of trials now is that the names preferred,
like Godless Jake or Stan the Global Terror
belong to Buntline, leaving but absurd
or commonplace, prosaic crumbs of names
for all us junior sons of sin and error.

If you can coin a blazon that proclaims
my nature one for ghouls to emulate,
with ravin but the mildest of my aims,
you'll help to raise me from my low estate
and launch me on the felon's road to glory;
but now, the disinherited of fate,
I speak when hailed as Johnnie." "Red'll do,"
was Conner's capping of his fellow's story.

"So here's to crime." "*Skoal, prosit* and *salut*,"
the outlaw pledged. They battened down the hatch
upon the toast. "It's horseshoes meeting you,"
Red mumbled, sucking light from Ringo's match.
"The eggs that hatched the Jayhawks here were rotten;
the coons can't wait to itch before they scratch."
"Subtract the barkeeps," Johnnie said. "For, lo,
I'll air a sooth I would not have forgotten:

no matter what misanthropy may sow
in Yankee exclaves, east away or west,

the gentle hearts will never be our foe,
provided we have pence. Should I request
another round to drink all Yanks perdition,
except for tapsters?" "Do it." Conner stressed
concurrence with a nod. "By God! we'll shell
the scorpions with corkscrew ammunition—

but missing barkeeps, which we like too well
to spare the Devil." "Spoken nice, and thanks,"
Detroit rejoined, "but I've done been to Hell
and got the bounce along with other Yanks
who couldn't make the grade, as they'd recruited
so many Rebels that McSatan's ranks
was overcrowded. Still I like you gents
for hoping I won't go where you'll be booted,

so I'd admire it, if you'd show some sense
and check your hardware like the signs advise
before a peaceful officer indents
your conks with grooves of pistol barrel size.
Now look, I don't hear much but Texans talking,
which means a bonus fact for fifty lies;
but they allow to wake up buffaloed,
because a marshal found you armed and balking,

don't really help a head in which you've throwed
a quart or so of bug juice." "Oh, I saw
that item from the local legal code,"
said Ringo, "but I've passed another law
which furnishes the privilege of beating
the sheriff or a marshal to the draw."
"I knowed a man who claimed he had such rights,"
Detroit agreed, "and we all held a meeting

and shoved him underground to see the sights.
Now if you live to hear the court's decree,
and while you're calaboosed them days and nights
for packing loaded hog-legs on a spree,

remember I said nothing. Here's the bottle.
Let's do it proper now. Have one on me."
Yet reason was so far from taking wing,
it counseled steam control and easing throttle,

so both agreed to gear their present string
of driving rods with food as balance wheels.
They left to clamp this safety on their fling;
but when they felt the walk beneath their heels,
they stopped appalled. The working day had ended,
aside from slowly ripening cattle deals;
and night and folly, dark's unblushing bride,
had yet to come. All living seeemed suspended—

as both appraised the city, sombre-eyed—
except for rattling plates and kitchen sounds
which emphasized the emptiness outside.
"It's quiet," Red pronounced. "The camping grounds
at Appomattox were a cheerful riot
compared to this," said Ringo. "*Sacre!* Zounds!
This town is like a fat and purring cat.
Men shouldn't doze, enveloping their diet

in torpor like a snake that's caught a rat.
We ought to stir them up." And as he mused
on ways and means of swiftly doing that,
the outlaw found that Homer's measures cruised
about his cerebrum and tuned its humming,
so thoughts of instant action now were fused
with Armageddon and a harried fleet,
the roaring charge and Trojan horses drumming

the march of doom with fiercely beating feet.
"I've got it, Red, my lad. We ought to stage
an act to lift their minds from what they eat
and make them choke, with luck, upon their rage.
What goat's your preference of the bevy yonder?"
"You mean hooraw the town?" His try to gauge

the ethics wearied Red. "Let's go," he grinned.
And, taking Ringo's lead, he seemed to wander,

as aimless as a bug before the wind,
across the glistening tracks to where were hitched
a brace of bays. "I think I'm being skinned,"
said Johnnie. "Call me Sherman, if I've snitched
so sad a nag since boyhood." "Hit the leather;
the sooner she is rode, the sooner ditched."
"Correct; but now to wake the living dead."
Astraddle, neither looked to notice whether

the eyes of owners marked them as they fed
the rowels to bolting mounts, with hunting whoops
and panther screams for music as they sped,
exciting dogs which swarmed in eager groups
and formed a claque. The loud, applausive barking
aroused the townsmen, tumbling out on stoops
or crowding window sills to trace the noise;
extending necks like geese in eager harking—

to squawk like ducks betrayed by near decoys
and disappear like cuckoos of the clocks.
For guns were aimed, and not as idle toys:
a bullet spiked a loaded packing box,
another left a drainage barrel leaking,
a sign descended, broken out with pocks,
and crashing glass announced a shattered pane.
These, for the cautious, put an end to peeking,

but scattered patrons, drovers in the main,
emerged from sanctuary in saloons.
Responding cordially to terror's reign,
they cheered the raiders. "Hoopalah! He-coons!"
a hunter yelped, and fired his mighty rifle,
as long and ancient both as Daniel Boone's,
to give a chimney-shaded cat surcease.
It gave a screech the bullet failed to stifle

before exploding into blood and grease,
its epitaph in sand the owner's howl
of grief and hate. "We've yielded them release
from lethargy enough to snarl and growl,"
called Ringo, slackening gait into a canter.
"I heard 'em." Red was pleased. "We've raised a yowl,
but all from this here side. Let's hop the rails
and look-see how the others like our banter;

them folks ain't met us yet." "And custom stales,"
his partner mused, "the sharpness of desire.
A meteor is wise because it sails
but once athwart one welkin, trailing fire.
So lope where we'll be news." They swiftly loaded
across the track from cheers and cries of ire
in tribute to their regional renown;
and galloped. Conner gloated as he goaded

his mount anew to speed. The sweep of town
appeared a soaring oriflamme, unfurled
in beauty like a rocket, tossing down
entrancing sparks, to string a rainbow world
for war against banality. He shouted
the glee of life triumphant, as he whirled
in Ringo's dust and drilled a phony front,
to shake a house whose frenzied tenant spouted

a satisfying fury at the stunt.
But as he turned from laughing back, there loomed
before his sight a sign which served to shunt
the casual out of mind. His pistol boomed
and kicked some splinters from a hostile banner,
educing Joe, upon whose features bloomed
such elements of rage as could combine
with shock at loss. Maniacal in manner,

he shrieked while pointing to the fractured sign,
then shouted even louder, arm outstretched

indictingly at Johnnie. "Valentine!"
he cried; and jumped as recognition fetched
a slug which missed his foot, though closely shaving,
to back him from the spot thus crudely etched
with crawfish swiftness. Watching his retreat,
Red saw him block a man who wasn't raving

but sure and sharp in motions toward the street—
a knife-marked, hunting man whose eyes were spun
of flashing readiness. He caught their heat
and saw behind the merchant's bulk a gun.
Then all were left behind. "The scarface fellow
looked mean enough," he called, "to kill for fun.
And, say, the storekeep swapped you for a guy
and yelled his name." "I heard the peasant bellow,"

said Ringo, "which is why I wiped his eye."

5

No Cheers for Hooraw

While Red and Ringo bartered treat for treat
and had not yet enjoyed the noisy jape
which others loathed from onset to recheat,
a colder move for fun was taking shape.
For Happy Jack, albeit with intention
to rob a rook and tax a queen's escape,
had planned a gambit handy for a thief
who had policeman's wages for subvention.

He way-stopped at the office of his chief
in time to beat his fellows, gathered there
by custom later on, to get a brief
of local torts. He warmed the look-out's chair
he'd earned with foresight while the others blathered.
In bearing half asleep, he was aware
when someone passed the summer-opened door
of Ellsworth's city hall, his features lathered

with sweat, but still a yearning carnivore
en route to Beefsteak Nat's—a fact which meant
Melinda, free to bargain, kept the store.
When Morco's stub of cigarette was spent,

he mimed a yawn. "The stores'll soon be closing
unless the sun is hustling for its tent
ahead of time. I got to buy a shirt."
Untaken in by patent, flimsy glozing,

his colleagues winked and laughed, but there was dirt
commingled with the mirth. "You heard him wish,"
said Brocky Jack. "He hopes to buy a skirt."
"He'll never sink his hook in icy fish,"
Long Jack opined. "Why she could freeze a river
in Hell or here by passing by it—swish!—
the way she does a man." "I smiled polite
at her," said High-low Jack, "and caught a shiver

I ain't yet lost a month ago tonight."
"A masher mashed, eh?" Morco laughed. "I'm glad
she moved up wind from *you;* it shows she's bright
as well as classy." "Gander for a lad
named Ringo." Brocky Jack had finished grinning.
"You've met or heard about him. Fast and bad,
the posters say; tall, educated, slim,
good looking; good at plain and fancy sinning,

with Valentine for play name. I knew him
in Abilene, and once I seen him brisk
his funeral stick—but never mind. The guy,
if twice a wolverine, is worth the risk.
A grand is on his carcase, see, for killing
a teller who objected to the frisk
in Kansas. Then he made some Texas hay,
but now he's back, they think. I got his billing

this afternoon, and Jess is on the way
to spread the news." "I'd button up the word,"
said Morco. "Jesus, Jack! For that much pay
the hurdy girls'll quit, to bag this bird,
and sink the town before I've finished pressing
that shirt, you know." He heaved a sigh and purred,

"I'll miss you boys." Though halting once to whet
with drink the lust which had become obsessing,

he strode to Joe's assortment store and let
the bell proclaim his advent. Randy-bold,
he waited till Melinda's eyes had met
his smiling ones above a mouth that told
their mouse and cheese relationship. Though longing
for all releases starving lives enfold,
she wore the aspect of a winsome child,
with innocence to make her right for wronging,

and so desired. With cunning she beguiled
the sadist in a man who tasted joy
at thought, she sensed, of modesty defiled;
and hence she double-acted sweet and coy.
"Well, here I am on deck," he murmured, winking,
"in case you know a gent I might annoy
by opening the can his cash is in."
"Oh, good, and thank you loads!" she whispered, linking

her fingers and unclasping them. "I'd been
afraid you'd be too busy or—" "Not me,"
he told her, with his scar-extended grin.
"The promises I pass are stickers, see?
You don't yet really tag me, do you, honey,
or savvy why I'm keen to set you free?
That's funny, for I'm glass to understand.
There's things I'll do for friends I won't for money;

are you that way?" The simple question spanned
all doubts, if any had been entertained,
that she must pass to freedom through his hand;
but this she'd picked for fact, and having gained
acceptance, faced it not with courage only
but with a gustiness. For long enchained
to continence by widowhood, her urge
for womanhood fulfilled had forced her lonely

desiring past repugnance to emerge
as yearning for such seizure by a man
of Morco's thews. And though she'd tried to scourge
her conscience, brooding merely served to fan
the fire she hid from him. In seeming frightened,
she widened eyes incredulous to scan
depravity. "You mean?" "One guess," he mocked.
"I'll tell you, if you're right." His smiling tightened.

"Or don't guess, sweets, but keep your door unlocked
and maybe you'll surprise me in the dark
with just the ticket. Go ahead; be shocked
and stay in Ellsworth slaving for this shark
you're begging me to rob." "All right," she yielded,
her hand upon her throat, her look so stark
with shame at her submission that he seethed
with bull elk glory in the power he wielded

and made his chest a barrel when he breathed.
"We've cinched a bargain. Lead me to the box
your uncle calls a safe, the nut! I teethed
on tin like that, so if it's full of rocks,
you're Boston-bound inside the next four-twenty.
Let's have the pitch." "I'm checking clothing stocks
against my books tonight." "That listens good,
if Joe's away," he nodded, "and there's plenty

of dust on tap. I've always understood
that merchant johnnies pile it in a bank."
"Not Joe," she said, "although you'd think he would;
but that's a point on which he's been a crank
since he was witness when a banking teller
was told with bang and bang. We have to thank
a man called Valentine for Joe's belief
that banks draw bandits who'll ignore a cellar.

He buries cash in his, when space is brief
in what you dub a can, but there are sacks

of coins now and bank notes by the sheaf,
and so— What's going on?" Revolver cracks,
their echoes mixed with yells, evoked her query.
"Oh, nothing but some work for all us Jacks
tonight," said Morco. "Shooting up the sky,
I'd rate it, by a Texan, whiskey merry;

but back to turkey—never mind that guy—
I'll come at midnight. Listen for a scratch,
like this, upon the— Jiggers! Let it die!"
he whispered, as he heard a hand unlatch
the door behind him. Weasel-swift in turning,
he leaped, but barely had the time to snatch
a shirt and eye it like a customer
ahead of Joe, his arms and temper churning.

"You, loafing here! I might have known you were.
The anti-Christs are shooting shops," he roared,
"and all you do is lallygag with her!
Police aren't paid for that. When lead is poured
along this street by rogues in need of hanging,
their trail's your only place. But help me board
my windows first; and then they get the clink."
"They will in time," said Jack. "This ain't a ganging

of Jesse James's boys. It's just a gink,
or maybe two, that's soon at getting stiff.
Forget the blinders for your store. He'll think
you've stuck a bull's-eye up for him to biff;
besides, you won't have time. It's *two,* and coming
like buffalo stampeding off a cliff.
Stand back!" But Joe, unheeding, wildly dashed
to mark the damage, when a bullet, humming

in transit to its destined target, crashed
upon a spike which held his sign aloft.
The hit enlisted Jack; his pistol flashed
its challenge and, supporting it, he coughed

an order whose alternative was battle.
But rump-directed toward him was the soft
and weighty bulk of Joe, who'd lost his will
for forward travel toward the lethal rattle

of side-arm fire, when Ringo shot to drill
the plank on which he'd stood. "Well, granny, who's
the scut that scared you so?" asked Morco, chill
with scorn. "They're only mounted tanks of booze,
and so I had no call to hoist my bristles
myself, I guess. I'll get 'em when they lose
their speed and gimp to hooch. But spill the news:
the past of that galoot, the salty one,
who answers to his name with bullet whistles."

"He's not a cowboy triggering for fun,"
the merchant snapped. "He's followed Quantrill's path.
I saw him borrow money with a gun!"
The thought of how a bank had suffered scathe
so sickened Joe that, trembling hands uplifted,
he vented hatred in a squeal of wrath.
"He's Valentine!" "He *is*?" Jack cupped his hands
and spat within. "Well, ain't it nice he's drifted

to Ellsworth, then? A mort of beaver stands
upon the hairpin's head. Why just today
they dangled the reward, and now he lands
inside the loop I'll tighten on the jay;
a thousand I can use. So now I'm riding
before some other marshal gets the lay
and tries to brand my steer." He eyed the girl.
"I ain't from Wales, and so your sale ain't sliding;

I said I'd buy a shirt." She forced a curl
upon her lips. "With buttons that will shine?"
she asked, remembering Red. "We've amber, pearl
and—" "Milky like your skin will fadge me fine,"

he muttered to the door, as it was closing.
Meanwhile the man whom Joe called Valentine,
and Red, concluded they had had their glut
of monkeyshines. "The town's no longer dozing,"

said Ringo. "Let us hie from here and cut
for cover by the creek till evening smokes
a screen for our return to eat the nut
we've now but cracked." "My hunch allows the folks
want holiday from hooraw," Red admitted,
"and some had green-persimmon looks." "Oh, jokes
and pleasantries, however small, inflame
the huckster soul," said Johnnie, as he fitted

a heater in its holster; "if the name
of soul applies—if you can call it such,
on which no other passion stakes a claim
but snudgery. And Ellsworth might begrutch
our fun enough to spring constabulary—
for towns retain such vermin—from their hutch.
We'll lose them, should they follow, in the maw
of boskage, then return, though not to harry

but to admire." "You bet, for I've not saw
that Prairie Rose," said Red, "and until then
I won't quit town for liquor, love or law."
And as he spoke, the youngster felt again
the pocket near his heart where lodged the billet
expounding Rose's charms. "I swore it when
I drawed my pay today, and I won't flunk."
"It's jumping in combustion from the skillet,"

said Ringo, as they left the trace and slunk
in shadow up the stream, "but I'll, too, make
the pilgrimage to see that bale fire sunk
in Nauchville stews; although with William Blake
I wonder at the guts of God to shape her.
That job of being deity must take

a pedlar's conscience. Yes, we'll both abscond
from reason and, ahungered, watch her caper;

moonrakers seeking treasure in a pond
that's as empty as skull eyes. But, Red, her ways
have schooled her graces so they best respond
to midnight's turn. Co-resident at Hays,
I found that Rose a dark of the morning flower.
And so before we watch it blow and blaze,
we've time to find another posy patch,
where blossoms not so baneful in their power

await: lane daisies, lacking thorns to scratch,
or back lot buttercups. Though later on
we'll gaze at Prairie Rose and dare to catch
a glimpse of what it means to be in pawn
to love and all damnation, now my leaning
is mill-run nymphs, desirous of a faun
and chicken-simple. Can you guide me, Red?"
For moments Conner fished the words for meaning.

"If nymphs are girls, I'm in the know," he said.
"A filly asked me to be certain-sure
to join her at a shindig when I'd fed;
a pretty one, and nice." "Well bred, demure;
I see. And in what musical bordello
does she," asked Johnnie, "waft a sinecure
to some deserving pander, for the boon
of sleeping with him off and on; eh, fellow?

She must have pointed out her pet saloon,
so you could squander mopus there." Red looked
as though he'd spied a lightning bug at noon.
"You reckon she's a flopsy-Sal? I'm spooked!
But no, she ain't; or if she is, I'm sorry.
I kind of liked her." "Well, as you are booked
as mortise-bolt, you rather should be glad
of amity. When mining such a quarry,

a special zest for it is nothing bad;
a fondness speeds the plough; hold on to it,"
the outlaw counseled. "As a hearty lad
who'd also like some kindliness to knit
my corporal self to that of some fair doxie,
I'll trust her sister trulls are every whit
as lovable as she of whom you spoke.
And, unlike Standish, I'll eschew a proxy

when seeking an erotic fire to stoke."

6

The Nymphs of Nauchville

By dusk as restless as a licking flame,
Rose waited at Van Wyck's for Jack's return.
The minutes left as empty as they came
and drab as ashes in a burial urn;
but yet their blankness nurtured heat so searing
it pierced to spark a subcutaneous burn
which fizzes, double-strength but sugared sweet,
could not allay. It waxed with bootless peering,

transmuting love to hate. "That short-bit cheat!"
she breathed. "He'll belly-creep before I'm through,
and when he breaks, I'll laugh to hear him bleat."
She raised her voice. "Say, Dick, have I had two—
since chow, I mean?" "Well, Rose, it ain't in writing,
so I can't call for sure the count on you,
but I'd say two was low." The tapster grinned
in answer to the winsome facial lighting

which bounced his pulse. "But you ain't really ginned,
in case you mean your glass ain't had enough."
"No, two is all I've had, and them so thinned,"
she told him, "that I couldn't swear the stuff

was swimming in the mix. Uncork a favor
and stir me one that's more than half a bluff;
I like enough damn gin to drown a brick,
not just a pigmy jolt to give the flavor.

You make me know I've had some liquor, Dick,
and then I'll be a good girl and go home
and get so prettied up that when I kick
the longhorns from the sagebrush hippodrome
that's Texas won't be only on the cattle."
The barkeep served her ice afloat in foam.
"This ought to help your kick. Say, honey, how's
it happen that you're giving booze a battle

alone before you see that Texas cows
are matched for umpty-ump. Where's Happy Jack?"
"In Boston with his beans, and hunting sows
in hopes of finding one upon her back
and get a piece of pork. He ain't expected
in Kansas till he's had that codfish snack,
so I won't wait." She reached the dregs in two
protracted pulls before she turned, directed

resentment at the clock and left to chew
the cud of rage. Meanwhile the man she missed
was kicking dust and catching evening dew
in quest of men, unmindful of his tryst
with either woman. Though the ground was printed
in palimpsest with tracks, the older grist
that others ground, he'd swiftly gauged his line
and followed it to where the river glinted—

a sunset spectrum—swallowing all sign.
Across, he scoured the prairie in an arc,
with beagle sureness that he could divine
the spoor as soon as found. Alike a shark
which hunts a fishing ground, he turned to double,
though ever farther out, on flats the dark

had thinly fogged. The eyes that had not failed
in midnight thievery had trifling trouble

in ascertaining that the hoofs he trailed
had scuffed no earth in flight athwart his course.
At length he peered where light from Nauchville paled
the sky to northward, giving up perforce.
"The rannies must be waiting in the willows
to fox it back," he said, and gave his horse
a quirting to abet its feed bag rush.
A league away, their saddles used as pillows,

the pair he sought reclined amongst the brush
as he suspected, while he searched the plains.
But next, arising in the darkling hush,
their thirst renewed, they loosed and caught the reins
of tethered, browsing mounts. "A Tam o' Shanter
scat for base astride ill gotten gains,
and then we'll shed them," Ringo said. "I've cash
that says you'll place. An eagle rides the banter,

or twenty, if you'd rather." With a splash
the outlaw left the bank and spattered spume
aslant the stream, itself a winding gash
of pallor in the woodland, forcing room
for glimpses of the sky. As rashly eager
to trample gleams atwinkle in the gloom
of muddy ripples, Conner lacked a gust
for high or sunken stars. He eyed the meagre

perimeter of light which arched to thrust
above the warp of tree and woof of shrub
that screened the stream. It tantalized his lust
to see the glimmering spokes demark the hub:
the building where enchantment had its bower.
The bosky pierced, they pounded through the scrub
and reached the clear, their race the charge of moose
which hear the mating call and spend their dower

of might and speed, compelled to make no truce
with obstacles. Before them now a flag
of light revealed an outpost for the use
of first and final drinkers. "Get your bag
of rustled bones to move or I'm in clover,
and you're the snail that buys the spider juice,"
said Conner, gaining slightly in his surge
to best his comrade. But the thirsty rover

of outlawdom was equal in the urge,
and spur-inspired the beast he rode to dredge
what bottom it retained. Upon the verge
of losing, now of eking out an edge,
they each foresaw defeat would lie in stopping
without the door. There met, each pressed to wedge
his mount ahead and make the other eat
the booby prize of crow. Within, and dropping

before their horses, braking with their feet,
could skid to halts upon the puncheon floor,
the saddle-stiffened rivals lunged to beat
contention to the bar, so keen to score
they all but knocked the fixture from its mooring.
"We win!" said Johnnie Ringo. "Vassal, pour
a pair of laurel crowns." "Now listen, son,"
the barkeep, Baldy, counseled, neatly pouring,

"you'd ought to learn to figger like I done.
You four come in together. Don't be cheap.
Or if the broncs ain't joining in the fun,
they plumb ain't welcome here. Dry horses keep
the drinking ones away by looking sour,
like that one there of yours. I'd bet a heap
he's took the pledge; I read the marks on him:
he'd close this trap, if it was in his power."

"The other, too," said Ringo. "He's as prim
and straight and narrow as a lightning rod,

I thank your trenchant eye. *Both* look as grim
as swindling tradesmen egging on Lord God
to strike a roisterer dead. We'll oust the mammals,
eh, Red, *mon vieux*? The horse has not been shod
whose blue-nose cant can wither me with drouth.
Equines they call themselves? They act like camels;

so let's abase their gall and bounce them out.
My fanes are few, but drink is one of them,
an isle of faith amidst a sea of doubt;
and heresies to scuttle it which stem,
as instanced now, from Calvin's curse on gladness,
I'll fight while blood sustains me. Come condemn
your mount with mine to outer darkness, Red.
These enemies of holy Bacchic madness

are placeless here, as has so sagely said
this priest of Dionysus." "Meaning what?"
While squinting at him, Conner scratched his head.
"No, let me guess. You mean the hay-stuffed mutt—
the horse; I never slander no bar tender—
is acting like a sinker in your gut
which ought to be coughed up. I'm with you there.
I never took a cayuse on a bender

that wouldn't belly-up before, I swear."
He strode and slapped his goat. "Go on; get lost,"
he barked. "Let's all," said Ringo, "brave the air."
Outside a moment later, Conner tossed
a pebble at his steed and grandly swaggered,
a friend beside him, toward the lights which glossed
the shacks of Nauchville, turning weathered boards
to walls so rich in texture that they staggered

the mind which tried to visualize the hoards
of treasure they enveloped. This was it:
the shouts, the clatter, laughter, joyous chords
of music, each contributing its bit

of harmony to blend with girlish voices
and make the world melodiously fit
for happy giant blood to revel in.
Assured he had the pick of all good choices

the cosmos stocked, he lifted up his chin
and gave the wolf howl, calling for the kill,
as easement for the glee which manned his skin.
A minute later longing had its will
amid a nimbus where the famished senses,
their wireless at work, could reach and thrill
to womankind en masse. Now making haste
to scrabble money, having sloughed pretenses—

a trout fly pose—of being shyly chaste,
they sparkled of Priapic ecstasies
and swarmed in shapes and shades for every taste,
some drunk, some merely feigning it to please
and lure the ear of lechery by squealing,
betokening abandon. "If we'd ease
to gee or haw, we'd find how it'd feel
to sidle close to one," said Conner, stealing

a look askance while voicing this appeal.
"I'd— No! There's Nan's place, Johnnie, over there;
The Happy Cattleman." "I'm at your heel,
Odysseus, and you'll find me game to dare
as much as any wight with any Circe,
though certain of my fortune in her lair;
for I've been there before, it comes to mind.
Yet I have no more sense than she has mercy,

so—oink!—lead on, my boy; though she may find
that I'm a razorback and not a sleak
sty-mansioned porker." Blushing, acting blind,
Red sidled in the den with but a peak
at harlots on display beyond the entry,
and shambled toward the bar in back to seek

the courage that he lacked but hoped to buy.
Yet here was posted one venereal sentry,

alert to catch the hesitant and shy:
a slim brunette, she caught him by the sleeve.
"I go for Texas red tops and for rye,"
she told him, "and I'm Scranton Mary Reeve."
"You thirsty now?" he asked, delighted. "Very,
and no one will believe me." "We believe,
and we would fight to buy you whiskey, ma'am;
eh, Johnnie?" But he was marooned with Mary

and, searching, witnessed Ringo pinch the ham
of buxomness that shrieked and grabbed his arm.
"He seems acquainted, so we'll take our dram
as deuce not trey," he said, in some alarm,
"if that's your bid." "I won't ask mama, sweetie,"
said Scranton Mary. "There can't be no harm,
or me, I wouldn't do it. Pass the runts
for deep ones. Hey, a pair of ryeballs, Petie,"

she told the tapster. "Skip the funny stunts.
My sugar just come off the Chisholm Trail,
so open up your special stock for once
or you and Fatgut Fred will find my tail
another deadfall's bait." The barkeep shuddered.
"I'm Davy's coon, for business sure'd fail."
Above the greying mice his eyes were grave.
"Now where's that extra special stuff?" he muttered,

while studying his shelves. "I try to save
the best for friends of yours: like Old Death Song
or Buzzard's Pal or Bottled for the Brave,
but Fatgut Fred keeps—nope, I done him wrong.
Look here; a neckfull quart of Ancient Jitters.
You're sure in luck tonight. It's pretty strong,
the one or two that's lived to tell me claim,
but good for nerves. It shrivels 'em to fritters,

and after that you keep a steady aim,
if you can see." "The price is rotten large,"
said Red, to make an ante in the game,
"unless the funeral costs are in the charge.—
Miss Mary, do you dance? The music's calling,"
he coaxed, when lees were left him. "Oh, I barge
around the floor, if some one wearing pants
will swing me— Hey!" She staggered, nearly falling

from onslaught by a lass whose furious glance
encountered Conner's startled one, a girl
who flounced between them, martial in her stance
and also in the tones she used to hurl
a challenge. "You ain't tough enough to diddle
me," said Nan. "Put that in your spit curl
and twist it every day. I found this man,
and no bad check is getting in the middle;

so beat it, chiseler!" Having voiced her ban,
she whirled on Red. "You came because of *me*,
now didn't you?" "I reckon so, Miss Nan,"
he mumbled, shocked at his disloyalty;
"but then I missed your sign at the beginning,
and there she was—" "And here's she's sticking, see?"
said Scranton Mary, in a shrilling burst
of fury. "Men ain't anthracite, for winning

like mines because you found and staked 'em first.
And, bed louse, they ain't steers, that you can brand
and keep as yours till cowboys lose their thirst
and hickville bags, too prissy to get canned,
can learn to hold a joe." "I'll show I'm able
as well as coal-pit tramps." A darting hand
inflicted then a raking slap that burned
no brand, indeed, but still a vivid label.

In backing, Conner saw the blow returned
and hairpin levies letting loose a flood.

For Mary, from her scouting fingers, learned
the mark upon her face was pricked in blood
and snatched her rival close for savage beating.
She struck but once. The sequel was a dud.
From fighting cock she turned to fleeing hen
as metal flashed which made her falter, bleating,

"Oh, Jesus, Nan; don't cut me!" "Cheese it, then,"
the other said, "until you're sick of life.
You think I scrounge in Ellsworth just for men
to buy you red-eye?" Bosoming her knife,
the victress fixed her ruined hairdo, gazing
at Red with such a smile as any wife
might give her husband, watching as she primped.
He goggled back, dumbfounded by the blazing

of battle over him, until she'd crimped
her plaits and curls in place with dainty speed.
"Would you," he queried, in a voice that limped,
"have really gutted her?" "Oh no, indeed;
I faked it just to scare her, silly." Smiling,
she quashed the subject. "What I know we need
is drink before we do-see-do." She tugged,
a playful kitten, at his belt, beguiling

the youngster so he let himself be lugged,
half-hearted, to the bar. "This friend of mine
is highball dry, but I don't want him slugged,
because we aim to dance. The usual wine."
But Conner had redoubled his intention,
the templet of his primary design,
to find the lodestar of his firmament—
its sheen above the spit and claw dissension

of which he'd been the fish. "I never meant
to see but Prairie Rose; I bet *she's* nice,"
he told his spirit, as his elbow bent.
His mind on gracious charm, piquant with spice

to liven it, he sipped what Nan had ordered,
ignoring her till she, unanswered twice,
had seized the arm he doubled when he drank.
"Let's join a set," she pled, in tones that bordered

on tears at his reaction to her prank.

7

Sixes and Sevens

While others so made hectic holiday
to hurdy-gurdy tempo, Boston Joe
was happy at a foreign style of play:
the totting of his gain. The jet ink flow
so overmatched the red, his mood was tender.
"Knock off," he urged his niece. "Go home and sew
or knit or wash your hair or read a book."
"Afraid the serf will die and make you render

the coffin fee?" she asked. He shrugged and took
a coin his fingers kissed, while she returned
to checking clothing stocks with hands that shook.
"I can't relax," she said. "For all I've learned
is work, since mining salt at your direction."
In fear that he would note the eyes that burned
frenetically, she bent them toward the shirts
in front of her. "I'll tally this collection

of odds and ends, for self-enamored squirts
to wear and give the looking glass a shock,
before I quit. Though parting from them hurts,
why don't you pet each darling in your flock

of eagles roosting bartering devices,
re-pen them where they're safe behind a lock
and then retire to dream of selling trash
to bigger fools for more outrageous prices?"

He smirked, too dedicate to mind the lash
of scorn applied for what he so adored,
and tenderly he lifted stacks of cash
he fondled for good night as they were stored.
Melinda half seceded from the living
for fear that he would linger with his hoard,
but Joe, though slowly, closed and locked the door
and dragged his hand along the metal, giving

the trusted Fafnir, made in Baltimore,
a last caressing. "Wind the business up,
as long as you have corner-stoned the chore;
and here's a nickel, if you want a cup
of coffee when you're done." His hat and Bible
in hand, he spoke again. "And keep your pup,
the mashing marshal from—" "House break your talk,"
Melinda warned, "or I will sue for libel."

At thought of damages, he paled to chalk
and found in horror courtesy of tone.
"I mean to bolt the door, to keep the gawk
from pestering, as lately he's been prone
to do, you know. Of course, he's not invited;
I know it, dear." He left her then alone
with hopes which might not keep their votive faith,
but sighs or growing nervous-grouse excited

were not her ways with unencountered scathe.
She did the work, and did it well besides,
before she snuffed the lamp and sat, a wraith
dismembered and awash in murky tides
of darkness where—their pallor shimmering dimly—
her face and folded hands alone were guides

for prowling lust, if it would snatch the lure.
But at the time the man she baited primly

indulged another appetite. So sure
the men he chased would double to the stews
of Nauchville, Morco counted them secure
in brothel trammels, knotted tight by booze,
if given leisure in the hours that followed
to snare themselves. With this relaxing ruse
to tide him, having drunk, he munched a steak,
his thoughts as tasty as the food he swallowed.

The night ahead was promising to make
all prior ones, by contrast, profitless.
In time he'd hire some deputies and take
the golden scalp his colleagues didn't guess
to be in town; and then he'd swoop on treasure,
involving, too, a variant claim to press.
From where he sat, he couldn't see the grey,
lane-hugging cottage where he'd take the measure

of prudery. His mind went up the way
it fronted on, however, to the jail
where Valentine would make a trifling stay
before a hempen noose could raise the bail.
But while he chewed and mused and smiled, the lover
he'd dropped from thought had made revenge her grail.
She smoked with fury, soaking in her bath;
the clouds of steam which rose from it to hover

were not more tropic than her mental path;
and when, anadyomene from suds,
she rose, it was erupting, naked wrath.
She stamped into the brief, salacious duds
the can-can called for, yanking at the laces
which promised but withheld from yearning bloods
the rainbow's end. She jerked the stockings on
which led the eye to interstellar spaces

where gaudy garters peeped from frills of law:
the whiteness of false day with, just beneath,
the warm reality of rosy dawn.
Her tresses in a gold madonna wreath,
she poured and gulped a final belt of liquor,
as though she rammed a dagger in it sheath,
and shot the looking glass a torrid glare,
the herald of a hard, triumphant snicker,

Medusa sure of power in her stare.
"He'll want it back," she said. "He can't resist
a soldier's home like that. I'll have him there."
She stretched her hand out, opening her fist.
"And then, by God!" She made the squeezing motion
foretelling Morco's fate. And in a mist
of dust the moon had made the shade of straw
she coursed the alley toward the tried devotion

of men to whom her dance was cosmic law.
They caught the loveliness without the taint;
if full perfection lacked, they saw the flaw
no more than art admirers eye the paint.
Aware they got the essence that they wanted
and didn't ask, as bonus, any saint,
she entered through a rear guard gambling room
and slacked her pace. When she had roused and taunted

the players tantalized by her perfume,
she swept into the star's retreat beyond:
a box which held a table, chair and plume
of candle flame, reflected in a pond
of cloudy glass. There was a branding iron
upon the table, too, and with this wand
she banged the wall until a hearer yelled,
"You ready, Rose?" "For hell or breakfast, Byron."

The fiddle ceased to skirl, the banjo quelled
its thumping cords, the trumpet hacked a cough

and matched the silence which the drum, too, held;
the dancers stranded on the floor got off,
and one by one the gabbling voices muted.
"You drinkers raise your muzzles from the trough
and watch some catchy steps, the cutest fun
since Eve got tight, saw snakes and hootchy-scooted

from Eden. Folks, I'll tell you what we've done.
We've brought you beauty's gift to the frontier,
the fairest flower beneath the Kansas sun
and Ellsworth moon, who'll do for you right here,"
the lanky barker stamped the floor in speaking,
"the dance that Paris, France, 'll lose this year,
and all the Eastern swells are going to miss,
poor bastards, though they'd all fork lightning, streaking

for Nauchville, if they knew. She's passion's kiss,
she's whiskey neat, she's pay day night in town;
she's Prairie Rose and watch her prance!" At this
a cow hand whooped, his consort hid her frown,
a gong was rung—and Rose came with its clangor,
kicking the scarf she'd let go drifting down,
to land it on the bar. Her face serene,
except for eyes like leopards' when in anger,

she braced the band about the coming scene.
"For once forget to copy hungry goats
and scramble something fast and sweet and mean,
like me." The leader tried a run of notes;
he signaled, and the chords began to rollick,
all lilting, skipping, jaunty antidotes
to starched decorum; fitting harmony
for satyrs, partly tone deaf, on a frolic.

And, bouncing with it, bawdry on a spree,
she worked to win an optic wanderlust;
contortionate of ankle, hip and knee,
or bending, thus to introduce her bust

to dazzled eyes, which left it for the cocking
of hoisted leg that kicked as soon as thrust
to heady heights—to give a vision then
of pinks that winked above a raven stocking,

no sooner seen than they were gone again.
She was Salome dancing for a head,
the darling and the certain bane of men;
a wrecker siren, singing as she sped
the blood of youth around the horn, and boiling.
Her legs were swords to stab all reason dead:
excaliburs that flashed from out a mist
of petticoats provocatively coiling

about their symmetry. Betimes she kissed
in pantomime or swiveled grinds and bumps,
or feigned to bare a breast, then slapped her wrist
and whirled to flounce her skirts and turn up trumps.
And while she anticked, songs of chaste devotion
belied the tunes which paced the flashing pumps
that spelled her hate of Morco. So she danced,
a range fire, searing men with sensual motion;

but Conner was not one. For he, too, pranced,
his glance alight with glee, his heart with song
as he retreated, jigging, or advanced,
an athlete in a jumping, stomping throng.
He'd not forgotten Prairie Rose, the peerless,
and swore at each new set to move along;
but Nan had blurred the memory of blows
and of the knife whose play had left him cheerless

for minutes first. For having had the nose
to sense the attitude she had evoked,
she'd wooed him back to liking with a pose
of schoolgirl hurt—with onion tears that soaked
a tiny handkerchief—and didn't bumble
the task of being ardor's tinder, cloaked

as maiden comradeship. Impinging art
too veteran to miss the way and fumble

a second chance, she gaffed her pickerel's heart.
Good sport, she joined him gaily when he quaffed;
good friend, she found him debonair and smart;
good bait, she used her body fore and aft
until he strutted like a courting pheasant.
So there he stayed, a tribute to a craft
which furnished him with concepts of himself
as novel to a bashful youth as pleasant.

Wherefore while Rose put love on Borgia's shelf
for poison in a beautiful disguise
and was herself a pantomimic elf
that vivified the close of Paradise,
Red, too, was agile. If his rugged romping
inspired no whistles or admiring cries,
he yearned to have no moths around his lamp,
shine though it did. Cavorting, swinging, stomping,

he shouted cheers himself, for all the camp
to hear or not. Meanwhile he flouted laws
of rhythm till his dusty shirt was damp
and trickles from his Stetson pearled his jaws,
and joltingly his pistol jounced and wiggled.
His pinwheel spurs were musical for cause
while—flatter echoes of his protean prance—
the glasses on a nearby table jiggled

as Conner clicked his heels and slapped his pants
or lunged or flung his arms about and jumped.
He danced the warring wapiti's advance,
the bison challenge, swaying as he stumped
with outthrust head; or, straightening and slowing,
he aped the randy rooster, stiffly rumped,
or next the bear walk, fiercely on the prowl,
to find his prey in Nan. He grabbed her, throwing

such verve into the act, she gave a howl,
not wholly feigning fright at being caught
in such a gale of manhood. But a growl
which left no space for mock alarm besought
return to realism. "Reach, God damn it!
You—Valentine!" The brusque command was fraught
with possibilities for all and each;
and mass reactions to it ran no gamut

but had one goal. With sputtered oath or screech,
they hit the floor or scudded, deft of foot
behind the bar; or farther out of reach
in corners now as swarthy as the soot
from lamps which shots had floored and stopped from
    flaring.
Yet one, its chimney broken, hung to put
a jaundiced finger on the crouching form
of Johnnie Ringo, scorpion-poised and glaring

at three remaining pat amongst a swarm
of headlong fugitives. A fifth stood fast
behind one move to duck the making storm;
for Red, about to breeze, had found, aghast,
his jolly partner was the threatened quarry
of closing hunters. One looked set to blast,
so, drawing, Conner whizzed a slug his way:
an either hold fire warning, or be sorry.

He saw the fellow glance to catch his play
and twist the mouth on tether to a scar.
"You take the cowpoke, Ben," Red heard him say.
He wore a badge, though not a sheriff's star;
but Red had little time to guess its meaning,
for when the fellow spoke, there was a jar
from Ringo's gun. In clangorous collapse
the final lamp, sent spinning and careening,

went down and out. And shots tore yellow gaps
in blackness, now suffused with acrid smoke;

and, hearing zooming bullets, Red took snaps
at firing back. "Oh, Christ! the bank is broke!"
a gasp declared. "They drilled me in the chowder
and I—" The groaning ended in a croak.
Then shooting slackened off as Red, for one,
regretted moments, happier and prouder,

when he had drained his arsenal for fun.
He felt for shells in desperate, futile haste,
yet dark and loyalty forbade to run.
He cursed the folly of his wanton waste
anew when light was brought to cast ungainly
galanty shows of furniture misplaced
amid the glassware, smashed or overturned,
and blood upon the floor. But Red saw mainly

the scarfaced man, his gun, his eyes that yearned
for killing. "Up 'em! Reach, and reach 'em high!"
he ordered. Red obeyed him, having learned
that instant what it was to wait to die.
His captor cat-stole closer, meanwhile speaking
to his companion. "Ben, I'll hold this guy;
how's Stevie doing?" "He don't do. He's dead."
The squat man bent above the slain one, seeking

the fatal wound, before he raised his head
and squinted through the drifting powder screen.
"The angle that he got it from," he said,
"was squeegee-wise from you two, which'd mean
the one that plugged him was the one that skittered,
and not the kid there, Jack." "For half a bean
I'd shoot the doughnut center anyhow
for butting in," the marshal raged, embittered

at thought of bounty money, vanished now
with Ringo's self. "You backed his play," he fumed,
"and screwed the law!" "It's wrongish, I'll allow,"
said Red, and fought for poise where terror loomed,

"but natural." He gulped but steadied, shrugging
as Morco's eyes informed him he was doomed
to give the state wergild. "You went for him,
and so I guess I kind of started tugging

my cannon out, to paddle with the swim.
Old Johnnie is my friend." "Not pal enough
to side you now," the one called Ben said, grim
of tone and feature. "Yeah; the going rough,
he wanted out, but he'll come running, maybe,
to watch 'em string you up for getting tough
with me and my two men; and one's thrown craps.
The camp has just the cage to hold you, baby,

for murder," Morco said. "Your tune is taps."

8

A Celebrated Wager

A youthful drover jailed to wait the rope,
a rogue escaped, a deputy shot down—
such table talk was normal to the scope
of gossip in a railhead cattle town.
Their man for breakfast meted satisfaction,
with mourners seldom. "Yankton Stevie Brown?
I bet the chigger was too mean to bleed.
Up ten," a rancher said. "The man wants action,"

a buyer murmured. "I'd have guaranteed
that Steve'd turn somebody up to dot
his eye with lead. I'll stay." "The lousy breed!
It always happens when they brag a lot,"
the capper said. "Besides, he'd took to fanning.
I'm whipped." "I bet old Happy Jack is hot."
The man he shilled for grinned while being deft
to palm a card. "They say the cuss was planning

to win some wampum with the pelt that left
just when he had it where the hair was short,
or thought he did. A straight, and don't say 'theft';
I got an orphan grandpa to support."

The gambler raked the pot in, eyelids lazing,
and laughed. "If Morco comes, let's raise some sport
by asking why he turned a bandit loose.
His fuse is short and easy set ablazing,

and that should give his powder charge a goose
which ought to take his head off with the blast.
I hope so, for I never had no use
for marshals anyhow. Not quite so fast;
you'll get this nice, cold deck too hot to handle."
But Happy Jack, while cards were being passed,
was huddled by a metal box, his face,
educed from darkness by the guarded candle

which made a death mask, in suspense in space,
of still Melinda's features. "Yeah, I'm geared
to work without much light," he said, "in case
you're worrying." He cocked his head and peered
at his companion, chuckling. "There's occasions
when I can work by touch alone." He smeared
a key with wax, to slip it in the lock
and draw it out, for shaping where abrasions

were signs to gently file or deeply nock.
"Some crackers work with wedges and with pries,"
he told her, "when they open up a crock.
A cricket squeak like this don't draw the flies,
though I admit the noisy way is quicker;
but keep the love light shining in your eyes,
and you can bet I'll spring you from the state
before the sheriff puts it on the ticker

to watch for you." "I've waited, and I'll wait,"
Melinda said, "but try to finish soon.
The train won't linger for me, if I'm late,
as it would do for steers." "I'll have the spoon
in trim to dish the gravy from the platter
a watch before the whistle's starting tune.

You won't get left, and neither," Jack declared,
"will I, my little bunkie, for that matter.

It's hand-on-Bible fact. A raspberry haired,
cow-nursing son of a Texas weasel's louse
unloosed my line and got my eel unsnared
already once tonight, and I don't mouse
for nothing very often. Sit it pretty,
which you can't help but do, and we'll red house
ahead of time for us to stage the clinch
you're counting on." But as, acerb and witty,

he pleased himself by yanking on the cinch
he'd thrown about her, tightening as he filed,
a pair at the Alhambra didn't flinch
from wondering if Rose could be beguiled
to keep the promises of more exposure
she gave betimes, but slapped her hand and smiled
to see expectancy reduced to gloom.
They yearned for beauty freed from the enclosure

of even bonds designed to seal the doom
of chaste desires. Aware, she rang their knell
by prompting hopes—consigned then to the tomb;
yet held the hopers. "Taken from the shell,
I bet she'd shine," said Pecos Bert. "The stitches
will maybe split," said Bronco Billie. "Hell,
I've give up faith in them. She sews with steel,"
said Pecos, "or she'd bust this side her breeches,

the way she kicks. She'll have to wait to peel
before we get a bigger eyeful." "Bert,"
his partner said, "we'd ought to rig a deal
to make her bet she'll shed her underskirt
or skin her stockings off or ease the laces
which hitch that— Well, I guess it ain't a shirt
but—" "Can it, Bronco; here's my honey-bun.
Stop thinking, too, or else you'll be in places

my mind has filed a claim on." "Stow your gun,"
the other counseled. "We don't need to feud.
Invent clean thoughts, and I won't crowd you none."
But while the twosome wished her clothes unclewed,
Rose danced a second time with such a flaming
of passion that the glance of all was glued.
Yet none that peered, bedazzled, through the haze,
a mulligan of fumes too mixed for naming,

possessed the sight her choler longed to braize,
for not a pair were recreant Morco's eyes.
"He's with her now," she thought, and ground the
    phrase
beneath her feet and slashed it with her thighs,
as up they sliced and down. "He's got her bedded,
the gutter mink. He must have, otherwise
he'd check this trap—he always has—to see
that I don't cheat and get my needle threaded.

Well, I've been straight, and now he thinks no key
will fit my lock but his. One easy could,
but that's no odds. He's got the drop on me
at diddling, and I've got to whip him, good,
not match his hand. I need a whitened poker
to burn it in the blockhead's rotten wood
that I'm a lay that any pair of jeans
would sell his mother's body to the croaker

to bed roll. I ain't like the quick-jump queens
they bait the gin joints with on pay day nights;
or like the other sort. Nobody leans
when *her* kind passes, rubbering at the sights—
the Christ's-my-Savior, pulpit-hugging bitches
who tumble backward when you douse the lights.
The boys would never pay good dough to perch
on chair rims just in hopes *she'd* rip some stitches;

but he don't seem to know he'd have to search
in dreams for other does that make the stags

as bucky as I can. She goes to church,
and so he thinks she's platinum. Hell, the bags
that scrounge for nickels in the nooky lodges
have, lots of them, more class. He don't know rags
from fine embroidery, so he's got to learn
my grade of silk, the mutt. There must be dodges

that I can use to teach him; then he'll burn
to let all Kansas know whose wren I am.
The slug'll find I'm mine, when it's my turn."
She spoke for ears then. "Switch the noise off, Sam;
the gents have seen enough to make 'em dizzy."
Bemused, she sought the bar. "I'm buying, ma'am,"
a towhead told her. "Bronco Billie Deems
they call me, if they catch me. Ugly, busy

at looking like a mule, ain't what he seems;
he's worse. You see his gun? He'd kill to flirt,
if making ghosts'd help his hellish schemes;
so as a friend, I warn he's Pecos Bert
and packs a grudge for you." Responding duly,
from actress habit, she portrayed her hurt.
"Why, Bert?" "You're holding out. I like what of
I've *saw* of you," he answered her, and truly,

"but shucks! Them doodads fit you like a glove,
but if the glove was taken off, I think
I'd like you *all* and be complete in love,
instead of just in spots." Upon his wink,
his ally took the buck. "It's dry wash fishing,
so clam and use your mouth to sluice your drink,
original sinner. Why she wouldn't dare
perform the way I hate to think you're wishing;

and scaring women ain't upon the square.
Besides, there'd be a diamond mine stampede
to take this town apart, if she'd go bare
a smidgin more'n now. My heart'd bleed

for poor old Ellsworth, if I wasn't sprinting;
but I'd be busy keeping in the lead."
"You'd tail me," Pecos told him. "That parade
is one I'd captain, man." His green eyes glinting,

he sighed. "But she's ascared." "It would've made
this graveyard," Bronco said, "a little sport,
but Prairie Rose is prairie dog afraid,
and I can't say I—" "Don't," she cut him short.
"Let's get it straight, before you bust out crying
because my nerves are of the yellow sort:
I ain't afraid of no man ever whelped
in wedlock or in Texas." "We ain't buying

a brag," insisted Billie, "never helped
with doing; and I know you won't make good
by shucking any duds, like Pecos yelped
he'd yen for you to do, the snake. How could
a man commit his thoughts? Oh, you ain't scary
with me to shotgun guard you, understood;
for I won't let him touch you, bless your heart."
"But still," said Bert, "she wouldn't." Tense and wary,

the dancer eyed him. "Wouldn't what?" "Oh, start
and maybe finish peeling," Pecos purred.
"Forget it, Bert." "For why?" "It just ain't smart,"
said Bronco. "If the corpses got the word,
Boot Hill would rally up and come aspooking;
and more'n that—" "What now?" "Why ain't you heard?
The town is full of deacons." "Worse'n studs,"
conceded Pecos. "Get so hot from looking

at plews of girls, they froth with mad-dog suds
and spring at 'em. On second thought, she's right
to be ascared to part with any duds."
But while they spoke of how the godly might
reply to nudity, a plan was minted
in Rose's mind. She saw with hard delight

she'd lance to Jack the jolt that was her aim
by covering the bet her baiters hinted.

She grasped the chance to reaffirm her fame
and crowd the town with chatter of her charms.
By flaunting beauty innocent of frame,
she'd start a fire to call for four alarms,
a draw for men as strong as steel for lightning;
and no cheap ruse of seeking other arms
would cut the fun of watching Hapless Jack
endure the rack which others would be tightening

by praising her. She threw her fair head back
and slugged the whiskey down. "You looning simps
could beat me down, if bets were paid in clack,
but acting's how you tell tall men from shrimps.
You yawped I'd be afraid to shed more cover
with rannies standing by to grab a glimpse.
But back your words or go and jump a pig,
if any gilt's so hard up for a lover

she'd take you on. I mean it! Crawl or dig.
I'll bet you fifty bucks, each yap of you,
that I'll parade a Main Street in the rig
that's hand me down from God; the sun up, too;
and not just any day but right this morning."
She hitched her skirt to dazzle with a view
of bills in gartered escrow. "All through town,"
she emphasized, but not without a warning.

"I'll likewise bet the first ball bearing clown
that tries to touch me winds up in a box.
So cork your mouths and get mazuma down
or find Red Riding Hood or Goldilocks
to kid next time." So swift in their compliance
their hands were trembling, reaching in their socks,
the cowmen sealed the wager. "We ain't crawled,
so you can't," Pecos said, as though by science

to make the bargain hold. The barkeep hauled
the stakes the ranchers pressed on him away;
but, smiling crookedly, the dancer called,
"Hey, Shorty!" Eagerly as Old Dog Tray
when noticed, seven feet of Texan hurried,
a donkey answering a jenny's bray
by instinct, not an exercise of wits.
"You love me still?" she asked. He grinned, though
     flurried,

"You know I do!" he cried. "Well, here's two bits.
You amble yonder, will you, sugar lump?
and hold this high as you can stretch your mitts.
I've made a bet," she fudged, "and you're my trump.
You got a ten foot reach?" "About that, honey."
"Well, try to touch a rafter of the dump."
He did so while she peered, her eye slits thinned,
to gauge the angle of the piece of money

from where she stood. Abruptly then she skinned
the gun from Bronco's holster, gave a twitch
that flipped it over, caught it, drilled the wind,
and watched, through clouds of powder, Shorty pitch
face downward, though unharmed—unlike the quarter
he'd held like New York's torch of hope, and which
was shattered by the bullet Rose had sent.
She laughed. "He'll find his fingers aren't shorter;

and, hating blood, I showed before I went
that no galoot should sidle up and bug
an eye at me he wants to keep." "I meant
to tell you," Pecos said. "I'll *think* my hug,
but Bronco here may—" "Nope, I heard her talking,"
said Billie, "though I'm laying off the jug,
aside from this one snifter, just the same,
to clear my eyes for good long distance stalking."

"Of what?" a cowboy queried. "What's the game?"
And so the grapevine linked the town's saloons,

electrifying Ellsworth with the name
of daring Prairie Rose and two gossoons,
deserving monuments of precious metal,
who'd badgered her until she bet doubloons
she'd be unfurled beneath the rising sun—
a morning glory, packing, though, a nettle

designed to limit joy to optic fun
for all who shied from bullets in their spleens.
The tale of how she'd fired a juggled gun
to blow a smallish coin to smithereens,
and whiten Shorty's hair, matured a story
which waggled jaws, in time, beyond canteens
and even reached the jail where Conner scanned
the face of loneliness. "They swear, by glory,

it's true!" the jailer chortled. "Ain't it grand?"
He shared the news with Red because, alone
of all within his keep, he'd understand.
The others slept or waked to writhe and groan,
the victims both of booze and buffaloing;
but separate from the tank where they'd been thrown
was bondage for a prisoner of the state.
Its inmate, for his fortune's sorry showing,

Red heard the warden's encore: "Ain't it great?"
and merely grunted in his threatened throat—
as little caring now what Rose might slate
as baffled Nan, who saw herself the goat,
no matter who might die of hemp or firing.
"What stinking luck!" she fumed. "They came to tote
that chub away when he was good and hooked."
At odds with fate, malicious and conspiring,

she glared at irony. "And I'm self-cooked.
A cowboy army's here, and what I tout
is one that shoots at marshals and is booked!
And now the night is shot or just about,

and every easy mark is tagged for rolling."
But on the verge of barging off to pout,
and damn a night that hadn't let her score,
she noticed Ringo, back again and lolling

against a wall convenient to the door.
Not merry now but dangerous and mean,
he beckoned Nan. "You're Conner's has-been whore."
His voice, too, rubbed to hurt. "And have you seen
the other livery stable mare, the tailing
I loitered with?" "She swore she's turning clean
on your account," said Nan, her tone a sledge.
"She saw she was a piker after trailing

behind you when you sloped, and took the pledge
to give up hustling. How's the yellow streak
you flashed for us tonight?" He met the edge
of bitterness with lips that twitched in bleak
acknowledgment of tropes he granted graphic.
"I left in haste, I'll own." His voice was meek.
"But yet I don't regret the action, since
delay was death, and living called for traffic.

I'm here, however, anxious to convince
the law that though it may have used its seal
to ostracize me, wench, I still am prince
of where I am and duke of how I feel,
the palatine of what I prize in doing
and regent of the only commonweal
for whose decrees I am at all concerned:
to wit, myself. Decided on renewing

my tilt with vice, I have, you see, returned
from Elba, so to speak. Now where's my friend,
my heart's companion, Red?" "In hock," she burned.
"He didn't welch like you, so now they'll bend
a rope around his neck—and who will pocket
the wad I worked all night for, in the end,

Hell only knows." "He's in the calaboose,
and with a murder charge upon the docket?"

He frowned. "And you're the one should get the noose,"
she told him. "Fairly stated, I suspect."
"And they will roast and baste him with his juice
for siding you," she hammered. "That's correct."
He slowly raised the glass his quaffing lightened.
"I always like to see the law cold-decked,"
he said at length. "I'll spring him from the box,
if you'll do what you'll flunk if acting frightened."

"I'm game," she said, "if I can get his rocks.
He'd pay as much to keep his neck, you'd think,
as rent my roost." "Why yes, by all the locks
which love has mocked and put upon the blink,
I do," said Ringo. "Never time was riper
than when a man beholds the mortal brink,
to bleed him of his final, shop-thinned dime.
As it's a choice betwixt you and the piper,

you'll find he squeezes easy as a lime."

9

Of Opening Doors

The pass-key worked the will of Happy Jack,
who turned it in the lock with artful force
until the tumblers let the bolt aback.
The door was now a check he could endorse
and cash, obtaining ducats packaged neatly
by Boston Joe, who loved them. Now the source
of Morco's joy, they changed from wealth to swag,
along with specie. Silently and fleetly,

he fed the total to a buckskin bag
before he held the candle up and peered
at money's captive. "Now's my time to shag
and rig an alibi, so I'll be cleared
in case somebody wonders how a heifer
could crop these oats alone." Erect, he leered.
"You take the loot—and then a lover's leap
between the sheets; and it won't be no zephyr

that blows in later. You won't oversleep,
I promise. Then we'll divvy uncle's moss,
and you can stone-roll east. And don't you keep
the coop shut when it's time to come across

or I will nail a cross for you that's double
by finding that you robbed your poor old boss
and jugging you." She reached to snuff the flame,
dissolving light, a silent, bursting bubble.

"Go on," she said. "My mind is still the same,
so if you wish, you'll find me." Darkness-mewed,
she hugged to her the winnings of her game:
her pledges of release and life renewed,
as Morco vanished. The erotic duel
on which his will was fixed she largely viewed
as something correlated with escape,
a ticket for her train. Till then the jewel,

the prize too wondrous in its grace and shape
to have a name but "freedom," was her world.
She lived in it when stealing home to drape
her form with scant attire before she curled
upon her cot, to dream, the while of waiting,
of Boston and the sea-born mists that swirled
around its heights and spires, as writhing trees
swept skies where seagulls cried without abating

in wheeling back and forth. No inshore breeze
then swayed her door, a hair line off the latch—
or lanced the salty spume of choppy seas
about the heavy, moon-cast shadow patch
beside the jail where Nan and Johnnie, lurking,
held council in the stillness. "Now we'll hatch
our squab from out this egg, if there's a man
for warden, not a dud," said Ringo, jerking

her sleeve to hone attention. "Here's my plan
for sesame: you—" "Rap?" she asked. "Don't knock,"
he growled at her. "Keep still and listen, Nan.
Just giggle through the key hole. If he's rock,
no scheme will flummox him, but if he's human,
he'll have to sidle up and spring the lock

to keep from wondering each night afresh
what charms he'd spurned." Unburdened with acumen

in matters less connected with the flesh,
she saw this point at once. "O. K., I'll try;
but what will you be doing while I thresh
that wheat for you?" "I'll wait until you pie
the jailer's brains, and then you'll see some action,"
he vowed. "Now clear the track." Her mating cry,
a teasing chuckle, pert and bold and sweet,
was polar in its power of attraction.

Alert beside her, balanced to delete,
the outlaw heard the clicking of the bolt
and waited for the latch to leave its seat
before he smashed the door ajar to jolt
the warden, now aghast to find the filly
he'd looked for supplemented by a Colt.
Part stunned and full amazed, he stood astare
as Ringo said in tones that were as chilly

and harrowing as dead flesh, handled bare—
but yet were not as icy as his look,
"My writ of habeas corpus has a pair
of uses, if I wish a goose to cook.
The red haired fellow: take us to him, mister!"
"I guess I will," the pudge declared, and took
small time in doing so. Within a cell
whose rankness seemed of heat enough to blister,

the prisoner paced and sweltered in a well
of woe too frantic to be called despond.
He blinked, uncomprehending, when the spell
of darkness lifted showing him the blond
and curly head of Nan, and the magician
who'd brought her there. Now Ringo waved the wand
he'd conjured with, to swing the door and prod
the jailer, giving pills to the physician.

"Here, hayseed, try the feel of this your pod;
it's foul enough to suit a midden creep
who'd cage a man—though hoisting first his wad—
to wait the butcher like a fattening sheep.
Now hold him, Red." "How long?" "Until he's folded;
my rod will rock this bantling—see!—asleep."
"Come on!" breathed Conner, then "Tear off his shirt,"
said Johnnie, "and be sure a sock is molded

around his tongue to hold the thing inert
until we leave—unfortunately chaste
but never parched, a fate I'll now avert
by enterprise. Although I've never cased
the one on hand, if I know calabooses
(a point on which I'd rather not be braced),
he's pilfered booze enough to burden pails
from sundry captives laden with the juices

before whose might the power of darkness fails.
There'll be all ilks, so what's your favorite brand?"
"Just bring it, and I'll drink it, heads or tails."
Red chuckled as he stooped to clap a hand
upon the warden. "Cops lift more than liquor.
This horse fly pinched my cash and said he planned
to buy a suit, the son of a lap dog bitch,
to wear the day the sheriff swung his kicker

and dropped me down in shape for spades to pitch
the sod atop." "I'll give *his* pants a frisk,"
said Nan, who all the while had quelled her itch
to yelp for her reward. Her search was brisk
and final. When she'd cleaned her fish completely,
she clutched the guts. "I'll keep it for my risk
in springing you," she said. "Your roll, I mean,
as well as all the rest." She cached it featly

while daring him with glares to intervene.
"It's coming to you," Conner gulped. "And thanks."

But as he spoke, she darted from the scene,
his stare her trailer. "Off she trips, or clanks,"
the outlaw said, "her bosom silver plated.
I must remember where the damsel banks,
in case— But that's the future. Let's inspect
the hostel's cellaret, as stipulated;

or I will. Find your field piece and collect
the lead to render 'stiffs' the proper noun
for catchpoles." Working meanwhile to effect
an alibi which wouldn't let him down,
Jack publicized his presence to the clients
of that saloon, a distance from the town,
whence Red and Ringo earlier had bounced
the horses holding Bacchus in defiance.

No crier of the news had yet announced
in this shebang the wager made by Rose,
so, witless of her wrath and how she'd pounced
upon a chance to ram it up his nose,
he happily was oiling up his plumbing.
Attracting notice by a tipsy pose,
he treated three to drinks and stressed the worth
of each's bawdy anecdotes by summing

the points aloud; and so obtained a berth
in each's mind that would endure intact,
he felt. But, sheering off from phallic mirth,
he left to press toward jointure with the fact
of human coupling—three-dimension vital
instead of comic shadows of the act.
Yet just before he reached the rendez-vous,
a lasso length away from lust's requital,

he dallied at the jail to turn the screw
on Conner's nerves. "He's so," Jack grinned, "afraid,
his shakes will goose an earthquake at my 'boo!'
and jounce the bed to help me, getting laid.

And waiting more will give the doll the jitters
for fear the Clam Express will load and fade;
if scared of Peter, she will jump for Jack,
and cold and heat will mix like gin and bitters

to make her fun to stretch upon the sack.
Besides, there's always liquor in the jug,
and one more snort will help to brace my back
so I won't disappoint the lady bug
before she flies for home and codfish chowder."
But while he hitched his horse, an oily plug
was worked by Conner's borrowed cleaning rod,
to purge his gun of clogging, frittered powder.

"We've whiskey, Johnnie?" Ringo gave a nod
that told his satisfaction. "Both the kinds,
including, Red, the wrath and wraith of God,"
he answered then. "The lesser of my finds
is dragon spew, unless I'm far mistaken:
Jove's bottled levin, rending as it blinds.
The other, though, is Nibelungen gold,
or like the kiss valkyries use to waken

the warrior dead: good rye, my lad, and old
when Pharoahs herded sphinxes up the coast
and painted Tyre cerise." His eyes turned cold,
responsive to a knocking. "Here's a ghost
that haunts hick jails of nights to win his quittance."
He stole, with Red behind him, to a post
beside the knob, wry-smiling at the note
of eagerness in calling for admittance.

"Collapse him with his yell yet in his throat,"
the outlaw coached in whispers. "Crack his skull
before he sees to flinch." "You whiskey-boat,"
cried Morco, born to sea terms, "move your hull
and open up this hatch for Texas waddies.
I want a peg, if you ain't made a cull

of every flask you've hijacked from the boys
we've conked tonight." "There's plenty for some toddies;

quit beefing," Ringo growled above the noise
of fumbling with the lock. Content, if grim,
Red held his gun aloft in equipoise
and harked the tones which once had promised him
a gallows rigadoon. He froze, till, blinking,
the marshal strutted in. He flipped the brim
of Happy Jack's sombrero, laying bare
his pistol barrel's target. "Sinking, sinking

and sunk; but don't," said Johnnie "leave him there
unanchored. Truss him when you've watched me pick
the trash of pocketbook which won't impair
his honored name." "I wish it was a brick,"
Red snickered, as he rammed a footwear muzzle
in Morco's mouth. "Confinement makes me sick;
an old affliction," Ringo said. "Come on!"
They passed the door. "I'll rig the bulls a puzzle,"

said Red. He shot the bolt and used his brawn
to send the big key whizzing through the dark,
then blackening from rubbing close to dawn.
"Who's in; who's out?" he asked, a muted bark
of glad defiance, as he stood attested
a man of will again, his temper stark
for staying free. Yet now there was no sound
or gleam of light nearby, for Ellsworth rested;

and even Nauchville was no longer crowned
with glare but seemed a cooling coal that glowed
his side the setting moon. But Conner found,
once having reaped what red-light brilliance sowed,
the silent darkness high in his affections.
"God bless the still from which this soma flowed,"
said Ringo, sighing. "Take Orion's belt,
and then we'll split the breeze in two directions."

Though startled, Conner made the liquor melt.
"I kind of thought we two would string along
as pardners, Johnnie. Hell, you saved my pelt
and well—" "Suppress the burlesque opera song
your granny taught you, or a mad coyote."
The outlaw drank. "The meaning might be strong
if nickel novelists had had the choice.
But Heaven baldly mocks a Don Quixote;

so piety enjoins you to rejoice
that hearts are not of sugar-coated gold,
although—sound boxes only—some must voice
the bedlam mottoes idiot aunts have doled
to custard brains, deluded with the fancy
they hear the Holy Ghost. Drink up! Don't hold
the bottle like a palsied missing link
or shy away from it like some Miss Nancy

with temperance tracts for bowels." Within a wink
of flaring anger, Red recalled the deft
and daring rescue, when he'd eyed the sink
of hemp infinity, no hoping left;
and then this man had come. He swigged the liquor
he also owed to Ringo, through his theft,
and felt the creature stealing from its shell
to boost a chilling heart and move it quicker,

renewing kindliness. "Well, go to hell,"
he told the other, summoning a laugh.
"But still it's not by talk that you can tell
what's under hat. Take you. You stood the gaff
when I was roosting lonely on my coffin,
so you're my friend." He watched the other quaff.
"It doesn't bug me if you've done a hitch
or maybe more, for I don't care how often

you couldn't tell which end of law was which.
I only know tonight I needed luck

when none was likely, and I struck it rich
because I'd somehow had the sense to chuck
a spree with solid wool. Ride your direction,
and I'll fork mine; but don't forget, my buck,
you've found a throat to side you any day
you catch another thirst." "By my election

I never," Ringo snarled, "hear burros bray
or drink twice with a fool. I don't have thirst,
for that means wishing something which will stay
the appetite when found. You're witless, first,
to think negation has the power of craving;
and priggish, next, for deeming that I nursed
the will to aid you. I'm against John Law,
and when I break his guard, he gets a shaving;

but spare me any further ass's jaw
about the phantom boat, good fellowship.
If you must grab for nothings, try a straw—
or hereabouts a steer or bison chip,
as commoner, is nearer to the letter
of something apt for silliness to grip
while sinking in a cesspool unpoliced
by reason or theistical abettor

of candy ethics." Ringo's rage increased
until his tone had waxed a furious rasp.
"You said, before your flux of nonsense ceased,
you liked me. Choose a fer-de-lance or asp
as targets for your mawkish, calf-souled doting;
or condor, rank with carrion in its grasp,
not me. Why, I would sell you for a dime
to buy the grease to give my boots a coating

or murder you for practice any time
or— Give me that!" He snatched and corked the quart
and spun away, a moving blur, to chime
with blackness. "Well, it's time to cut it short,

at that," said Conner, sagging shoulders shrugging,
"before the jailer or the scarface sport
spits out a sock and yelps I've done a bunk."
Emerging from the entry he'd been hugging,

he tried for stealth but clumped instead of slunk
and lurched, asway from weariness and booze,
along a lane he felt must meet the trunk
of Ellsworth streets. In sloping down, it sunk
through moon-abandoned mist, betokening dawning,
to turn his flight into a shambling cruise,
his jib the touch of buildings, to assist
in limping home to port. He smiled in yawning,

however. "You won't leave the missing list,
if darkness keeps a hat like this on, pard."
Relaxed, he rubbed his whiskers with his fist
and mused upon a holiday so starred
with craps and passes. "You saw Ellsworth, fellow,
and had the turn near called on hock for card."
He reached to touch a cottage. "Nauchville, too.
I guess you pawed the ground and raised a bellow

and helped yourself to what there was to do,
except see Prairie Rose. You missed her wide,
and that's a fall. But still you sluiced a slough
of drinks and shook the wrinkles from your hide
by do-see-doing Nan. She's kind of stunning,
though Johnnie's right: you could have had inside
her petticoat and not the calaboose
with any luck; and yours was mighty thin
to let a pack of marshals come agunning

an inch before you'd cinched her for a win.
But never mind the lost. You had a night
and came away with all your hair and skin;
and Johnnie, though he sours some when tight,

is aces in your deck—and, partly potted,
there never was a fellow more all right.
So I'll for—" Here his guiding fingers felt
a door which failed to bear the weight allotted.

He gasped and staggered as it seemed to melt
and suck him into murk. He nearly crashed,
but as he floundered, some one gripped his belt,
and next he found a welcome body mashed
against his own. "Be quiet, now, and hurry,"
Melinda urged. Then as he gulped, abashed,
she said, "You're awfully late, so please be quick;
you see I'm ready." Rattled by her flurry,

he tried for words but found his tongue too thick
to but repeat, "You're ready?" "Promptly now,
so doff what you find needful in a flick.
I'll guide you to the cot." "But holy cow!"
he husked. "You couldn't know—" "Dispense with
    teasing,"
she snapped. "If I'm untaught, instruct me how,
before I miss my train. Just don't be rough,
and I'm your woman, if you find me pleasing.

But not to fool with; there's not time enough
and— Now will you get busy?" With a shrug
she slipped the robe which left her in the buff
and pressed anew against him, firm and snug,
to put an end to need of more persuasion.
He wrapped her in a bruin's wrestling hug,
amazed that flesh could feel so fresh and sweet,
and felt his manhood rise to the occasion

as with a whoop he snatched her off her feet.

10

A Glimpse of Prairie Rose

It was not either dark nor blossomed dawn
when Prairie Rose, enfolded in the cloak
which was her only sheathing, stood in pawn
to her engagement by The Charter Oak,
the knock-me-down shebang, no longer painted
which marked an end of Main Street. When she spoke,
no auditor received the throbbing croon
of syllables, by dire intent as tainted

as any ever voiced in the saloon;
they welled like acid, fizzing out to scorch.
"I'd rather sleep with puke in a gobboon
than him again. He's romped upon her porch
enough to wear it out; but he'll be shagging
about this time, to bring his fizzled torch
to me, as full of lies as boils of pus,
and swaggering to prove his back ain't sagging.

Well, he won't even get my fud to buss,
though first I'll act as though I thought he was
G. Washington, the cherry chopper, plus.
I'll let him gas as long as he can buzz

before I hint I smell a wood-pile nigger,
a bastard one, and then see how he does
to try to show that polecat isn't skunk.
He'll sweat then, swapping giant lies for bigger:

he stood me up to sit beside the bunk
of one of Quantrill's dying apes, afire
with fever-blab about a boodle trunk
my lovey-dove was hoping to acquire.
Oh, he'll be rich, and I'll allow him ticket
to cake walk to the middle of the wire
before I knock the props from under. 'Hon,'
I'll ask him, quiet, 'how'd she like the picket

you staked her with?' " In promise of the sun
the east horizon flushed a dusty pink,
so Prairie Rose took thought to check a gun
and its envenomed mate. "I hope no gink
with tender ears will get afraid he's dreaming
and wriggles close enough for me to think
he aims to back his peepers with a feel.
I'll give the jughead's lug a bullet reaming

that ought to sell the show as strictly real."
She felt a hammer with a twitching thumb
and sniggered as she saw some figures steal
behind a car. "I hope that yancing bum
will see the house I draw. He'll blow his boiler;
and so will I unless the sun'll come.
It needs another stoker, that's a cinch,
or else some better service from the oiler;

it sure is slowing up." But while the pinch
of deadline waiting wore on Prairie Rose,
Red found that light was spreading fast, to clinch
the certainty of day. "Retain your pose,"
Melinda said, "of greeting dawn. I'll hustle,
so in a minute I'll be in my clothes,

and then we'll halve my earned but borrowed cash."
Complying, Conner hardly heard the rustle

of cloth aslide on flesh. "I ought to dash
before the town's awake," he thought, aghast
to see a whiteness wedge a widening gash
in skies that had been grey. Yet what had passed
between him and this hot, impetuous stranger
demanded courtesy; so he stood fast
and brooded, next, on fortune's Christmas gift,
bestowed on him, an unexpecting ranger

of urban darkness. "Gosh! it pays to drift
around a city, pard," he mused. "I've learned
that much at least in Ellsworth." "Help me lift
the mattress," said his hostess. As he turned,
the strengthened light vouchsafed the silhouetting
of thews she unexpectedly discerned
and didn't know. "Where's Happy Jack?" she shrieked.
"I never met the gent," he told her, netting

a strangled gasp. "He can't have gone!" she squeaked.
"Why only now— I mean I saw him here."
"No, ma'am," said Red. "I swear nobody sneaked
to spy on me and you." "Let's get it clear,"
she whispered. "You're the person I've been treating
so—" "Yes, and thank you kindly." Stepping near,
she conned his features silently. "My God,
I think you mean it! Would you mind repeating

the newsy item I find also odd:
you haven't seen a handsome scarfaced lout?"
"I heard," said Red, "that one was heaved in quod
for acting up, and so he won't be out
for hours yet." In hope but disbelieving,
she breathed, "But he's a marshal!" "Turn about
is fair, they say." He coughed. "I'm sorry, ma'am,
if—" "Crocodiles and I will do the grieving,"

she said. "Now lend a hand." In haste to cram
the plunder Morco once had thought to split
within her carpet bag, she helped him slam
the bedding back and grabbed the bucksin kit
while Conner, mildly flabbergasted, hovered.
New England common sense had seized the bit,
and hers had weighed embarrassment and swag,
to find the balance favored her. She covered

the springs whence wealth had hung and closed her bag
and coolly met the stare of circumstance.
Her fellow thief had gone to prison stag
yet not neglecting her deliverance,
for which she'd paid, as promised, with the error
that Morco's lecherous duebill had, by chance,
been cashed by some one else. Well, she could blot
those debits from the books of moral terror,

for Boston wouldn't know. "Now I'll allot,"
she pointed, sensing Red was hers to use,
"the heavy one to you, sir." From her cot
she caught the satchel which she mustn't lose
and hastened into light. Not till he'd followed
where curiosity could now peruse
the features gloom had blanked was each alive
to strange identity. He gulped and swallowed,

remembering the spittle she'd let drive
to douse his friendly feathers in the shop;
and she, abashed at last, could not contrive
to stem the semaphore that told it. "Chop
the service short." She glared while speaking, waiting
for him to don a smirking grin and drop
a load she must abandon; but he bowed
and gravely met her agony of hating.

"I'll tote your luggage, ma'am, if I'm allowed.
What really counts is how a meeting ends,

not how it starts. I knew that I'd be proud
when first I saw you, if we could be friends;
and now we are." "Beyond all refutation
I've made you more than generous amends,"
she said, when sure his earnest wasn't joke.
"But now let's hasten—*friend*—and reach the station."

Some minutes later Boston Joe awoke
by reason of an engine which aroused
an echo with each huff and puff of smoke
erupting from its stack. He stretched and drowsed,
contented with the thought his debt to Heaven
would not that morning see him stiffly housed
beneath the steeple of the tin brick church,
killing the trading day of one in seven:

he smiled and slept. The engine gave a lurch,
retrieved the slack and bore away his niece,
descrying with a final, scornful search
the hated town from which she'd won release—
the hated plains and hated cars for cattle
the hated riders brought. Although at peace
with life, she shook her head and grimaced then
as, like in stance to scouts approaching battle,

there came to view some crouching, peering men
and then some more: a crowd of them somehow
alert so late, or else so early, when
the night had surely skinked them all. Yet now
they all seemed sparrow-lively, meeting morning
with quaint maneuvers she could not endow
with any purpose known to her. "The West!"
She made a face to underscore the scorning

engendered by a region at the crest
of rugged youth. "Perhaps they've found a steer
they haven't yet tattooed." She sighed and pressed
her head against the cushion. But if fear

had dropped from her, it rode her recent lover,
dismayed to see a host intent to peer
along a street he'd hoped to course alone.
He swerved to parallel it, seeking cover

behind the dowdy buildings, in the zone
of privies, carriage sheds and cord wood racked
for seasoning. Fearful yet of some one prone
to cry the chase at word that he had cracked
his penitential safe, he found the stable
where he had left the pinto which had packed
expectancy to town. But there the fruit
of folly, like the rubric of a fable,

upreared to mock his conduct with the hoot
that Nan had fleeced him cleanly in the course
of lightening the jailer of his loot.
And so he couldn't ransom out his horse—
a fact put out of thinking by his flutter
but must foment another risk perforce,
when smooth escape had seemed to be in sight.
As furtive as the rats he sent ascutter,

he tiptoed in the stable. Wrong or right,
he had no future then without a mount,
and he had learned when bursting bonds that night
that raw necessity could be the fount
of savage competence. So while advancing,
he drew the means of settling his account,
his forty-five, prepared to more than bark.
But, thinking Rose's actions more entrancing,

the hostler wasn't present to remark
Red's gun or movements, as with practiced hand
he swung his saddle in the semi-dark
and cinched it forward of the Mabry brand,
then whisper-loved the horse to still its stamping
when walking forth. "It's snoggering but grand;

I wonder where he's sawing wood?" said Red,
while loping rearward, past some ponies champing

the gleanings of corrals. He turned his head
and saw, above the ground, the molten sun
upsurge, releasing rays which swiftly spread,
enveloping the town. "We ain't yet won,"
he chatted to his steed. "We'll find an alley
and scout the street before we cut and run.
The mob may still be there, so take it slow;
but if they've gone to breakfast, don't you dally,

for we have toured this Jayhawk burg, you know.
We didn't come to fight these Kickapoos,
but since we had to, what we dished was woe:
we lifted hair and counted plenty coups,
while them, they ain't got ant-hill grounds for crowing.
They never scratched our hide and so could use
another shot at us. Oh, we ain't scared
but tired of whipping townies, so we're blowing

before we have to hurt some more that's dared
to paint for war with us. Not only game,
we're merciful; and so the rest is spared—
if we can dodge 'em." Shortly then he came
to where an alley shouldered shacks asunder
that fronted Main and eased his aching frame
with caution to the horseshoe harrowed earth.
He peered around a building at a wonder

which made him doubt his eyes, yet prize their worth
that they had skill to compass such a sight:
a treeless dryad, clothes her other dearth,
advancing like a lantern in the night,
the one thing to be seen. Her comet tresses
defined horizon shoulders with their light,
a strand excepted. Seeking ports more dear,
it dangled, indolent in the caresses

it gave the pole star of one hemisphere.
The rumor he'd ignored while in duress
returned to tell his gaze that in its weir
was revery confirmed, in ampleness;
desire in motion, manifest unbidden,
to prove imagination's might was less
than stark reality's. Near walked the grace
he'd come to worship from afar, unhidden,

a keepsake miracle of form and face.
"It's Prairie Rose!" he blurted, in a voice
which carried clearly with its vibrant bass
to Rose herself. Though Happy Jack, for choice,
would then have been her target, here, offending,
was some one ire could punish and rejoice.
She'd warned the town to be discreet, at least,
and not to haunt the footlights while attending

her lone, undress parade; and there had ceased
her obligation in preserving fools.
She saw in gaping Conner but a beast
whom lust had made adenoidal; venting drools
and bold as mating drakes, subjoining staring
to calling her by name. As she'd the tools
for scotching impudence, she moved to wing
come-uppance through his hat and one ear, flaring

enough for her to drill it for a ring.
She cocked her guns but just as promptly stepped
upon a lurking splinter, primed to sting
from board walk ambush. Triggered hammers leapt
to blast the bullets through the barrels' rifling;
but wincing rendered mastery inept,
and neither ball was true when on the loose.
For one, divergent through the splinter's trifling,

beseemed the chaser of a feral goose
in flight above the crown of Conner's hat;

the other skimmed his jerking neck, to sluice
the crease it made with blood. Enraged at that,
as representing both intention thwarted
and vaunted skill defeated by a slat
when least she could abide to be withstood,
she cocked again—to find that she was shorted

of anything to rend but dirt and wood;
yet heard the hoofs respond as Red used spurs
to race away from furious womanhood,
and leave by any other way than hers
whose path he'd come to cross in the beginning.
Past dumps and clumps of ripening cockle burrs,
he laid his road along a tortuous route
until at last, the line of buildings thinning,

he angled toward the trace again, to boot
the paint, free footing, toward the Smoky Hill.
There Brill awaited, saturninely mute
till Conner joined him. "Well, you met the bill
with just a quarter of a jiffy over
to prove you done it easy. Had your fill
of cities, so that maybe for a change
you'd like to work a spell as dogie drover?"

"I might," said Conner, careful to arrange
the neckerchief again which hid his wound.
"You look like a disease that's got the mange,"
he greeted next the stocky hand who mooned,
in drowsy aftertaste of dissipation,
beside the foreman. "Got my fiddle tuned,"
the other said contentedly. "Did you?"
His mouth a prune, Red signified negation.

"I might have had a drink, or maybe two,
but cutting didoes ain't my style in town.
I came to see the sights and saw a few
but ducked the cribs I bet you didn't, Crowne;

so I could stand trick now." But while he boasted
to cover up, his force was ebbing. Down
the strength of mind and body sank until
he reached the pale of consciousness and coasted,

a mil away from sleep, by drive of will.

II

The Trail Once More

Some faecal fuel, pallidly aglow,
was heaped beneath the chuckling coffee pot
a chore boy settled with a careless throw
of tepid, muddy water. Near the spot
the outdoor kitchen occupied, a fetid,
bedraggled spring leaked water down a slot
between the willows—dusty, stripped by cows
and dwarf at best—whose wretchedness abetted

a scene that Dante might have picked to house
a man he owed revenge. It held more dung
than brush, or grass for steer or mount to browse,
and, climbing fast, the sun of summer flung
its beams to paint the cheerless panorama
in microscope detail. Unmoved among
the optic horrors, though, of Pawnee Spring,
the Major watched a bit of comic drama

with dry amusement. "If a horse will bring
the last man in, I'd swear it saddle-broke."
He saw the fellow start to fall and cling
with lolling head; then, smiling, rolled the smoke

he dragged upon until his nearing riders—
an able man, a used one and a thing
they'd brought along—reported. "Howdy, Seth."
The foreman winked and glanced at buzzard gliders

on watch above the spring. "He's still got breath
enough to groan and play he's still alive,
but them there birds ain't conned, for they know death
on horseback any time. We met at five,
and he was warmish then; but he's been cooling,
so just his ghost'll finish up our drive
to feed the Shoshones." Jim hit the earth
while Red forlornly listened to his fooling,

so far below all aptitude for mirth
he didn't know why Brill and Mabry laughed.
He knew two things alone had any worth,
and these were food and sleep, if he'd the craft
to reach the ground. He saved himself from falling
by bracing rocky legs and with a daft
and vacant look he staggered toward the fire.
The breakfast beans which he had found appalling

the day before entrammeled his desire
so strongly that he snatched the teeming plate
from proffering hand. "A weasel paid good hire
to raid the inmates of a chicken crate
might work as fast, but Red would get my money,"
the rancher said. "I don't suppose he ate
unless he chewed the bottles of his booze,"
the foreman shrugged. "And here's a thing that's funny:

there's blood on his bandana. What's the news?
There's some, for you're in camp with just the kid."
"A wheel on cookie's wagon made us lose
repairing time, so Tom affixed the lid
to breakfast beans, in case you hadn't eaten—
which one of you had not, I'd guess—and slid

up trail with me to meet you, as agreed."
The Major turned to Red. "Your shirt's too beaten

to be the new one, surely, that you fee'd
a merchant for in town?" In part restored
by food and coffee, Conner slackened speed.
"A fellow there," he mumbled, "can't afford
a shirt, as living takes your every nickel."
"I'll bet it did," said Brill. "You tanked and whored
and never saw a shop. And how about
the golden dame you went to town to tickle

your peekers with, and sun danced with the shout
you couldn't live unless you watched her kick?
You missed her, too, I'd bet you." "You'd be out."
Red gave his spoon a final, thorough lick
and tossed it on the battered metal platter.
"I saw a lot of her." "The Good Book, quick!"
the foreman cried, "to see if he will swear."
He spat and drenched a lizard with the splatter

of ambered nicotine. "And would you care
to stretch your conscience clear to Idaho
and say she noticed you or flies was there?"
"I'll Bible it, as long as it was so;
she dealt me such a personal attention
I couldn't take no more and had to go."
He turned to Mabry. "Now I'm primed to fight
my weight in work, but since I heard you mention

the herd ain't here, I'll soldier with a mite
of shut-eye." "Day's when night hawks always nap;
enjoy yourself?" The rancher's tone was light,
but where the neckerchief was snugged to cap
the trifling flow of gore from Rose's bullet,
he marked the blood which caked this dusty wrap.
"Why yes, sir, thanks. I minded manners fine
and found myself as welcome as a pullet

in Roosterland." Red hitched his belt in sign
of casualness. "The only thing went wrong
was this: I had to sneak that paint of mine
from some corral. I'd gone on spending strong,
you see, and outright couldn't pay the stable—
an end I'll square the next time I'm along."
They watched him drag his saddle from his mount
and stumble with it, bent legged, barely able,

to where the scrawny willows were the fount
of shadow pools. In one of these he fell,
paralysis. "I guess I'll take the count,"
said Crowne. Then, worn from yielding to the spell
of wagering on pasteboard pips and faces,
the foreman tossed the sponge. "Just give a yell,
if you can use me, Seth." For hours then
the rancher paced or sat, to brood on places

he'd never seen, where badlands, flood, Cheyenne—
or springs in name that, found, could only parch—
perhaps were minting obstacles for men
with double-trouble cattle, on a march
to dwarf the great Ten Thousand's; only trusting
to skill and fortitude to take the starch
from hazards, Thule-distant and unknown.
But finally he paused to note a dusting

not born of wind. "How come you're here alone?"
the cause soon asked him. Coffee cup in hand,
he added to the Major in a tone
that spoke of ancient friendship, "Ain't your brand
on any critter live-awake?" "I've others,"
said Mabry, as he shifted stance and scanned
the south. "They make and eat the cloud of dust
that's moving north to cheer our redskin brothers

who live—though this I've had to take on trust—
in Idaho. You heading now for home,

old timer?" "Yep, it's Rio Grande or bust."
Leander Crawford doffed his hat to comb
his salt and pepper hair with mighty fingers.
"I sent my crew ahead, unfree to roam.
Some tinhorns sucked me in a poker game,
and I was two days pulling out their stingers.

But I was glad it broke so, all the same;
the town was hot last night." "What happened, Lee?"
the Major asked. "Well, Johnnie Ringo came
to Ellsworth." Crawford paused to sip. "And he
and some long red top took the camp to pieces.
They drove both sides of Main Street up a tree
on horses stole in sunlight—cool as that."
"A long red head, you say?" Enquiring creases

striated tan below the Major's hat.
"It's how the word went, Seth, but anyhow
when found with hurdy girls, they turned a rat
from officer to low grade maggot chow."
Leander chuckled here. "Well, you know Ringo;
he gopher-holed, but like a snorting cow
which guards a dogie that you try to burn,
he stuck around to help long Red, by Jingo!"

"To help him how?" Seth asked. "I've yet to learn
the red top needed succor." "Oh, I meant
to say they'd jugged him, but he grabbed his turn,"
said Crawford. "After Ringo came, they bent
a shooter over Morco—he's a marshal,
in case you didn't know. And then they went
and locked *him* up, and snook the key away.
And that ain't all Red done, for he was partial

to this here girl who robbed the store. They say—"
The Major checked him with a hand. "*What* store?"
"One Boston Joe's. His niece decamped today
and cleaned him like I cleaned them tinhorns. Moore,

the railroad agent, saw a tie-sized ranny
who smashed the chicken's baggage just before
her train eloped. He didn't see him clear,
but tootsie didn't cuddle with her granny

last night," said Crawford. "Sifting out her gear,
they panned the proof." "How's that?" "Red hair was
　　found
embroidering her pillow." "Did you hear,"
the Major queried, studying the ground,
"the red head helped the lady with her looting?"
"He couldn't have, for he was in the pound,"
the other pointed out, "till nearly day,
according to the jailer. Some owl hooting

strong box wrangler led the lock astray—
the jill could not have jobbed the safe alone—
then fiftied, say, and cut for hideaway.
Well, she blew, too, of course, but hadn't blown—
still waiting for the train, you see, and idle—
when out of hock, with some oats not yet sown,
the red top comes—I love that kind of cat—
and finds the filly answers to the bridle,

then helps her on the train and tips his hat
and gallops off for Texas on a horse
that's maybe his. I didn't see all that,
and neither did nobody else, of course;
but that's the way that Ellsworth's got it figgered."
"I see," the Major said, "and I'll endorse
the findings, Lee. Did other odd events
enliven town?" "Yes, one." Leander sniggered.

"That Prairie Rose was bantered by some gents
to take a *pasear* naked, which she done,
and all the boys was peeking through the fence
to case her. That I know, for I was one;

though none of us was beauty-loving nearer,
for in each fist she held a bullet gun,
the others said. I didn't watch her fists.
Well, some rhinoceros had to see her clearer

than us that was polite, so he insists
on scootching close to her as us to Jim;
and now he's lucky that he still exists.
A guy that saw her sling the slugs at him—
I couldn't see the play from where I scouted—
reported that she give his cream a skim,
for snoopy hiked his hand and felt his neck.
But he had peeped his fill and right-abouted

and hopped upon his bronc and, once on deck,
he kicked the irons nearly to the hilt
and didn't admirate another speck
of Rose's petals." "Bullets tend to wilt,"
the Major said, "the stand of adoration.
You want that cup of coffee there rebuilt?"
"I pass," said Lee. "I've got to catch my crew,
at least what's left of it from celebration,

and that'll take from here to dusk to do,
unless I find 'em foundered on the trail
with liquor flasks for headstones. Watch the Sioux.
You'd look like hell without some hair to nail
your scalp in place." Alone a moment later,
the Major flushed a flock of fledgling quail
while sauntering to stand above a youth
in seeming neither man of blood nor satyr

but wedded to the decencies of truth
and trusting as a happy-hearted pup.
The rancher sighed. "Not cut a wisdom tooth
and in the larva stage of growing up,
he rides eight hundred miles to mix with evil
to last a man a life-time. Who'd he tup

that robbed her uncle's store? And how'd he meet
the niece of any sharking, boomer weevil—

no hurdy-girl—while scrambling in retreat
from durance that he'd passed to the police?
Or one of them. Another has a beat
in Boot Hill now and can no longer fleece
the lads who compensate for harsh denial
and lonely work by smoking whiskey peace
with all the hungers. Conner got away
without indictment binding him to trial;

and those that gun for steam released to play
collide with chance; and chance allows for loss.
I'll guard my own, as partisan as they,
and keep him secret till we push across
the Smoky Hill and into chartless regions
where there are neither laws, nor sprees to toss
by kicking colts. But Johnnie Ringo—Christ!
A *loup garou,* and worst of all the legions

of killer thieves, as viciousness is spliced
to cultivation, spawning a despair
I'd hate to neighbor; but the rabid feist
was chosen by my pup to make a pair
for fun and gun! When Gabriel blows his trumpet,
I hope to learn the story, so to square
a circle which would never have been drawn
if Red had not had pipe dreams of a strumpet

he found at length with but revolvers on
and nearly lost all games. But here he's back
with large exchanges for the hours gone,
which all don't get, and doesn't look more black
of soul than when he left. True innocences
are proof perhaps." The Major found his sack
of crumb tobacco, rolled a cigarette
and paced away. Meanwhile the imminences

of peril or of evil didn't fret
the mind of Conner. Now and then he smiled
as in his jumbled consciousness he met
redactions of his recent exploits, filed
within his mental stock room helter skelter;
a part of him but loose and running wild
in dream's Walpurgis Night. But once he frowned,
as some intruding pressure pierced the welter

of pleasant visions playing hare and hound,
to sugar sleep. An irritating hump
was somewhere his disturber till he found,
by fumbling, he was prone upon a bump
composed of something folded in his pocket,
a shirtfront one. He growled and threw the lump
away from him and was again in sleep—
unmindful of the dust which thronged, to rocket

and dash his way, a whirling, dodging heap
of particles a twisting wind had wrought
and rushed along. It missed him in its sweep
but not the thing discarded, which it caught
and whipped away, and as it whipped, unfolded.
A scrap of paper (battered, torn, but fraught
with images so framed that they might stir
to action further young retrievers, molded

to find in loveliness a lure and spur),
it first met straining mules whose sweat glands leaked
while plodding through a dust as soft as fur
and thick as feather beds. A broken beaked
and lone-eyed cook, his buckskins crudely mended,
rocked grimly with the vehicle which creaked
abaft them, bound for Major Mabry's camp.
Behind a league, the giant cattle wended

their aimless way or took a stand to champ
the foliage of a stunted prairie shrub,

or showed by lowered, sweeping horns and stamp
of pawing foot resentment at the rub
their keepers gave in forcing forward motion.
Unhurriedly and gentle with the club
they wielded—that of bootstrap human will
to make of goals a continent in the ocean

of time and space—the riders used their skill
with seasoned ease. The spit of indolence,
it hid the hardihood required to drill
a thousand feral beasts, devoid of sense
but rife with fitful humors. Their indenture
to industry, all alien to their bents
of wildness, was in keeping with the trail:
a Marco Polo bridge which spanned adventure

for men whose sober load was goods for sale.

THE SACK
OF CALABASAS

I

Big Game Up Wind

With only buzzards watching as he went
a man jogged up along the Santa Cruz,
a stream whose winter flow had long been spent;
southward he rode, unarmed except with news—
two stringy yards of man hunched up astraddle
a donkey lost beneath an army saddle,
threading a trail which smoldered like a fuse

in winding past the Arizona hills,
as barren as sheet iron in the heat
they caught and threw, or crossing braided rills
atwist amidst the cactus and mesquite;
no water troughs, but each a dusty furrow
to mock the thirsting of the weary burro
and of the one for whom it made a seat.

He was that Western miracle, a man
with neither kindred, ties, nor name, nor past;
each time he moved a different life began
which kept no consulate within the last.
Meanwhiles, as now, he was a formless power,
waiting until the force of his next hour
should cram him in a mold to be recast.

He went because he had no need to stay:
as self-sufficient as a rolling rock,
he had the strength of nothing to betray,
nothing invested, nothing put in hock
to fortune by ambition or devotion;
he only recognized that life was motion,
desired or forced. Behind him lay a stock

of fifty secret, disregarded years;
ahead lay rawness counting on renown
which drew him as a spring entices steers
that smell it from the hills and trace it down.
It took new worlds to greet new life and nourish
its sudden growth and give it space to flourish,
like this, the Border's most ingenious town.

Bonanza camps were often known to bloom
like cactus blossoms, blowing over night,
but Calabasas had the goofiest boom
the sagebrush ever saw. Where men alight
to build, some wealth has elsewhere been in season,
but this was tossed together for no reason
except a rumor, bought for truth on sight.

Gold raised up Wickenburg and silver put
Tombstone upon the mesa of Goose Flats;
Bisbee was built by copper under foot—
for men have always swarmed like swamp-hole gnats
at twilight to the site of buried metal,
afire to scoop free treasure out and settle
and throw up walls in which to hang their hats—

but Calabasas, Spanish long ago,
revived for someone guessing out of turn
about the railroad's route to Mexico;
he talked, and footloose rogues rejoiced to learn
this greasewood patch would be a national sentry,
a shipping point, a mart, a port of entry,
where men of parts need scarcely strive to earn.

And so the frontier gave the place its best:
the boom-town planets, faded by this moon,
paid tribute in the coinage of the West
by losing shifty citizens, till soon
the classic cast of gunmen, whores and gamblers,
land speculators, thieves and loafing ramblers
were gathered in the Golden Fleece Saloon,

whose elegance was covered by a tent;
the Grand Hotel was canvas patched with duck.
The cash was yet to come which would be spent
by tycoons there to parlay skill and luck
and for a side dish order up a city
whose denizens could eye New York with pity.
So much was sure, but destiny was stuck

till rail officials should at length concede
that what they must do, they could not avoid:
the line would use the valley—thus to lead
the tracks through Calabasas. Though annoyed
by stalling due to nitwit indecision,
the townsmen did not let it cloud their vision
of better days, when they would be employed

in palming off domains of real estate
and shaking greenhorns down with joyous ease
for everything they used or wore or ate,
or fleecing them with cards, the badger squeeze,
and many another tried and ancient swindle,
some used to make new settlers' purses dwindle
since Jamestown planters watched beneath the trees

for suckers sailing from the mother isle.
So as the rails rammed nearer, spike by spike
en route from Benson, southwest mile by mile,
they schemed and skinned each other. Or belike
they talked of how Tubac would be deflated
and how Nogales would be populated
by ghosts alone when facts approved their strike.

Or else they took impatience out in death
and dropped on Railroad Street amidst the gore
which turned its dust to mud, or kept their breath
to brag and challenge others. For the roar
of shooting irons, fired in reckless fury,
was all their warrant, sheriff, judge or jury;
they killed for cards, for insults, for a whore;

but most of all to hold their place among
a pack where weakness never met with ruth.
Theirs was a city of the knowing young
where violence was the arbiter of truth;
yet while engaged in rank, wolf-hearted scheming
they could not keep from softer styles of dreaming,
and that, too, saddle-galled their angry youth.

This was the prey—this hot and ready stag,
this strutting cock whose spurs were set for blood,
this bull whose charge would never wait the rag,
this rearing stallion, savagely in stud—
this was the game the riding man had scented
and now was tracking to its torrid, tented
lair amidst the swirling dust and scud

of wheeling tumbleweeds. He had no plan;
he did not know how he'd confront his prey
or what that prey would find in him, a man
whose only passion was to have his way,
because he had the force of wit and knowledge
of things beyond the scope of church or college,
which he must use until his mortal clay

was part and parcel of that other earth
whose purpose is less wayward and more sure,
where questing restlessness must find a berth
and make its peace with stillness and endure.
But now, emerging from a mesquite thicket,
he first saw horses, hobbled or at picket,
and then the tents which meant he'd struck his lure.

2

Death on Railroad Street

The year was eighteen hundred eighty-two,
the month July, the hour was first-drink time
on Sunday morning, and Sedalia Sue
prepared for breakfast with a gin and lime,
while Deuces Wilde and Longhorn Charlie Durben
gnawed quietly at tumblers full of bourbon
on either side of her. Cards, lust and crime

must wait the issue of the crucial strife,
or rather ritual of somber peace,
when drink, the moon, won back the tide of life:
meanwhile their spirits, pending their release,
lurked motionless within or foraged, stalking
some shadow of the past. There was no talking
as, grimly waiting for the ebb to cease,

each leaned upon the Golden Fleece's bar.
The nearest to the door was Deuces Wilde,
remembered by his kin as Hamilcar,
though none could then have seen in him the child
who'd tired of Illinois and chores and schooling
and said, "I'm going West," and wasn't fooling
some twenty years before. His eyes were mild,

but so are fishes', when the fish are dead;
the only difference was that his would blink
the lids whose stubby lashes once were red,
though they had long been bleached a mushroom pink,
the match of the moustache which blurred concession
to what his mouth might yield toward an expression.
He stood beneath his hat and eyed his drink

as if it were a hand he meant to fill
by bottom dealing, angling in his sleeve
or kindred prestidigitative skill;
all men have credos: Deuces' I believe
was luck was for the crooked and the ready
to palm the derringer and hold it steady
and neither ask nor proffer a reprieve.

He wore the gambler's black, but just beyond
a sworl of color was his foil and more.
Sedalia Sue was blonde as brass is blond;
her hair shown like a polished cuspidor.
The purple gown below it was a litter
of precious stones, or near enough to glitter
and advertise a first-line frontier whore,

though she was now the seller, not the sold,
postgraduate in harlotry, a bawd,
a matriarch of tarts, purse-proud and cold,
whose rugged dignity was seldom thawed.
Her smiles cost more, they said who'd tried and counted,
than lesser heifers charged for being mounted;
though few essayed her smiles, for most were awed

by either Sue herself or by her mack:
one Longhorn Charlie, dark as she was fair,
and more convincingly. A muddy black,
his eyes took in all comers with a glare
which spoke of energy leased out to meanness;
the face they glowed in was not wrought of cleanness,
though he was not the one to know or care.

The body which it topped showed wide and thick
beneath the gaily colored, open vest,
yet he could move demoniacally quick,
which he had proved all up and down the West
as rustler, sheriff, robber, pimp and marshal;
but some said—not to him—he wasn't partial
to shooting ready gunmen in the chest

when backs would serve as well. So there they stood,
morosely silent till a woman screamed,
"You fishfed bastard, now I'll fix you good!"
And on the instant did as she had schemed
by firing at her enemy or lover.
No matter which, he fell for blood to cover,
while he stared up and neither saw nor dreamed.

The incident destroyed the moody hush
of first-drink time. The gun-schooled clientele
ducked out the side flaps, jostling in the rush,
or hugged the ground themselves till they were well
assured the frenzied wench was through recruiting
for Boothill's silent witnesses to shooting.
Yet, Deuces, Sue and Longhorn scorned to yell

or dodge or even start. This stuff was old,
and they had seen it often and survived.
Besides, they'd counted five full shots, which told
no more were coming; wherefore they contrived
to gaze with boredom, not unmixed with pleasure
at showing rock-ribbed poise, to prove the measure
of three who'd seen the elephant and thrived.

Deadwood they'd known, Tascosa, Leadville, Dodge,
Fort Griffin Flat and Tombstone and what not:
the roaring chapters of the master lodge
whose high degrees they held. Yet, of the lot,
they swore that Calabasas was the roughest,
its citizens the slickest and the toughest,
who dubbed in what the Devil had forgot;

so in a moment Longhorn shrugged and grinned.
"Call in the buzzards, boys; he's drawing flies.
Who is it?" "Schooner Blaine, fresh out of wind,"
said Deuces. "Oh?" Sue looked her mild surprise.
"The dude who's fixin' up the Gloucester Palace
but ain't yet got his stock? Don't worry, Alice."
This to the murderess, whose widened eyes

showed dawning fear. "He didn't have no friends;
he hadn't bought a round yet for the house."
"He'd ought to do it now, to make amends,"
cried Deuces. "Go ahead and frisk the louse!
He's your corpse, Alice; see he does his duty."
And Alice, brightening, took and used the booty,
then tucked away the balance in her blouse

while all the others cheered her, overjoyed
at sharing in this corpse-is-treating wake.
Then Longhorn slapped the bar, his spirits buoyed.
"We've had our man for breakfast; let's have steak.
You coming, Sue?" "You fellows feed your faces.
I won't swap here," she told him, "for no places
until I get my cut of this whore's take.

You hear me, Alice?" But the girl had turned
to watch two bouncers readying to eject,
forever, Schooner Blaine. "I guess I learned
the son of a bitch," she mumbled, "to respect
a lady— Oh!" And then she started bawling.
"Shut up!" said Longhorn. "Hell, the sky ain't falling
because you plugged a man." But the effect

of tears at death, now passing in review—
as Blaine was leaving, soon to be beyond
all reach of fellowship—was to imbue
the moment with the matter of despond,
and quiet put a crusher on their revel.
But Deuces noticed, as the corpse drew level
with him and Longhorn, that the dead was fond,

or had been, of cigars—a taste they shared—
for two fine, long cheroots were sticking out
of Schooner's waistcoat pocket, unimpaired
by blood or bullets. Like a fly-sucked trout,
the gambler's hand moved, snatched them both, and darted
to place a smoke between the slackly parted
jaws of Blaine, wherein it rolled about

as he was hustled to the tent's rear door;
while Deuces snapped aflame a lucifer
to fire the stogie he had mouthed, before
he called, "Well, thanks, and don't get lost, now, sir.
I didn't think to offer matches, knowing
you'd easy find a light where you are going.
But don't you take my roasting place, or fur

will fly when I drift in." Longhorn guffawed
and, forcing more than he, the others laughed;
now keen to show they were not overawed,
they drove their stalling mirth with studied craft
until it gained momentum and recovered
the ground lost when the wraith of horror hovered
so close they'd felt its presence like a draft.

But Deuces' offhand mockery of the cult
of death and mortal sinning's just rewards
had steadied them again, with the result
they once more knew themselves the ribald lords
of antiworlds which outlawed moral beauty
and recognized apostasy as duty;
for by their will they'd severed all the cords

which bound them to the world of ordered homes,
religion, and the hangdog decencies,
the fool's gold some had mined for once, as gnomes
enslaved to trades or universities,
before they'd found true wisdom on the Border.
So, seeing that their own house was in order,
the gambler and the gunman hit the breeze.

3

The Creation of Abimelech Jones

Along the dusty length of Railroad Street,
symbol of all that Calabasas hoped,
Deuces and Longhorn minced with booted feet
toward Dan's—"The Best Meat Rustlers Ever Roped"—
until their way was blocked by some who'd halted
to watch a traveler, not much exalted
by perching on the animal which moped

down street, a ratty donkey, tired and small.
The man aboard looked glum as he was long,
somehow more helpless, too, for being tall:
a pilgrim born for rougher souls to wrong.
He called no word and got a Western greeting,
a chorus of blank stares to chill the meeting,
daunting the weak or challenging the strong.

The rider seemed the first. When none gave ground
to let him pass, he whoa'd; the mount obeyed.
"Hello," the stranger said, and blinked around,
uncertain certainly, perhaps afraid.
"Is Calabasas far?" he asked then, pitching
his voice so high it cracked, and meanwhile twitching
a long and bony nose on sad parade

beneath the reaches of a floppy hat.
In time a man asked gently, "Far from where?
It's far from 'Frisco or Mount Ararat,
the realm of Prester John or Herald Square,
the Shannon or the Mississippi Valleys;
but not so far from Tubac or Nogales,
and nearer to a jackass. Do you care,

or were you only asking?" For a while
the other seemed to ponder, then his lean
and wrinkled face lit feebly with a smile.
"I think I understand, sir, what you mean;
this place is Calabasas. I am *in* it."
He looked about him, wide eyed, for a minute,
while winks and snickers were exchanged between

the men who watched. But he who waited felt
the surge of life creep through his nerves and veins,
heating his substance till it yearned to melt,
plastic to circumstance. He took no pains
to force the onset of an inspiration
but made himself a blotter for sensation
as he observed the street awaiting trains

and then the townsmen with their edgy air
of having chewed damnation, fruit and pit,
and fattened on it. Yet he grew aware
that some had shaved, had even spruced a bit
in dim response to what was once a habit
of honoring the Sabbath, though a rabbit
could now match mystic faith with any there.

The rider sensed the place then, also those
who poured in it the force to work on him;
he felt the current tugging at his toes
and guessed it deep enough for him to swim.
The time was near, he knew, when he must wallow,
trusting his genius for what next would follow,
but now, still uncommitted on the brim,

he gauged the speed and temperature. At length
he cleared his throat and spoke. "I'm very glad.
The name is Jones." His voice acquired more strength.
"Abimelech." He paused as if to add
those elements, and then he started over.
"The Reverend A. Jones, a humble drover
of straying sheep, though none, I hold, are bad."

And so this western Proteus took the form
which he would use and settled in that shape,
but anything so foreign to the norm
of Calabasas left the rest agape:
a rattlesnake that rode a dromedary,
a Gila monster sipping Tom and Jerry,
a grizzly banking faro for an ape

would not have startled them a half so much
as this that solemnly returned their gaze
and looked paternal for an added touch.
"Aw, nix!" a watcher mumbled from his daze.
"Go 'way! I just ain't seein' it—a parson!"
But neither man, nor ass he had his arse on
would vanish, so one tried a different phrase:

"I met a fellow back in Vinegaroon
who told me how he once saw General Grant
raped by a Flathead squaw in a balloon,
and I believed it all; but this I can't.
A minister— Ah, hell! A goddamn preacher!
A sin-and-liquor-hating Bible teacher
turned loose in whore-and-rye-land with his rant—

it just won't wash!" "It's true; it has to be,"
a third declared. "It's written on his phiz,
and it's a thing, like trainer to a flea,
a man don't claim to be unless he is—
he'd never think of it. There's no use squawking,
for facts don't lose their patents through our balking;
we've got a shepherd, and this flock is his,

so let's see what he wants." "I guess I'll ask,"
a fourth said. "Reverend Jones, what's on your mind?"
"The bearing of the Word is all my task,"
the rider told him, "so if I could find
a tent or shack—I don't expect a steeple—
where I could give the Message to you people,
which I am duty bound to give all blind

and erring souls, my work here will be done.
Is there a place?" But each one shook his head,
till Deuces laughed and answered, "I know one,
if you don't mind saloons." "I do not," said
Abimelech. "A barkeep is my brother,
I humbly own, as much as any other."
"Well," Deuces purred, "a man called Blaine is dead

of cheating on a whore, or some such thing
which he won't do again. He had a bar
he'd not yet opened called the Gloucester King—
no, Gloucester Palace. It's not very far.
Just back down Railroad Street and read the banners,
and when you find the tent, don't stand on manners."
"The Lord," said Jones, "is still my guiding star,

but who will guide me now to a hotel?"
The rest swapped looks before a fellow spoke:
"The Grand should do him." "It should do him well,"
another man agreed. "And if you're broke,"
a third said, "why just tell the Chink your troubles;
he'll bust 'em for you, smooth as poppin' bubbles."
At this some hid their knowledge of a joke

behind a hand, bandanna, or a cough;
but Reverend Jones said, "All men here seem kind."
And, after getting bearings, he was off
to find the Grand Hotel; and there to find
the landlord, Ah Chin Honk, a most unplacid
Oriental, wizened, shrewd, and acid
to all but wealthy patrons. Some assigned

his own wealth to the fact he had the trick
of squeezing coins, not merely till they yelped
but till each eagle yielded forth a chick;
while others claimed a Chinese idol whelped
gold ingots for him while the joss was burning.
True tales or not, his one-track, no-switch yearning
so owned his mind that it could not be helped

if now he marked Jones "enemy—he's poor";
and so he did not bow but sat and shrugged.
"Five dollar cash for bunk; we gots not more
of any rooms." The parson sadly tugged
upon a lip but didn't voice resentment.
"I find that heat infringes on contentment,
don't you?" he asked. And with the words he lugged

a handkerchief in view, as though to mop
the sweat from where his hat had left its mark;
but coins came with the handkerchief to drop
upon the hard-packed floor. And as the dark
is shriveled by a lighting lamp and ceases,
just so did heavy, shiny yellow pieces
erase Ah Chin Honk's gloom. A friendly spark

warmed up his eyes before he rose and bowed.
"I have forgots," he said, "my best of all.
Will you allows me?" "You will be allowed,"
the parson said, and soon was in a stall
with tarpaulin walls, wherein a brazen, burnished
bed stood fast, if hardly level, furnished
with bolster, spread and quilt against the call

for warmth in desert dawns. There was a stand
for washing and the pottery attached:
four pieces. To the glory of the Grand,
the pitcher, bowl and pot and slop jar matched:
beauty in porcelain, brave with princely towers
seen in the distance through an arch of flowers
whose very stems were gold. The parson scratched

a scar beside his nose as he admired
each separate ceramic work of art.
"No more," he said at last, "could be desired.
Have you a cook?" "Damn goods and velly smart,"
the landlord nodded. "Tell this clever minion,"
the parson urged him, "that in my opinion
fried eggs are best; say, four eggs for a start

and then we'll see." Ah Chin Honk saw and sighed,
for Reverend Jones was diligent and ate
as warrior ants do, not to be denied
while food remains. At length he mopped his plate,
however, with a biscuit. "Now I'm able,"
he said, "to make a temple of a stable.
Great ventures must be met with strength as great."

4

Readying for the Pitch

With dignity Abimelech set forth,
slow as to step but quicker with his eye;
the barren hills ran south, the dry stream north,
and in between them, sat on by a sky
which glowed like brandy flame, the boom town squatted
amid the dust which coated it and blotted
all color out. The lanes dispersed awry

through dust to tent, bare camp and wickiup,
or from such residence points they turned and curled
toward Railroad Street, where Lil's, The Gutter Pup,
The One-to-Spare, and Trips-around-the-World,
The Louvre, Beefsteak Dan's, and Dot's-from-Dallas
were all near neighbors of the Gloucester Palace.
Reading the painted bunting there unfurled,

the parson left the street and slowly crossed
the doorless threshold, stopped, and peered around.
The empty bar—where never man had tossed
a snifter off, and never gun had downed
a customer, or gambler proved his slyness—
seemed waiting any claimant to its dryness:
content but not yet sure of what he'd found,

the parson pottered aimlessly about,
gazing at pictures, fixtures and spittoons,
the jars for hard boiled eggs or sauerkraut,
glasses and corkscrews, jiggers, stirring spoons;
but these were messageless, and so he ambled
to tables, custom-built for those who gambled.
He neared the one for craps and read its runes

indifferently before he next perused
the faro table's layout. There he stopped
to fiddle with the dealer's box, bemused
by flaring lips that snarled and fangs that chopped:
traditional, a raging tiger guarded
the thirteen spades whose pips and features larded
the felt expanse. His hands arose, and dropped.

But up the sun climbed, fiercer as it soared,
and Calabasas, yielding to it, drowsed,
except for one pledged servant of the Lord,
intent to see his congregation housed
as suitably as will and work could make it;
if he had thirst, he didn't pause to slake it,
this not withstanding all the dust aroused

by sweeping out the place. He pushed away
the gaming tables, making room for pews,
and sought out Ah Chin Honk anew to say
he needed extra chairs, could even use
the boxes emptied by the trained and artful
chef when cooking beans. There was a cartfull,
and when they were installed, he bent his thews

to beating out the dirty canvas flaps
which walled The Gloucester Palace. Though the sign
that styled it so he'd shredded into scraps
with which to scrub and make the fixtures shine
behind the bar—of which he'd wrought a chancel—
with rags to hide the buxom nudes and cancel
the posters billing whiskey, beer and wine.

And when the legacy of Schooner Blaine
had all been hid or drafted for the church,
the parson, not content to slave in vain,
endured the sun of Railroad Street in search
of souls to save. So girls and macks and matrons,
barkeeps, barflies, the gamblers and their patrons
were startled and amused to see him lurch

within their purlieus, drumming on a pan
and crying, "Sinners saved at half past six
in Blaine's old place, next door to Beefsteak Dan,
the rustlers' friend. Beware the Devil's tricks
and learn instead the orders of the Master
from Brother Abimelech, your loving pastor;
admission free." And with the word he'd fix

some listener with a smile and then move on.
But those who heard him only grinned or laughed,
mocking his godliness when he was gone;
or didn't wait for that and crudely chaffed
him to his face with taunts and counter-drumming.
At first, it was agreed, no one was coming
to hear a man so childish and so daft

that he would challenge sin on its home stand.
But still they talked of him and prized a joke
so different from the Border's common brand;
and finally a notion stirred and woke:
the thing to do was not to dodge the fellow
but follow up the fun and hear him bellow;
then get his goat till he went up in smoke

and lost his pious air, or lost his nerve
and quit the game. The idea spread and took—
not fast at first, then jumped upon with verve
by almost every killer, whore and crook
in town, which meant the cream of Calabasas
would swarm like yellow jackets on molasses
to watch the sucker struggle on the hook.

Sedalia Sue and Longhorn had a spat
about the matter. "Sure, I want to go;
it might be fun," she urged, "to hear him blat.
And trade won't start till dark." "Aw, honey, no!"
he told her. "If the Devil heard you praying,
he'd quit the job he's got and take to playing
an end man in a traveling minstrel show

so he could spread the joke." "Is that a fact?"
she asked. "Why, you dry gulcher, I'm as good
as any slut for which you ever macked;
and if I don't do everything I should,
you ain't the one to say so, when you're livin'
on what my girls are makin' and I'm givin'."
"Giving!" he laughed. "You'd keep it, if you could;

but you need me, like I need you. All right;
this ain't a reason we should have a split:
we'll pick up Deuces when we've had a bite,
then watch the pilgrim throw a holy fit.
If he ain't spry enough, my Smith and Wesson
will give the boob a fancy dancing lesson
to start him going like his pants was lit—

it might be fun at that." And so it chanced
that as the hour appointed marked the clock,
Sue with her escorts trailing grandly pranced
inside the tent, now crowded chockablock,
and made for the front row, then calmly waited
till three seats in the center were vacated
when Longhorn showed his gun and slapped the stock.

So all were there but their evangelist,
whose whereabouts nobody could discern;
though at the outset he was hardly missed,
his congregation was so keen to learn,
by dint of signs and gestures, winks and whistles,
just who had brought along what noisome missiles,
produced in handy sizes from the stern

of hens long since or horses, a la carte,
to name two favorites. But the moment came
which brought impatience for the show to start;
the huntsmen started calling for their game
to break from cover. There were shouts and stamping,
whoops, and the imitated snorts and champing
of mustangs not yet ready to be tame,

so like themselves. But Deuces rose and held
a slim cigar aloft until the din
was hushed a little. "Blast your hides," he yelled;
"You'll scare the vicar clean from out his skin!
This is a church, remember, not a riot—
not yet." They got the point then and were quiet,
trying to lure their holy quarry in.

5

The Gospel of the Pips

Deuces had hardly lighted his cigar
when, straightening, the man of God upreared
from where he had sat hunched behind the bar.
He mounted it, while Calabasas cheered,
then stepped upon a box with "Beans" for label
which humped its back above a faro table
to form his pulpit. From this height he peered

a moment at his chuckling flock, then clapped
his hands as loud and sharply as a shot;
and when all jumped, he raised his arms and snapped,
" 'Keno!' you'll cry and claim the doomsday pot
of good or ill, when death calls out your number
and at the end you wake again from slumber
to take your winnings, liking them or not."

Addressed in their own tongue, his hearers stirred
but quieted and dropped their nether jaws.
So Brother Abimelech was clearly heard
as he went on with but the briefest pause:
"I quote no Bible text to start my sermon,
for rather I let where I am determine
the subjects of my little talks, because

no matter where I am, the spot is God's;
and so all places offer me a text.
A temple or a railway stop—what odds?
He sponsors both, and I am not perplexed
to find His power upon a depot landing;
I read His word wherever I am standing—
a gaming table now. Should I be vexed

at what it tells me? Rather the reverse;
the layout there below is near akin
to all of life, for better or for worse.
The tiger which we buck, my friends, is sin;
the Devil deals, and we must back or copper
on every turn he thumbs from out the hopper;
nor can we welch or quit the game we're in

until our stack is gone." At this the throng
who'd come to heckle found each other's eyes,
nor hurled the ancient eggs they'd brought along
nor laughed nor mimicked Jones; and there were sighs
from five or six whose recent fatal traffic
with faro made his parable too graphic
for hearts to bear without protesting sighs.

"You who are gamblers!" Brother Abimelech
next shot at them; and every one sat straight.
"You each have Bibles, if you know your deck.
So learn to read, before it is too late,
the message of the cards you handle nightly;
then, as you play, you will be guided rightly
and be prepared of soul, in case your fate

should overtake you, as it sometimes does
in games of chance, unsparingly and quick."
He showed them cards and waited for the buzz
of talk to quiet. "This is not a trick;
it is the tale of man and sin and glory,
with pips instead of words to tell the story."
He took a card and, giving it a flick,

he let it fall upon the layout. "There.
I played my trust in God. It is my ace."
He dropped one more. "My deuce. God made a pair
of Eve and Adam in a state of grace.
My trey. There stole a third into the Garden,
creating sin past any earthly pardon.
My four. We have four helpers in the race

for our salvation. Matthew, Luke and Mark
and John, who daily pray for our escape
from Satan's clutch. My five. You ladies, hark:
of some ten virgins of a lovely shape,
though five were wise, yet five were vain and silly,
which means we are not punished willy-nilly
but damned for what we do, and if we ape

the ways of Hell. My six. There are six days
for us to gad and jape and do our worst.
My seven. The Sabbath is our day to gaze
upon the sins in which we are immersed,
then choose a better course." The words came slowly,
spoken in tones as soft as they were holy,
but yet all heard distinctly. For a burst

of smoke no longer stemmed from the cheroot
in Deuces' hand, Sedalia Sue was flushed
and motionless, with no desire to hoot,
and Longhorn merely moved a hand which brushed
a fly away—his gun stayed in its holster,
as harmless as a chicken-feather bolster;
and all the rest were leaning forward, hushed

and wondering, while they watched the falling cards
as though they'd never seen a deck before.
"My eight," the parson said. "You have eight guards
against misdoing, and you need no more:
You have two eyes to tell the right from evil,
two feet to crush the serpent head's upheaval,
two hands to thrust temptation from your door,

two ears to sift from Satan's lies the truth.
My nine. Nine days of falling fast divide
the Enemy from God. My ten. In youth
you heard the Ten Commandments; but abide
by these, and Paradise is your assurance.
My knave. The angel fallen into durance:
the Prince of Hell, the Devil, horns and hide.

My queen. It is the Church, my children dear,
a royal mother, warding you from harm.
My king. He's God's own mightiness, to fear
and love forever—if you take alarm
in time to earn forgiveness from Heaven
and soar aloft with angel wings for leaven.
Yet thirteen cards do not complete the charm

that's spelled out by a deck. My diamonds tell
salvation is a gem above all price,
my clubs say sin is punished down in Hell,
my hearts remind us that in Paradise
the Savior's beats for us, while spades give warning
our mortal selves must slumber night and morning
down in the ground, where worms with blood like ice

and carrion maggots wait. So that's four suits.
They tell us of the seasons we enjoy
while we are here and reap the earthly fruits,
so rich and numerous they never cloy,
which God has blessed us with." Abruptly dashing
the ones he still held down, his tones now crashing,
the parson cried out, "Cards are not a toy!

They number fifty-two to match the weeks:
and each week has a Sunday such as this,
when we can show we are not brainless freaks
by paying on account for Heavenly bliss.
I'll sing *Old Hundred* as I take collection.
This is your chance to show the Lord affection
in concrete terms—a chance you must not miss!"

6

Bucking the Tiger

The parson had a pleasing baritone
and lungs enough to fill the tent with sound,
though now and then he'd pause enough to drone.
"Let's all put in, to show we're Heaven-bound
and are not paying taxes to the Devil.
Use faro checks to fill the Stetson level—
if cash is short—before it goes around."

And Calabasas, hypnotized and awed,
reached in its money belts and pocketbooks
to give, with hearts rejoiced at being thawed;
while some, their fervor lighting up their looks,
took up the words that Reverend Jones was singing
and sent *Old Hundred* thunderously ringing
throughout the town. Yet if some softened crooks

forgot themselves and knew not what they were,
Deuces was made of no such flimsy stuff.
He saw a pot which set his blood astir,
and though he fed it carelessly enough
and won a smile from Jones by grandly throwing
a double eagle in, his eyes were glowing,
but then went dead, as when he meant to bluff

for major stakes. He watched the cash pile up
until the hat had made the circuit, when
the parson cried, "My friends, you've filled my cup
and that of God, who'll bless you all. Amen.
Now buck the tiger!" When these words were spoken,
the sacred spell he'd wrapped them in was broken,
to let high spirits back. They cheered him then

or whistled, clapped their hands or fired their guns
to let the twilight through the church's roof
and let the angels know who were the ones
that prized religion; then, in further proof
of zeal, they sped to drink to their conversion.
Some women made a similar excursion,
though others, left uneasy, kept aloof

to ponder soberly upon their sins—
made manifest by Jones a little since—
and swore they would not, for a thousand skins,
so lose themselves again. But no mere hints
that after death, that far and dim dry gulcher,
there'd hover Judgment Day, a dimmer vulture,
could alter Sue's intent or make her wince

away from profit. Off to work she went
at Trips-around-the-World, her place of trade;
while Longhorn sought his natural element,
the Golden Fleece. There Deuces also made
his gambling stand; but now the dealer waited,
to join the handful, reverently elated,
who watched the parson count. Then when he'd prayed

and given thanks for Heaven's charity,
these eager faithful flocked around to talk.
"By God!" one said, "you done converted me;
I'm harnessed to the Right, and I won't balk."
"You sure did cheer me up, sir," Deuces told him.
"You gave the Devil hell enough to hold him
but didn't draw too thin a line of chalk

for me to follow. How about a drink?"
The man of God was courteous with his smile
but shook his head. "Why, thank you, but I think
I'd best retire and meditate a while
in my hotel." "Aw, damn it, come on, vicar,"
another urged him; "just a round of liquor
to get acquainted on. We like your style;

besides, I think you ought to know the town
you're preaching in." "My son, I find you right,
on second thought," said Jones, "and I don't frown
upon a friendly glass. When hearts are light
they're nearer to the Lord, for Hell is sorrow."
"Don't worry till you shake your head tomorrow,"
said Deuces. "My treat, gents." No one would fight

at those words in a land of chronic thirst;
docile, they trailed him to his chosen bar.
"A pleasant spot," said Jones, and downed his first.
"A bird," said Deuces, "can't fly very far
on just one wing." "A witty observation."
Brother Abimelech took the next potation.
"And aren't tails needed, too?" "You bet they are!"

cried Deuces, slapping him upon the back.
"We'll have one more, then come and watch me deal,
unless you think you'd like to take a crack
at faro playing." "No, I hardly feel,"
said Jones, though hesitating, "I should gamble.
You go ahead, and I'll drink up and amble
to my hotel before I show more zeal

for worldly things than any pastor should.
I fear the whiskey's going to my head
or I should not be tempted." Touching wood
for luck, the gambler gripped his arm and said,
"Suppose you *won*, though, vicar. You could double
or triple your collection take." "The trouble,"
the parson told him, "is that I might tread

the path of folly till I lose it all."
"But think of what," said Deuces, "you might get.
You'll need a stack of check's that's mighty tall
to build a church with. Chance it, and I'll bet
you'll win enough. I've got one of my hunches;
besides, I know that good luck comes in bunches,
and yours got such a start tonight you're set

for quite a run." "But how about yourself?"
the parson asked. "My gain must be your loss.
Are you so large of mind that risking pelf
when certain that you cannot win the toss
is something you can court to please a stranger?"
"Oh, I am not that generous—no danger,"
said Deuces, "but a gambler learns to cross

the flats of luck—and I am in one now—
as quickly as he can; and never mind
just what it costs to shake the jinx." "I vow,"
the parson smiled, "you fill me with a kind
of admiration for the gamester's spirit—
unmoved by fortune's whims; Jovelike or near it—
I never thought to own. So now I find

my interest stirred; though you must show me how.
From Hoyle," he said, as Deuces led the way,
"I've learned the terms, but they're but phrases now."
His words were drowned in cries of "Look!" and "Say!"
"The preacher!" "No!" "Hell, yes!" Then everybody
picked up his shot or highball, beer or toddy
and ganged around, intent to watch the play;

among them Longhorn—well aware—who wished
he had a way to cut in on the game.
He'd watched them wistfully while Deuces fished,
tickling the trout until he'd made it tame;
and now stood waiting for the sudden killing,
half fascinated, also half unwilling
to view a prize on which he had no claim.

The fifty cards from soda down to hock
were slipped, and Deuces patiently explained,
while fumblingly the parson tapped his stock
of chips or added to it as he gained.
But on the whole, he found by careful counting,
that steadily his wealth in hand was mounting;
and he was overjoyed—though later pained

as fortune changed. "Perhaps I'd better quit,"
he said, on finding he'd sustained a loss,
though minor only. "Now's your time to hit!"
the dealer told him. "Show your luck who's boss
by crowding it. Just kite your bets up higher
and bring your money back upon the flyer."
"I'll try," the parson said, and reached across

to scoop the cards his way. "And just for luck
I'll make the deck, my son; I've got to learn.
If I'm to be a gamester, I won't duck
my portion of the work, and it's my turn."
His long, thin fingers dropped the cards and fumbled,
but in a little while he'd somehow jumbled
the deck together well enough to earn

a nod from Deuces Wilde, who cut and filled
the box; the bets were placed; the cards were sprung.
"The Lord," Jones murmured shortly, "must have
    willed
that I should win." The gambler held his tongue,
but as each card produced a new disaster
his well-drilled face had much ado to master
the urge to show the anguish of the stung

each time the parson gathered in the chips,
then raised his eyes toward Heaven to invoke
the powers there before, with prayer-moved lips,
he pushed out stacks so tall they sometimes broke.
They came back bearing gifts, but Deuces dourly

accepted chance until the other surely
announced the turn; and then his wrath awoke.

He yearned to kill. He almost snatched his gun
and shot the parson as he bowed to bless
his winnings; but he heard: "By God! he won."
"The angels do look after him, I guess!"
"He broke the bank!" "Why, gents, we got a preacher
I wouldn't swap, with boot, for old man Beecher!"
To slay this novel, popular success

was more than he could do and not be lynched;
so Deuces, bracing, made his face a mask,
and when Jones shook his hand, he hardly flinched.
"We'll play another time, that's all I ask,"
he said aloud, though in a voice that fluttered.
But in the reaches of his soul he muttered,
"I'll have your blood and stow it in a flask

to use instead of catsup someday soon."
But Reverend Jones was meanwhile on his feet
and called to every one in the saloon,
"My friends, I've taken note that it is meet
for winners to be hosts, and as a servant
of Heaven should be carefully observant
of cherished customs, it's the Church's treat."

7

The Squeeze at The One-to-Spare

The parson did not have to say it twice;
the invitation started a stampede
which even Deuces, lacking now the price
of soothing bourbon, joined to glut his need.
But Longhorn Charlie, though he blithely started,
in mid-stride left the course his thirst had charted
to sidle out the door and stride with speed

down Railroad Street to Trips-around-the-World,
the bawdy house of Sue, who was on deck.
"Wipe off your paint and get your hair uncurled,"
he told her. "This here Brother Abimelech
somehow won Deuces' roll, and now he's drinking."
They looked into each other's eyes, unwinking,
and then Sue nodded. "Well, get on his neck

and don't let go. I'll meet you at the Fleece."
But Longhorn shook his head at her. "Not there.
Deuces would spot the game and want a piece.
I'll take the parson to The One-to-Spare
and fill him full of buzzard's milk. Now hustle
and wash that goo off." "Tell it to my bustle,"
she counseled him. "Just go and hold him where

the hair is short until I come along.
Here, take this eagle." Longhorn did and sped
to seek the Golden Fleece and work the prong
inside the sucker's mouth before it bled
and warned him he was hooked. Now, as he reckoned,
the parson's guests were working on their second
so, easing into line by Jones, he said,

"A stool must have three legs or it can't stand;
my treat!" He bounced his coin to make it ring.
"Don't mind me, Reverend; I'm a little canned."
"Yet not too drunk," said Jones, "to say a thing—
that phrase about the stool—that's very clever.
Yes, I'll have one more drink, though I should never
imbibe so much." "Go on and have your fling,"

Longhorn advised him. "Reverend, what I like
about you is you're good, but you don't itch.
You let me know that Heaven's a lucky strike
and that the Devil is a son of a bitch
but still don't make me feel I am a bastard
for being just a man." "I have not mastered
myself," said Jones, "the dreadful urges which

impel a man to sin. I'm getting drunk
right now, I fear, and must be off to seek
my bed before I play the fool." "Aw, bunk!
You're sober as a stone, and you can't sneak
away," said Longhorn. "Look, the house is buying."
"Man strives and falls," said Jones, "but keeps on trying;
the spirit still is strong, if flesh is weak

which God perhaps will take into account."
"My flesh ain't weak," said Longhorn; "what the hell!
But still when I've took in the right amount
my shanks get tuckered. Let's sit down a spell,
when these are gone; not here in all this riot
but right next door, say, where it's kind of quiet."
"Indeed," Jones murmured, "it is just as well

that I should sit." He did not stagger, but
he wove a little, as they picked a course
outside and in again. "I'll tell you what,"
said Longhorn, "I'll just buy a quart, old horse,
and then we won't be always dry and waiting
for barkeep service." "How I will be hating
tonight tomorrow! though I'm past remorse

just now," said Jones. As Longhorn had declared,
The One-to-Spare was quieter in the sense
that rifle shots are quieter compared
to cannonading. Life was less intense
than at The Golden Fleece but bluffly jolly,
and Jones, admitting pleasure in his folly,
forebore to dwell on sin's sad recompense.

"You know," he said, "I even think I'll smoke."
And when cigars were brought, he proffered cash.
"Your dough's no good here, Reverend." Longhorn
     spoke
while paying out as if bestowing trash.
"No friend of mine can buy while I got money."
He turned, then looked annoyed. "Aw, beat it, honey!"
For Sue stood there; a different Sue, not brash

or wanton or aglitter with fake gems
but dressed in white, and shy, and bare of paint.
A tear-soaked handkerchief with lacy hems
concealed an eye. "Oh, please!" Her voice was faint.
"I've got to see you, Charlie—just a minute!"
"Go find a grave," he said, "and tumble in it;
I got no time for crying jags." "I ain't,"

she told him, "tight. Oh, Charlie, don't be mean!"
So Longhorn, groaning, rose. "Well, say it fast."
In pantomime they briefly sketched a scene
where he refused but yielded at the last
and came back to the table, looking harassed.

"That loco heifer there," he said, embarrassed,
"got scared this evening, when she heard you blast

at sin. You've got her thinking of the end
when Hell and Heaven bid in for our souls.
She's keeping hurdy girls but wants to mend
her cat-house ways so she won't fry on coals.
She says she's got to pray or she'll go crazy
and hopes you'll learn her how—ain't that a daisy?"
"She's right to think of death before it tolls

the bell for her," said Jones. He cast a glance
to where Sue filled the contours of her dress.
"It seems a very piteous circumstance
that such a goodly vessel should confess
the Devil's presence. Surely I must aid her,
but I could do no good with the Invader
right here in public; don't you see?" "Hell, yes,

and so does she," said Longhorn. "What she hopes
is that you'll go and see her in the dive
she owns—and so, of course, she pulls the ropes;
you'll have a private room in which to drive
the Devil out. But look, there ain't no hurry.
The Devil would get in, so let him worry
about the chance of getting out alive.

Let's you and me drink up." "Don't talk like that,"
the parson warned. "I'm drunk, but not so much
that I will countenance such callous chat
or share in mocking any one in such
distress of heart. And if she feels that learning
to pray will save a soul now doomed to burning,
I must not fail her, so I will not touch

another drop. Poor child! Where does she live?"
"At Trips-around-the-World, just seven tents
down Railroad Street," said Longhorn. "Well, then give
this message to her: I am hieing hence

to get my Bible, hymnal and my psalter
but presently will join her and won't falter
until I've taught her something of the sense

of my religion, friend." The parson rose,
somewhat unsteadily, and made the door.
Then Longhorn sprang toward Sue, who shed her pose
of tearful humbleness. "Just what's the score?"
she asked. "He swallowed hook and line and sinker;
what's more I filled him up, and he's no drinker,"
he whispered to her, grinning. "Why the poor

old nut has gone to get his praying books
so he can save the soul that you ain't got.
He'll meet you at your joint; and when your hooks
are in him deep, I'll jump him on the dot;
and there's our pigeon, cooked and carved and salted.
And he's a fat one!" Starting off, she halted.
"What happens, Charlie, if he don't get hot

and keeps on prayin' for me?" "What's the dif?"
he asked. "No matter how he moves, he's tagged.
A preacher in a whorehouse, stinking stiff,
and you ascreaming that he up and bragged
he'd do you wrong, and him afeared of scandal—
why he'll sweat money like a burning candle
sweats off its wax. Oh, he's as good as bagged.

Now this was my idea, but I'll be fair
and cut you in for thirty." "Ain't you nice?"
she wondered. "I'll take fifty for my share,
for doin' half the work, or it's no dice.
It ain't your brains that starts the poor hicks droolin';
it's what *I've* got. God damn you, I ain't foolin'!
I freeze the game unless I get my price."

8

Man Bait and Woman Bait

Assuring Sue her snack would be a half,
Longhorn returned and poured himself a drink
to brighten waiting time, but had to laugh
before he gulped. It tickled him to think
of Deuces Wilde and how his wrath would kindle
at learning that the hoary badger swindle
had snatched away from Jones the very chink

which Wilde had lost at faro, not to name
the church collection money. Longhorn's watch
was out four times before the minute came
wherein he judged it time to slink—a blotch
of deeper shadow on a midway brightened
by only lamplit entryways, which heightened
the darkness in between each gilded splotch

of rumpled dust. Apachelike in craft,
he slipped through these before some fellow's hail
could warn the victim of impending graft;
and sure, but careful still, he did not fail
to check his draw, so there would be no hitches
to rob him of this chance for easy riches.
He passed six tents, then turned to swing his trail

between the hither tent and that of Sue's.
He took three steps but did not take the next.
An arm choked off the oaths he tried to use,
its partner cured him then of being vexed;
it rose and fell but once, to end the scuffle,
and Longhorn's hair was thick enough to muffle
the sound of his revolver barrel flexed

across his scalp. The gunless gunman sank
in hushed acceptance of a passive part
in life's great drama—heedless while a lank
and aging parson found the harlots' mart
called Trips-around-the-World. He hesitated
but shambled in where Sue and duty waited,
the former with impatience. "Bless your heart!"

she cried. "I thought you'd maybe changed your mind
or figured I ain't good enough to save."
"Not so," he said, "but I am slow to find
my way in darkness." Bibulously grave,
he peered about. "Is this a dance hall, daughter?"
"We do lots worse things that we hadn't oughter
than dancin'," Sue confessed. She broke and gave

herself to tears she covered with her hands;
yet not so thoroughly she could not peek
to note he wore the slack-jawed look which brands
the owner as too lost in drink to seek
for ties of reason linking words and action.
She could spin fast, she saw with satisfaction,
and not alarm a fly with eyes so weak

he'd fail to see the web she wrought upon.
"Regret is half salvation," Jones approved.
"The sin you've learned to hate is all but gone,
and so the penalty may be removed.
But just what have you done that's so unlawful
and ill-beseeming?" "It's," she cried, "too awful
to tell of—but come here." His forehead grooved

with puzzled lines, he let her be his guide
past all the canvas cubicles but one;
and there she motioned him to step inside.
"Here's where I lost my soul," she said, "and done
it every night for pay." "But *how?*" he cried.
"It's not a time for mystery; speak frankly.
The name of sin can never smell as rankly
as wrong's accomplishment." "Oh, I have tried

to say it," she informed him, "but I can't!
I'm too ashamed; but I will show you how,
if you won't scold me." "Why, of course, I shan't,"
he told her, belching. "Well, then watch me now";
and Sue undid the fastening of her placket.
"A guy would come and say he'd like to shack it,
so I'd do this." The parson smote his brow,

collapsing on the bunk meanwhile. "And then?"
Sedalia Sue removed her skirt and blouse,
asnicker, thinking of the moment when
the cat would spring to pin the moron mouse;
for Longhorn, with long practice, was a master
at injured-husband roles and showed a vaster
enragement at the dalliance of his spouse

each time he slashed the canvas with his knife
and stormed, his pistol flashing, on the scene
to threaten the philanderer and the wife
whose honor only blood and death could clean;
though in the end he grudgingly would settle
for all the money—paper stuff or metal—
the man could proffer, borrow, beg, or glean

through selling his effects. Her shoes were off,
but still her partner did not take his cue;
and so the parson, blinking, watched her doff
her petticoats. "What further did you do,"
he asked her, "that was sinister and shocking

and fateful for your soul?" She shucked a stocking
and next its mate, then paused when she was through,

but nothing happened; so she hid a smile.
"Old Charlie wants the sucker dead to rights,"
she told herself. "O. K." So in a while
she'd shed her corset bustle, slip and tights,
to stand before the parson in a fashion
which hinted that she felt the call of passion.
"The serpent of temptation once more bites,"

the parson groaned and, rising, gave a shove
which stretched her out full length upon the bunk.
"If sin is wrong, yet it's divine to love,
or so the Scriptures teach." "You horrid skunk,
get out of here!" she mimicked scared confusion;
yet still there was no sign of fierce intrusion
on Longhorn's part. The fear that she was sunk

at last bored in, to make her really scared.
She moved to flee, but something fell to thud
upon the bedding. Furiously she glared;
and then her anger fizzled like a dud;
for in the lamplight, round and richly yellow,
there gleamed a coin—followed by its fellow
and thirteen more. And as a golden flood

once rendered Danae pliable to Zeus,
so now one did as much for Reverend Jones;
for Sue was prompt to see there was no use
in letting wealth abscond to other zones
of lesser worth. And so she fell back, crying,
"They never shot Methuselah for tryin'.
Get on, old horse; and don't break any bones;

but first turn out the light, so I can't see,
and maybeso I'll never know you're there."
So what was done was done nocturnally;
and light began retreating everywhere

as most, in time, resigned themselves to giving
that kickback, sleep, which death demands for living—
supine or sprawling, snoring in a chair.

Though some, their liquor turned philosopher,
sat leaned together, chattering like birds
in all but empty bars; or still astir
in open camps, they hunched in little herds
between the darkness lurking at each shoulder
and fires they crowded as the night grew colder,
to muse aloud on Jones and on the words

he'd handed down. By one such fire of dung,
left by the Spanish cattle, three conversed
beneath the outsize desert stars, which swung
slow-motion over looming hills. "At first,"
a man remarked, "I didn't want to listen,
but he made so much sense, I wasn't missin'
a word he threw at us before—" "The worst,"

another interrupted, "of the case
is that each one of us so damn well knew
that what he said hit home and found its place
as slickly as a foot goes in a shoe.
I say it's good he got here." "He was needed,"
the third man nodded, "and I hope he's heeded.
It's time that we gave thought to what we do,

and to the consequences, not alone
for our salvation but for what we owe
to future generations here. The tone
of any town is set by those, you know,
who are its leaders. Blast it, we're the founders!
And if we act like rotten, heathen bounders
the rest will follow suit." "By God! that's so,"

the first approved. "Well, they can count on me,
them future generations. I'll be straight
from this on out." Responsibility

so weighed on them, they passed the flask. "I'd hate
to have my kids," the second man admitted,
"raised in a burg like this has been, outfitted
with every mantrap on the Devil's slate."

"And with no place for God to swing his loop."
"You've called the shot; we got to settle down,"
the first averred, "as soon as we can scoop
our fortunes out." "Oh, when the tracks reach town,"
the third said, yawning, "that part will be simple."
"I'll find a blue eyed church girl with a dimple,"
the second stated. "Aw, not blue eyes—brown,"

the first said. "Man, if I was married now,
I sure would start my family tonight."
"The method would be pleasing, I'll allow,"
the third said, drinking. "That's my last. I'm tight
enough, I hope, to dream that Calabasas
is populous with pure and dimpled lasses."
They slept then as the stars and sky turned white

above themselves and others of their like:
hard as a loaded pistol, aimed and cocked,
ruthless in action as a hungry shrike
but young enough to keep their hearts unlocked
to hopes of tenderness. They went on sleeping
while down on Railroad Street a man was heaping
his plate so high that Ah Chin Honk was shocked.

9

The Sheriff from Grizzly Paw

The Golden Fleece, although it never closed,
was quiet at the hour of ten to six
on Monday morning. Scattered patrons dozed,
but one could not. His eyes like burnt-out wicks,
his mouth a bloodless furrow, Deuces wondered
about his losses: had he really blundered
within the hands of one more skilled to fix

the cards for paying off than he, or had
the parson hit a streak of bonehead luck,
as sometimes chanced? By then a quarter mad,
his mind could neither break nor cease to buck
the wall of mystery which hid the answer,
and one-groove thinking gnawed his mind like cancer.
He jumped as Longhorn staggered up and struck

the faro table, fumbled for a chair
and slumped in it. "I got to have a peg
and got no dough," he said. "Then we're a pair,"
said Deuces. "Jesus! who pulled off your leg
and hit you in the phiz with it?" The query
was not unapt, for chaos had made merry
with Longhorn's face, resembling now a keg

whose load of wine had leaked from seams and dried,
though first it had been rolled about in dirt.
His hair was long but not enough to hide
the welt upon his head, which throbbed and hurt
at every move; though quiet, too, was painful.
"Cork it!" said Longhorn, trying to look baneful
but mainly looking cross-eyed. To avert

this strain upon his sight, he dropped the lids,
seeking again to conjure up the scene
where, ambuscaded, he had hit the skids.
He could recall his ducking in between
the tents; but who had laid for him and strangled
his cry of protest, struck and left him mangled?
He searched his pockets one more time. "Picked clean,"

he mumbled. When he'd moaned as bankrupt, both
retired to private thoughts, the gambler still,
the gunman sometimes muttering an oath
inside the hands which propped his face, until
they heard, "Why here's the double-crossin' flivver!"
And Sue was there. "God rot your lemon liver!
You welched on me." But yet there was no chill

of anger in her eyes or in her voice;
she rather seemed at peace. "Oh well, I bet
you didn't go and let me down for choice,"
she said, "so what the devil happened, pet?
I couldn't sleep all night, I was so worried;
it's why I left the hay so soon and hurried
to look for you and—" "Get your whistle wet,"

said Longhorn. "Here's my alibi." He dropped
his hands to show the carnage. "Christ!" she gasped,
"who scrambled you?" He glared at her but stopped
because it hurt. "I don't yet know," he rasped.
"Shut up and buy us drinks around. I'm stony,
and so is Deuces." Nodding at his crony
returned the splitting pain. He bent and clasped

his hands about his head. "Well, I ain't flush,"
she warned him. "We sure done a sickly trade
after the parson handed out his mush
about reform. My punks was so afraid
of being damned, I hardly made a dollar;
but I can buy a round or so." "Well, holler
and tell the barkeep," Longhorn said; and stayed

as though in silent prayer until he heard
the glasses rap the table. " 'Nother round,"
he ordered, when they'd drunk. And on the word,
Sue bought again, and sighed when she had downed
the double shot. "You know," she said, "I needed
them drinks myself. I'm bushed." She spoke unheeded
and once again the silence was profound,

somber on their part, comfortable on hers,
until a horseman strode into the place,
dusting himself and jingling pinwheel spurs:
a long, loose-jointed fellow with a face
which told of readiness for fun or killing—
two things or one for him. Slim Parr was willing,
and his obligingness embraced more space

than Barkis ever dreamed of. He had been
on both the sides of law like jaws of clamps
and cherished views on statutory sin
which served him well. They told it in the camps
that he'd put in for mileage to the county
to chase himself, and pay himself a bounty
for catching up. With two bar-shaking stamps

he shed the dust, caressed the rail and crooked
an elbow, downed his whiskey with a snap
and wheeled to gaze; then chuckled as he looked.
"I know," he cried, "that alligator map,
warpaint or not. You're Longhorn Charlie Durben;
who you been fightin', what'll you have but bourbon,
and are you on the lam, or on the tap,

if I need deputies?" He slapped his star.
"Bring us a quart of forty rod!" he roared;
"I'm dry as buffalo chips in Hell." "Slim Parr,"
said Longhorn warmly, as the sheriff poured,
"it's good to see you." But he eyed the liquor.
His eyes were clearer now, his motions quicker,
the creature aiding. "Why it's been— Oh, Lord!

When did I see you last?" "Cheyenne, I guess,
after we pulled the job in Black Hawk or,"
said Slim, "in Silver City, maybe." "Yes,
a year before the Lincoln County War,
when we was deputies," said Longhorn, sliding
his empty glass across. "And now I'm ridin'
as one of John Law's hands again, unless"—

the sheriff winked—"you know a better pitch."
Longhorn and Deuces kept their faces blank.
"It's quiet here, and no one's getting rich."
Before continuing, the gambler drank.
"Whose traces did they sic you on, old timer?"
The sheriff swallowed half his shot for primer,
and then he laughed. "A bird that cracked a bank

in Bozeman, robbed a stage from San Antone,
and shot a man who recognized his horse
at Trinidad. His bill ain't really known
though I suspect he done them things, of course."
His hearers shrugged, for he described the masses;
what normal citizen of Calabasas
might not have such a history? Perforce

their thirst sought amity with such a host;
but he was with, and they were not, the law,
and that was that. They closed their ears almost,
as he went on. "*But* up in Grizzly Paw
the ranny set up shop as an assayer
and sold some salted claims to Smith, the mayor,
and that's who put me on him." "I ain't saw

no renegades in these parts," Longhorn said.
The sheriff grinned. "Each time you've stuck your pan
before a glass, is all. To scoot ahead:
I think I'm just a day behind my man,
because in Tubac folks was kind of bitter
at havin' found a nifty counterfeiter
had boiled a brass bed down to suit his plan

of mintin' double-eagles cheap. So—" "What!"
Sue lurched from lazy dreaming with a shriek,
unsnapped a little purse and spilled its glut
of coins upon the layout. There were sleek
and brightly yellow twenty-dollar pieces,
"In God We Trust" the double-ended thesis
embossed above each lordly eagle's beak.

With trembling hand she lifted one and let
it fall upon the table's polished edge.
It hit as socks do when they're soaking wet
to make a sound like dry and rattling sedge
instead of bouncing with a gladsome ringing.
"I didn't get a cent!" she shouted, flinging
the rest away. She beat the rounded wedge

between her breasts and let them have the news:
"He worked me over like I was his farm;
I ain't had such a go since Bearcat Clewes
blew into Medicine Bow." She flashed an arm
across the board to jab a trembling finger
at Longhorn, who recoiled as from the stinger
of a scorpion and blinked in the alarm

of one who's in the wrong but isn't sure
just why or how. "He got to travel free,
as if I was a pinhead amateur!"
She rose to scream her anguish at him. "*Me!*
A top price whore in Deadwood and Dodge City,
bought like a squaw with buttons—and I'm pretty
sure *you* helped the weasel rig my fee

and got one of your own from him." "From who?"
Longhorn demanded, goggling and aghast.
"The wolverine you sicked on me," cried Sue,
"and swore was swacked! The thievin' louse who passed
the queer on me! That son of a bitch, the parson,
who ain't none, any more than I'm Kit Carson!
You got that through your skull, or must I blast?"

10

Longhorn Makes a Noose

Deuces' and Longhorn's eyes made bitter tryst;
and only then did either one begin
to trust his ears. But suddenly the mist
of puzzlement which both had floundered in
was burnt away by truth so bright and searing
it hurt to face it. Knowledgeably peering
at each in turn, the sheriff wore a thin

and hardened smile. "I see you know my boy.
Where does he bunk, and what's his local game
outside of passing buttons to annoy
the hurdy girls? And what's his local name?
He's money in the bank for me." But shaking
his head, the gambler rose. "You won't be taking
the bastard back alive," he said. A flame

of savage hope now flared in Longhorn's eyes;
recovered from the shock of shame, he stood.
"We'll get a rope and steer him toward the skies
he likes to preach about." "You mean it? Good!"
cried Sue. A little calmed but still untrusting,
she eyed him as she gave her face a dusting
with powder. "Will you cut me in or would

you rather have me spill it to the town?"
"Oh hell, you're in, of course; we'll split three ways,"
said Longhorn. "Four," said Deuces with a frown,
in answer to the sheriff's cough and gaze
of cold reproach. "You see, it ain't the money;
it's just that I get feelin' kind of funny
when I let guys be lynched, and no one pays

my conscience back," said Slim. "To help, I'll pry
his boots from off him, so I can collect
when I get home and tell how him and I
swapped lead until I blowed his soul direct
to Hell with my last bullet." "Let's get started!"
the gambler barked. No longer heavy hearted,
Sue fell in step till, pausing to reflect,

she asked, "But where's the rope?" "Why, right outside,"
the sheriff said. "I got one on my bronc."
So first he led them with his rider's stride
and then was led by tented honky-tonk
and shop to where the Grand's imposing portal
showed—burning joss to spirits of immortal
ancestral kin—the landlord, Ah Chin Honk,

whose look of reverence vanished when his ribs
were larruped by the rope in Longhorn's hand.
"Show us," said Deuces, "where his pious nibs,
the vicar, camps. "The pleacher give command
when he come ins and eat so big this morning
that he wants sleeps and I must stop men horning
ins, and if he do, he pay me grand

when he rise ups again." The landlord bowed
but straightened when the sheriff grabbed his hair
and pointed to his star. Ah Chin Honk, cowed,
then shrugged and led the way in dumb despair
to where some canvas curtains, painted brightly,
defined the bed rooms. Stepping very lightly,
the landlord entered one and whispered, "There."

On tiptoe the avengers, one by one,
stole in, exchanging nods and woodchuck grins—
all teeth and rock-hard eyes, which gleamed with fun
at thought of teaching Jones indeed that sins
net retribution. So, as Longhorn knotted
Jack Ketch's tie to show their sleep-besotted
bamboozler that the world held other gins

than Satan's, they gazed, gloating, where was stretched,
beneath the jumble of a quilt, their man;
no part was showing, but the bulges sketched
the figure well enough to show the plan
from foot to head. The sheriff neared the latter
and jerked the cover off—to start a clatter
of crockery on parade. For in the van

there sat the pot; the jar was next in file,
the pitcher next, and last of all the bowl.
It held a missive penned in ornate style,
and while they cursed the writer, frame and soul,
Sue stretched a hand to find what had been written.
"My friends," she read aloud, "when fate has smitten,
to struggle is to earn a harsher dole

of agony. Be wise; forget, forgive;
though I will never reconcile myself
to one sin of omission while I live.
In Tubac two nights since a jolly elf
revealed a secret which he mightn't throttle
while with a man he honored—or his bottle.
Your town will be left high upon the shelf

where railroads are concerned, a fortnight hence
when line officials—conning the report
of him who lately drank at my expense
(though cards in turn left him a trifle short),
make known what they will give as *their* decision,
to prove that it was rather blind misprision
which led you here, not sense of any sort,

as I forgot to tell you yestereve.
My bottle crony was the engineer
who's laying out the road. There's no reprieve;
instead of switching southward it will veer
across this pearl of sucker-haunted valleys
and enter Mexico at twin-Nogales.
I grieve I may not offer better cheer

to you who proffered hospitality
to put the Good Samaritan to shame.
There was no thing which you withheld from me,
and so I'm richer far than when I came
in cash and memories—and better mounted:
I leave the beast that brought me to be counted
among the Calab-asses I could name

who fed me and—" What followed wasn't heard,
for Ah Chin Honk discharged an eldritch wail
like to the crying of a great sea bird
and bolted from the spot to spread the tale.
So pidgin English launched the tragic story
of broken local hopes of urban glory
and, sadder yet, of Jones and how his trail

had served to cancel out a monstrous bill
for meals to make an emperor stretch his belt.
The tale, progressing, then grew wilder still,
to end by showing that the teller felt
the sheriff-hunted, lynch-evading preacher
was no mere criminal but a darker creature,
a demon lurking in a human pelt.

But while the tortured landlord aired his grief,
the four he'd left behind, though also racked
by savage anguish, did not seek relief
in vain laments. "My bronc's been too long backed;
I'll need a fresh one," Slim said. Longhorn nodded.
"I've got to get a rod," he snapped, and wadded
the man-stretch rope till it was deftly packed

in coils to loop below the saddle horn.
"I'm heeled," the gambler growled. Sue drew the gun
her flaring skirt concealed from view when worn.
"I'd hound a saint to Hell for what he done,
to watch him when the lariat chokes his hollers
and starts him dancin', rattlin' them brass dollars."
"Well, side us if you can," said Slim, and spun

to glare at her, "but, missy, you don't get
to join no posse I'm the sheriff of."
"Oh, she'll get tired," said Longhorn, "don't you fret,
when she gets slappin' leather hard." "Let's shove,
before the breeze," said Deuces, "blows up stronger;
for if we let it dust his traces longer
he'll leave a trail like a Sonora dove."

II

The Slaying of the Parson

Out of the valley where the Santa Cruz
hitched aridly along the parson went,
leaving the city where his name was news
for parts which neither knew him nor his bent.
He left as he had come there, solitary
and taking nothing difficult to carry
except a sorrel Morgan, somewhat spent;

for, wild when mounted, it had lost its taste
for sprinting on the slope that met the ridge
to westward of the river. There it faced
anew the town, now tiny, and each midge
of mankind kicking dust around the city.
The watching rider's lips were also gritty,
and so he spat before he burned the bridge

which linked him to these folk—a big cigar,
one Longhorn Charlie Durben's parting gift.
Detached as though considering a star,
he eyed the town. Betimes he'd be adrift
without a bell buoy of the past to guide him,
but now while curiosity yet tied him,
he slowly smoked and watched the vapor drift

above the camps where men prepared to eat
before surrendering to the suction force
which soon would draw them all to Railroad Street.
But four then took a strongly different course
and left the street of manifold attractions,
to ride and stop and show by other actions
they sought the sign of either man or horse.

The lounging parson blew a ring of smoke
and nodded, but he did not move as yet.
"The dreamer waxes bitter, once awoke,"
he quoted. "Granted company, I'd bet
I know the names of three, if not the other—
who seeks me as I never sought a brother—
unless it's he to whom I stand in debt

for mount and saddle. There! They've cut my trail."
And as he spoke, the distant riders bunched
and started toward him, carrying the mail.
Not finished smoking yet, the parson munched
the cylinder and waited for their nearing
to give them shape and color. Grimly peering,
he found a stranger leading, riding hunched

to keep his eyes on sign, while just behind
Longhorn and Deuces coursed. Behind this pair
in turn was Sue, though mostly riding blind;
she'd shaken loose the pins which held her hair,
which swirled about her face, now seen, now hidden.
"She does not ride so well as she was ridden,"
the parson said. "She's losing ground. Ah, there;

she's turning back, perhaps to make my shroud."
And as he spoke, the ashen skeleton
of his cigar stub fell. His voice endowed
with crispness, he remarked, "That top's been spun";
and threw the butt away, as he was throwing
all thought for any act except his going.
He wheeled his rested horse to flee the sun,

still low above the valley where were pitched
the tents where dreams and viciousness had bloomed
and both alike had sent him off enriched—
and both alike were stricken as there loomed
the shadow of new knowledge. Up it towered
until the boldest read the truth and cowered,
as Ah Chin Honk, twice wretched, moved and gloomed.

His stories spread like ragweed, and which burned
their hearts more cruelly, they did not know;
for though their backs were broken when they learned
the railway line was lost to them, and so
their chance for easy money had been buried
in hope's boot hill—its murdered spirit ferried
trans-Styx to ghost town limbo—yet the blow

to pride was deep and festering. To think
that they, the tough, the wordly-wise, the fly,
had all been sold down river by a gink
who dealt in gold bricks; yes, and made them buy!
Rubes for a con man! Marks for a thimblerigger!
A flock of pigeons, brainless as a chigger,
who'd let themselves be plucked, then let the guy

who'd trimmed them live to laugh! All good had left
a camp where such a thing could come about;
the place was jinxed past salvaging, bereft
of any chance for better luck to sprout.
Prosperity could never round the corner
where Jones's memory, like a hired mourner,
abode to tell them what they had paid out

to shamming piety. It was too much
for sober men to bear with fortitude,
so all worked in a body for the touch
of Lethe that is found in getting stewed,
before they started pulling stakes or loading
their wagons, mules and horses, in foreboding
of Calabasas left and not reviewed

in pristine grandeur ever—vanished, lost
with Tara, Ur, Mycenae, Camelot, Tyre
and Gila City; Calabasas tossed
back to the dusty end of all desire
and crossed by tracks of drowsy lizards only,
never to hear the stirring, deep and lonely
hallooing from those other tracks, afire

with snorting engines, clanging with the vim
they used to bring the world to Railroad Street.
The town was ended, then. But what of him—
the one who'd wrought this Ilium's defeat
and forced its folk, Aeneas-like, to travel;
proud loafers now reduced to scratching gravel
or punching cows or hearing woollies bleat

in mines or ranges where they sought a berth
to make a stake and lick their gashes clean
in near or distant corner of their earth—
stretched east from Angel's Camp to Abilene
and from Canuck to southern border passes—
what of this nemesis of Calabasas?
Nogales, next as neighbor, was a mean

and unaspiring, boundary-straddling town;
but still it sat athwart the finest road
(a rugged relic of the Spanish crown),
which entered Mexico. The parson slowed
a rod before he reached this point of entry
and walked his horse to meet the barefoot sentry.
The latter called an officer, who strode

to block the passageway from Gringoland.
"This Mexico," he said. "What do you here?"
Ignoring first the truculent demand,
the parson glanced behind. As none was near,
he raised a hand as though in benediction;
then shook his head, to show a lost conviction,
before he dropped his arm and spoke in sheer,

raw desperation. "Are you loyal, friend,
to old Sonora and the governor
at Hermosillo? Can we both depend
upon your secrecy?" His pupils bore
upon the startled soldier's, who was blinking
and gaping as the parson stared, unwinking,
before he whispered. "I will ask no more;

I see you are a man whom we can trust.
I have a message for His Excellency
and him alone; and if I live, I must
deliver it—though I am trailed by three
who must not pass the border now. Devotion
to duty will assure you a promotion,
if we succeed. Here, drink to Liberty!"

He flipped a yellow coin toward the man,
who caught it on the upswing of salute,
and hastened onward with no other plan
than finding sanctuary to recruit
his shattered forces, now without a focus.
For by his latest act of hocus-pocus
he'd slain the parson, when he'd found him mute,

his piety unequal to the task
of squeezing past the border. Forced by need,
he'd sketched and donned a flimsy form and mask
to meet the moment's wants, but had been freed
at once of their demands and of their guiding.
An empty vessel seeking new providing,
his energies withdrawn inside the seed,

his name now Nemo—played completely out—
he blindly moved toward something to attack,
assured but of a truth unpocked with doubt:
there was no point to which he might go back
or wanted to. Then he was overtaken
by sleep at last and, slumping, did not waken—
so fiercely did his body claim its lack—

for miles along the winding road, south bound.
The horse, now pacing slowly, did not jog
the rider from his rest; he rolled around
but held his saddle like a sleeping frog
upon a pad that's teetered by an eddy.
Some miracle of balance held him steady
until he should emerge from slumber's fog,

prepared to build anew with circumstance.
He was not then; but in this middle while
did he recall the last bequest of chance,
that stricken victim of his force and guile?
It seemed he did so, signaled by a gleaming—
a bass that jumped and vanished back in dreaming—,
as now and then his nose bestrode a smile.

THE DEVIL PAID
IN ANGEL'S CAMP

I

The Strike

The Angel's Creek excitement, ripening late
as time was measured by the Forty-niners,
attracted veterans of their estate
of seeking gold more often sought than found:
a Terence Dade and sundry tangent miners
of Cibola. The first to sift the ground,
in patient league with Gordon Galloway
and Hercules, their hinny, Terence crowned

his many months of little to assay
with days of skinning claims that no one wanted
except the resident ants. "Let's pack, and flay
the pelts of neighboring gulches for a week,"
he said, "for if this blasted camp is haunted
by any angel, he has picked a freak
to foster, never true, deserving men."
And as they scouted, more were keen to seek

for treasure, or its finders. From a den
in Marysville, where he'd been banking faro,
Arbaces Brothers came, and brought the wren—
a daughter of Acadia, claiming France—

who shilled for him. And Olney Jones of Cairo
was hunting in a manner not for Vance,
who'd shucked his surname, aping fellow Hounds,
among the Diggings through the circumstance

that San Francisco now was out of bounds
for those who wished to live. Unlinked to labor,
the handful under Vance began their rounds
with practice-bred efficiency. They trailed
the wanderer from touch with any neighbor
and killed him, if he'd found or if he'd failed,
as silence, next to nuggets, was the gold
they coveted. These ganchers had impaled

some several on the spinners which they trolled
the area with, when Vance, the master ferret
among the mob, discovered tracks that sold
the whereabouts of Galloway and Dade—
whose stand as yet, however, had the merit
of being miles away. Beneath the shade
of fronds that balked the brightly falling sun,
they had no inkling that they were betrayed

to felony, and tried to squeeze some fun
from closing out a day of barren drudging
which stretched the roll of others that had none
but emptiness for name. So if dismay
was all the fruit of digging, packing, trudging,
their words were light. "We'll make this last essay
at robbing Mother Lode, and if the bitch
is once again too slick for us, I'll lay

my pick aside, and scorn to strike it rich
until— I know where Shakespeare's three tomorrows
were learned: the Swan of Avon had the itch
for California dew drops, and he found,
as we have to our more important sorrows,
that gold is for the future." Terence ground

that wisdom with his teeth and raised his pick
with lanky arms, above a countenance browned

where tangled hair the shade of yellow brick
did not conceal it. "Are you busy begging
your medicine to help me win the trick?"
he asked the man to whom he'd turned his beard.
"I've done it," said the other, meanwhile pegging
a stone from where he leaned: a tree upreared
to eagle-eerie heights. "Now where it lit
is where to sink your probe." Intent, he peered

to watch the swinging point descend and hit
a score of times, and rose to do the spading,
a standing grizzly of a man. "The grit
is full of nuggets," Gordon Galloway
announced, when he had scanned the shovel's lading.
He said it calmly, as a man would say
"a lily's white," because the lightning stroke
of luck was blinding, coming on a day

that had so many nights the hue of coke
for counterpoise. And Terence, rising slowly
from where he'd watched his partner through the smoke
he hadn't finished, came and saw and puffed
upon his pipe. "A frog would call it *jolie*,
if born in France." Abstractedly he buffed
a nugget on his sleeve. "Let's dig amain,
my wealthy friend." But when the pair had stuffed

their pockets with the pellets spelling gain,
the lid of shock blew off, to leave them grinning
and babbling both of fortune's long disdain
and of the life before them—now they'd crossed
the Wall of China separating winning
from wincing in a game they'd always lost.
"We'll have a frisk in 'Frisco, yea and dressed
in hats that beavers covered to their cost;

and bathe in *torrid* water." Terence stressed
the adjective voluptuously. "It's over,"
said Galloway. "We're finished with the West.
I never said it, but I thought us trapped
and— Jesus, Terry, I'll be back in Dover
in time to help when maple trees are tapped
for sweetness; and I'll be with Sallie May,
and this will not exist." With that he rapped

the ground on which he sat, and swept away
with an imperious, dismissing gesture
the gulch whose precious soil had made him gay,
the limpid waters of the central creek
and all the handsome firs which were the vesture
of both its banks. But Dade's assent was weak.
"We came to find the means to scurry hence,
as you remembered first. And so we'll seek

the land of yesterday for recompense,
as I suppose, for rigorous endurance;
or did we suffer?" "Gold has snatched your sense,"
his partner snorted. "Have I heard you moan
for home or not? And now that you've assurance
that you can go where tears were in your tone,
when speaking of it and a girl that's there,
what ails you that you talk as though a bone

were sticking in your throat? By God! I'm yare
for what you fill my crop with crud by styling
the land of yesterday. It's now! It's where
reality has staked its claim, not here,
where there's no other valid cause for smiling
than ours, for we can leave." "I'm coming near
your look-out point," said Terence, "but I'm slow
in self-persuasion that the road is clear

to— Oh, there is Penelope, I know,
as well as Sallie May; but it's been fiction

for many months that we'll contrive to grow
from shadows in the letters we exchange
to something other than the dream addiction
of opium drowsers. Let me get the range
of cloudland, and I'll bring it down to earth
and join you." "What the devil can be strange

about your girl, or place you've known since birth?"
said Galloway, who filled his pipe and drifted
with his desires.— But Dade returned to Worth,
the New York thoroughfare at which he'd gazed
for weary months whenever he had lifted
his head from ledgers alternately blazed
with black and damning red. That hitching rack
had held him when a fellow clerk had lazed

across the room to nudge him in the back.
"If I were you, I'd quit and take to picking
some California gold," he said. "A sack
is all the tools you need for the career,
and salaries run to millions." "Gold is tricking
your teeth," said Dade, a quill behind his ear,
"but honest Terence scorns an act of greed;
what California gold?" "You didn't hear?"

Delighted that he'd found a soul in need
of being posted on the gaudiest story
that Broadway yet had rung with, Robert Breed
had poked him once again. "The papers state
that gold encrusts the coastal territory
we won from Mexico, which now will hate
to taste that tardy news. No ancient myths
can top reality in Forty-eight,

for seeming chunks of mud have golden piths,
reports agree, and lumps that shine like butter
are in the streams, and bright as fires of smiths,
they glisten in the sun. It's true as tripe

and—" Here his racy spate became a mutter—
"the Vulture lights. So long." "The time is ripe,"
a voice cut in, "to warn, as twice before,
that both of you are proving of the stripe

that brands the ne'er do well: the man whose oar
does not propel the boat but crabs and splashes,
because he never wonders what's in store
for wastrels. Did you ever pause to think
of all the early hopes that lie in ashes
because of frittered days?" The nose was pink,
as Terence mused; a healthless, toadstool hue.
The eyes were spiral anchovies, ashrink

for lack of vital oil. The soul was glue
whose only function was a stale adhesion
to money. But though all alike were true,
he ruled the firm of Daniels, Sears and Quirk,
so Dade forbore to mention what a lesion
the fellow gave his bowels. If, though, to burke
his sentiments was politic, he boiled
the more for no release, and pressed to work

with inner eyes that saw existence soiled.
"I wasn't born to tend a tapeworm's coffers,"
he told the figure columns, as he toiled,
"so nature's outraged; yet I wish her rage
would prompt the proffer of befitting offers
of better parts upon a nobler stage.
Or if I had—" And then the word came: "Gold!"
He saw it heaped upon the ledger's page

and out the window, waiting for the bold
to garner it and join the bloods thereafter
who didn't crouch in silences when doled
the wisdom of a walking fungus growth.
And then there'd be Penelope and laughter
within the house he'd build to compass both—

if it was true. He conned the news at noon,
and it was so, attested by the oath

of one who'd seen: the gold was there to spoon
like clams from chowder, asking from the fishers
but enterprise to be among the soon;
and there was fortune. With it he could leap
the fence that penned a man among the wishers
and have fulfilled desire. A sudden sweep
of feeling, epileptic in its force,
so shook him that he could no longer keep

from telling what he knew must be his course.
"I'm going there; are you?" he asked his fellow.
"To where?" said Breed, who'd mounted no such horse
of dreams as Dade had done. "We can't go yet."
"To California, Bob!" His raucous bellow
delighted him and made the other sweat
with fear of retribution. "Box it! Hush!
He'll soar again. And what about Miss Brett?"

"It's all about Miss Brett, my heart of mush!
And sparked by you, who've none," said Terence,
    roaring
to startled Mr. Quirk, who'd come to crush
the insurrection.— "What's the laughter for?"
asked Galloway, emerging from adoring
the vision in his mind. "I closed a door
and felt so bold," said Dade. "I walked a street
called Worth, as though a pirate come ashore

with all the reivings of a treasure fleet.
My God! if I had known the range of valor
this country asks, or all the trails I'd beat
so bootlessly till now, I'd not have smeared
my braggadocio on the quiet pallor
of its security." His partner peered
at blue but deepening morsels of the sky
amidst the meeting branches. "Dusk has bleared

the light already underneath the fly
these firs provide, so eating is in order
for us and Hercules. I'll fix a fry
of something that Lucullus wouldn't cook,
if you'll conduct our vegetarian boarder
to where he both can browse and reach the brook
while staying put. He keeps a wanderlust
I lost in California." Terence took,

accordingly, that commissary trust
and led the hinny up the golden gully.
And meanwhile Vance, and others with a gust
for death and seizure, sifted through the trees
as softly as their shadows, printed dully
by fading light. Australia's criminal lees,
they lived and hunted by the law of packs
and clustered at a signal. "Here's the wheeze,"

said Vance, below the sound of Gordon's axe.
"There's two, and one ain't here, which nixes shooting
until we find his perch." "I'll nose his tracks,"
a stocky shadow caster volunteered.
"But use the knife, unless you hear me hooting
to tell you that this bandicoot is speared;
and owl me, Brock, if you have sunk your sting
before we bag this rat." His henchman veered

away from where the camp fire grew, to string
a veil between the eyes of the igniter
and those who waited for the dusk to bring
a thickening of the curtain. While they watched,
their fellow ranged for Dade, himself the lighter
for having left the hinny where it botched
the pruning of a shrub.— So once again
his mind was in Manhattan, where he'd notched

a victory to stump Apollo's pen
and wrapped the future in a jeweled rundle.

The bees were busy in the zinnias when
he crossed the lawn beneath the spearhead leaves
that drooped about the prickly chestnut bundle,
the freight of twigs—the tallest topping eaves
extending from a multichimneyed roof.
The dress was a meringue, and from the sleeves,

a froth so filmy that it seemed a spoof,
the slender arms were stretched to give him greeting.
"You're real." He pressed her hands. "I hold the proof;
I wish your lips were real." "Perhaps they are."
She pursed them. "But there won't be pudding eating,
to succor science even." "Let's not mar
my final evening here with such a stand."
"Finality's a bore," she frowned. "Or bar,"

he pointed out, "that luck can countermand.
Penelope, I've burned all boats and bridges,
including this, perhaps." He freed the hand
he'd still retained and smiled with brittle lips.
"I'm through with frittering amid the midges
of ledgerdom." "But there are partnerships
your work can lead to—and what could you do?"
she wondered. "Rise above the menial thrips;

I'll get enough to steer my own canoe
or not return." "From where?" Her voice was tiny.
"From California, orchard of the true
Hesperian apples, golden as your hair;
or else this ruby roundlet, small, but shiny
and precious, too, they say." He held it where
the light could plumb its coldly molten heart,
the while he searched for signs that hers would flare

with heat to match his own. He saw the start
of fire below the softly molded features
and in the gentian eyes.— And then the art
of conjuration failed, for someone spoke

who whisked all lovely, evanescent creatures
to Loegria, where they lived. "You got a smoke?"
The speaker was a blur in nearing night
that hovered close. "I'm hungry, lost and broke;

and still in California, ain't I?" "Right,"
said Terence, but in acquiescing noted
the voice was not an easy one, not quite,
though feigning it and more of heartiness
than suited speaking to a stranger coated
by gloom so deeply as to help no guess
at what his humor was. He paused and stropped
his memory, to find the right address

of some sib incident; and then there popped
the recollection of a different action,
the acting, though, alike and one that stopped
all time for him almost. He sprang aside,
to dodge destruction by an instant's fraction;
for Brock had charged and sliced the air, not wide
a centimeter. Terence saw the claw
the fist and knife made, as it rose to ride

from where his groin had been to where his jaw
no longer was. He jutted it, in lashing
with knuckles that were knouts enough to draw
a gasp of anguish from the mouth they banged.
For Brock had braked and sprung, again for slashing;
but knowing him so minded and so fanged
for rending, Dade had leapt within his guard,
and as he did so raised a shout that clanged

a warning. "Watch the dark for killers, pard!"
He caught the arm which would have upped and gutted
and rushed the concrete shadow, driving hard,
to keep from gaining balance, one who fought
with nails that reached for eyes, a skull that butted,
and teeth which tried to tear the shoulder brought

relentlessly to bear. So linked, they fell,
and Brock, the jolted cushioner, was caught

by hands which throttled mute his muffled yell
for rescue by the gang. His head was thumping
a tattoo on the ground, until his gell
of conscienceness was melted. When his grip
relaxed, the conqueror tried to rise but, slumping,
subsided to the ground until his ship
of needed breath came in. With that he rose
to shaky knees and felt the neighboring strip

of earth for both the dirk and gun their throes
had caused his foe to lose, but fingered neither.
"I hate to leave a tiger teeth to close,
and turn to him the nape he'd leap to bite
when finished with his restful, little breather,"
said Dade. Afoot, he stood above a wight
a minute didn't move. Wherefore his mind
retreated swiftly to another night

when he had eyed a man who was a rind
and nothing more: his thews and myriad uses
of muscles that a surgeon still could find
reduced to nullity. "He might have teeth
sequoia tall, and they'd be poor excuses
for dentals," Terence said. "He lies beneath
a tree in August, Eighteen-fifty-one,
the which is all the vault or funeral wreath

I can afford him, Arb." His thoughts had spun
a unit, in his semi-stunned confusion,
of what had been and was. Until he'd done,
and found upon his tongue a disused name,
he didn't recognize the past's intrusion.
He shook himself at that, and next became
aware again that stiffening would-be death
might have some running mates who'd try to claim

from Galloway his mortgaged loan of breath.

2

Three from Four Is One

In inchworm progress, as the fire connived
with murk and shrank his victim's vision, narrowed
with every lapsing second, Vance arrived
at pistol-finish range. And there he lurked
until the shadows right and left had farrowed
a pair of hulks whose careful creeping burked
the whisper of their movements. Still, they eyed
a man who dreamed as gravely as he worked

at cookery. For Galloway was tied
to California only in the body,
and while he hacked a rabbit's corpse and fried
the gobbets with a gallimaufry, mixed
of odd-and-end survivors of the shoddy
of bachelor repasts, his mind was fixed
on what he'd left and whom. While Vance's gaze
had found the saffron pellets piled betwixt

a fir root and a rock, and made assays
in estimate of murder's guerdon, Gordon
was reenacting deeds before the craze
for riches had abducted him.— His stare

was on the older boys who'd thrown a cordon
before the small academy. The dare
to enter it and teach had brought a jeer
from fry who garrisoned the school, a pair

at every window, craning forth to cheer
the leaders and to shrill their own defiance
with yapping-puppy glee. In every year,
the fourth for him, the rites of opening day
had so begun: the savage versus science,
protesting thus the death of summer play
and resurrection of the indoor drudge.
The sameness was a hurt, and the affray

was one reducing manhood to the sludge
of tadpole senselessness without the bonus
of knowing tadpole joy. A second grudge,
it was an aggravation of a third,
which nagged it back and charged him with the onus
of suffering this bout with the absurd
for peon pay. The hands that steered the school
belonged to men whose life was not deferred

for lack of pence; but they had eyed him, cool
as though he'd asked for alms, the while denying
his bid for betterment. An angered tool,
he'd beat the guard and stormed the inner keep
more roughly than was needed, so that crying
replaced the grins of some; so he'd felt cheap
all day on that account. And then he'd crossed
the path of Adam Brown. "I'd bet a heap,"

the school board chairman chuckled, "that you lost
those buttons in a tussle. Was you beaten?"
He hadn't laughed. He'd answered, "Buttons cost,
and you'll be billed for them." A silly threat;
but he was roiled and ruffed and hadn't eaten,
and buttons did cost. "You'll collect the debt,"

the burly boardsman said, in tones as cold
as he had used but harsher, "when you get

your second eye-teeth, son." He'd gotten hold
of Gordon's threadbare sleeve. "See here; if teaching
don't pay enough, there's California gold;
go get you some of that. It's lying free
for any one to grab who's tired of breeching
the brats of Dover, learning A, B, C
so he won't have to work." His wrath had turned
a loser to his curiosity.

"There's *gold*—and lying loose?" Excitement churned
his bloodstream as he spoke. The other blotted
a buttercup with spit. "I thought you'd learned
to read," he said. "It's in the paper, plain
for any one who can. The cricks are clotted
with nuggets, so if buttons are a drain—"
"Let go," said Gordon. "Let my sleeve alone."
He felt a leaping sympathy with Cain

but leashed his muscles till the other's tone
ascended to the storm zone also. "Listen;
I'll fire you, if—" The smack of fist on bone
had followed then, and Galloway had stood
to watch the crimson welling out, to glisten
where sunlight twinkled in it. "Gold, eh? Good!
Forget the buttons, Brown." He'd helped him rise
and left, already seeing bachelorhood

discarded and the glow of Sallie's eyes,
reflections of the house that he'd be building
when, nugget-burdened, he— The butterflies
and flowers of Delaware were swept from ken
along with scornful boardsmen and the gilding
that gold can give to dreams. He was again
in California, whisked there by a hard
exponent of reality for men.

a bellow: "Watch the dark for killers, pard!"
The Diggings had supplied him with a schooling
that never questioned warnings. On his guard
as quickly as a lynx, he dropped the spoon
he'd stirred with, kicked apart the torches pooling
their flames to make the camp a niche of noon,
and sprang from where the tilted pot had spilled
its steaming brew amidst the oddments strewn

by shipwreck of the skillet. Vance was filled
with startled rage to see a quarry fleeing
that he had confidently marked as killed,
an owl hoot only lacking. Twice he fired,
but he had blinked and jumped before so freeing
the lead which missed a man who'd been inspired
to scatter flames the coffee half put out.
The dimness spoiled the murder he desired

a third time; and although he heard the spout
of poison calling cards from both his fellows,
as diligent as he, he mourned in doubt
that any ball had bled a man who dove
through light reduced to flecks of reds and yellows:
a dimming shape, at home where blackness throve,
that blended with the night. "What's next to do?
By Christ! I never saw a gink who drove

a hole through air so fast before, did you?"
The whisper was to starboard. "Brock ain't sounded,
but just the guy that scared the kangaroo;
my Jesus, how he jumped!" The voice to port
went on. "If Brock ain't sung, it means he's grounded
in Botany Bay below, I guess." "The sport,
if that's the case, won't get to cut the cake
that we will," Vance declared. With that retort

he rose. "Be damned to Brock. He lost his stake
by botching, live or dead. We flubbed our killing

because he let his pigeon bellyache;
but skip all that. Our wallaby was scared,
and that one up the line can't spot us filling
our pockets with the nuggets that they aired
before they left. So neither coot can squeal,
when back in Angel's Camp, that we have snared

what no one begged us to." "This ain't a steal,"
the starboard speaker husked. "It's never robbing
to grab somebody's leavings, in a meal
or gold mine either one." "There ain't a sign
that says somebody'd mind, so this ain't fobbing,"
the other praised his logic. "If 'twas mine,
and I had left it all alone, I'd scratch
my name and gold's inside a valentine

I'd carve upon a tree. But this here batch
of nugget's cuckoo eggs that—" "Quit the chinning,"
said Vance, as they approached the shrinking patch
of lesser darkness where the scattered coals
were fading out like stars at day's beginning,
"and nudge the logs together. We ain't moles,
and gold don't whiff; we got to see the stuff.
And make it slippy, blast your duckbill souls!

I want away from here. So ditch the buff
and fix the fire, before the wombat handy
enough to handle Brock—he ain't a fluff—
is near enough to pipe what we're about.
A thing which ain't my favorite stick of candy
is being in the light while he is out;
it's just the gyp of luck I thought we'd dodge
by sending Brock to—" Meanwhile on the scout,

he stepped across the darkling coffee podge
and peered for what he'd seen—before the sounding
of Dade's resounding tocsin shrank the lodge
the flames had raised in night: the natural mint

of Galloway's and Dade's offhanded founding
between a root and rock. He caught the glint
of fire on metal then and leapt to seize
a thing he cursed and hurled, to make a print—

a fasces head—upon the shoveled lees
of nugget wine. "Stoke up the fire and hurry!"
he snapped. And meanwhile, back amidst the trees,
a man had stopped his flight and stood to brood
upon the turn of fate which made him scurry
away from what he'd sought so long, and hewed
from fortune with his hands that laureate day
of hundreds wherein thorns alone were strewed.

Was Dade alive? There was no one to say,
nor dared he call, for thus he'd aim a rifle:
his own or else his partner's, left to play
the turncoat, if the men of murder willed.
He matched the bitter groan he could not stifle
with twisting hands and stamped a foot that stilled
the trembling of his knees, and took a stride,
a slow one, toward the spot where hope had spilled

its chary radiance. The light he'd tried
to quench was now a small and fitful glowing
whose nimbus showed no killers yet inside;
but they'd be there, the filchers of his fee
to all that dreams had promised at his going
from all he cared about.— Disconsolately,
he beat retreat to Dover, where the gale
was westward winging, speeding from the sea,

and mountains did not ring a man like jail
to stunt his vision with their jagged gnawing,
and nature did not pattern on a whale
the landscape's furnishings. In Delaware
she'd found the golden mean, for neither sawing
nor adding on was needed anywhere,

and oceans knew their place, to wit: the east.
And in that rightness—verdant, douce and fair—

was Sallie, whose affections he had leased
but could not claim the option, being short
of wages by the board. "You hit the beast?
I'm glad," she said, "but California's far;
you're sure it won't take years, my love?" He'd snorted
disdain of that demur, for hope was par,
redeemable in gold. "Some weeks from now
I'll jump my ship, no more a jolly tar,

and find the Diggings, darling. That is how
they call the places where the miners shovel
the nuggets up. For that I will allow
a month, to play it safe, and then return,"
he glanced about, "to oust you from this hovel
and build a school where I'll instruct, and earn
as owner, honey." He had held the hands
which sewed too long all day to let them learn

that fingers can be soft, and kissed the bands
of wrinkles which not age but constant straining
had set above her eyes. "But foreign lands—
I know it's now America, but yet
it doesn't seem the same. I'm not complaining,
because you're doing what you must, my pet;
but California's strange, and you're my all."
He'd seen the brown eyes spring the tears, to net

the salmon freckles in that water fall
and course the tender planes which made her features
the heart beat of the world, albeit small
and pale for lack of sun.— But while love wept,
it faded from his sight, which showed him creatures
that separated from the dark and crept,
like maggots on a corpse, about the camp.
Somnambulist, he neared the two who swept

to concourse coals he'd left subdued or damp,
while one that whispered orders aped a beagle
that seeks a scent. He watched the fellow ramp
and snatch a thing he next refused to hold.
"A bloody axe, not worth a quarter eagle,
and had the glittering guts to gleam like gold!"
said Vance, forgetting caution in his wrath
and telling one who could not have been told

by darkness what an implement for scath
he hurled toward hostile hands. Anew enkindled,
the embers sired a glowing aftermath
which covered all the camp and bared the hoard
that Vance had thought to pounce upon when swindled
by shining baser metal. "Man, we've scored
a Montezuma bull's eye now!" he whooped;
and three men leaped. The duo in accord

were faithful followers of the leader, stooped
above the lambent nuggets, too enraptured
to mark the charging maniac who scooped
an object from the dirt and whirled it high.
And in so soaring, baser metal captured
a flash of fire it held until a cry
defined it as a bloody axe indeed.
It swooped again, to give the reason why

a hand that tried to shoot remained to bleed,
though gripping still a gun. But Vance, though dropping
his pistol in his frantic quest of speed,
escaped the bit which made a bid for him.
He joined the dark that saved him from the chopping
which split a head and made a feckless limb
of what had been a multipurposed arm,
belonging to a man whose hopes were dim

for fleeing, though he fled, the mortal harm
that is the end of hurts. While this was passing,

the man whose shout had sounded the alarm
had left a quiet terror of the night
and now was pressing through the murk, amassing
to slow the strides between him and a sight
he feared a certainty. For shots had stamped
a picture on his brain he viewed with fright

till firelight mushroomed, showing where he'd camped,
and there were cries and figures in a tangle.
He halfway clenched the fingers, which were cramped
from locking on a hairy throat, and sped
to where a man an axe had dived to mangle
was gore's minute Old Faithful. Gordon's head
was bowed till Terence spoke. "My God, they would
have cheated me of Dover! Is he dead?"

"And thoroughly," said Dade. "He's dead for good,
and one forgot his mauly. Were this couple,
and one who would surprise if he should
renew in any but a spectral guise,
the total, pard, or were there vermin supple
enough to dodge you, as you swatted flies?"
"It can't be funny," Gordon said. "That's cant;
for anything is funny, if it tries

to wipe you out and misses, and I shan't
dispense with such a test tube for assessing;
but were there more?" "Yes, one. My chop was scant,
as he unballasted his gun and, slick
as sand fleas, hopped from under. That's a blessing.
I've never killed before." "Well, you were quick
to join the crowd," said Dade, "by bagging two,
your spotless virgin effort at the trick.

I wish the coffee wasn't bolluxed." "You—
you've killed before tonight? But leave that hanging,"
said Galloway. He grabbed the hand and threw.
"I did that," he affirmed. "Almighty God!

I tossed a scrap of man and heard it banging
against a tree. What demon of the odd
contrived this country mirrored in a lake,
where all is upside down. I could have trod

the sward of Delaware till Doomsday's quake
and never found, in situ, like a mussel,
a hand without an owner." "Well, let's stake
this nob that's made our camp his catafalque
to privacy," said Terence. "Then we'll rustle
some touch-me-not of grub, to somewhat caulk
our gastric seams. What was the scoundrel like
that gave your hopeful battle axe a balk?"

"A dark and pock-marked mannikin, a tike
compared with this one." Gordon grunted, lifting.
"A nose like Punch's; pop-eyed as a pike;
I'd know him anywhere." "I would myself,
I think," said Dade, his fingers quickly shifting
on touching blood. "A hornbill, pitted elf
is one I'll watch for, pard." "We carry death,
and if its flask was Ghibelline or Guelf

we've no idea; or if he's Sam or Seth,"
said Gordon. "And tomorrow we will bury
a quondam mix of bones and soul and breath
but cannot—" "Not a single dud; a pair,"
said Terence, "but for Christ's sake be more merry.
You slew; and I made sure a shark won't bare
his teeth for me again, and that's not nice
as pastime, pard; but *he* is lying there

for worms to thank me for, while I'm a slice
of life as yet and find that food for joyance.
And we can name them—mine is Thotmes Price—
if that will cheer you up." "I think I'm glad
and wish my conscience mooned with more annoyance,"
decided Galloway. "To slay is bad;

you shouldn't have to butcher men like pork
to stay alive yourself, but here it's mad:

a stage set for the hump-backed Duke of York,
and we're the fifth act spearmen, a cadaver
our final-curtain burden. It's the cork
of everything that's happened in this land
of nightmare make-believe." They heard the slaver
as jaws in darkness carried off the hand,
and winced. "Let's leave the dummy here," said Dade,
"and hope the wolves I hear won't countermand

all sleep for us." "I fear the serenade
connotes they've scented Thotmes Price," said Gordon,
"but we will pile the firewood when we've made
a tidbit that a wolf would shudder at."
"Or if he ate, he'd cross the River Jordan,"
amended Dade, "in twenty seconds flat;
a wolf's not got a Forty-niner's craw."
Their hunger, for a little, silenced chat

till Galloway, remembering, ceased to paw
the biscuit dough. "You've never talked of killing,"
he said. "In places it's against the law,
but that's not why," said Dade. He frowned and
    shrugged.
"You don't talk of a woman you've found willing
to face the sky; or one you've merely hugged,
I'll add. Those things are privacies, and so
is any man whose mortal coil you've bugged.

It's not a thing concerning which you'll blow,
as you will learn, I think. Arbaces Brothers
and I abstained from gossip of the show,
although we both were actors in it, pard,
and Arb's a wight whose word no subject smothers;
or was, I mean." He eyed his knuckles hard
then raised his head to hark the wolves that howled
and neared his latest kill. "I'll turn the card

tonight, though, since tonight we both have prowled
a mystery I never thought to finger
when parting from a lady gowned and cowled
in gossamer. Was that myself or this,
or can the two be one? But I won't linger
in Knickerbocker's fabled isle of bliss—
a seaport in Bohemia to allure
a Mendelssohn to tune it to a kiss;

for soon I'll play a different overture."

3

Even and Sometimes at Odds

Sabrina lolled beneath her parasol,
a pantaletted figure in the fashion
of Godey's sweet and swooning paper doll;
and then she spoke. *"Mon dieu!* If you had minced
with no more Matterhorn of mining passion
than that poor claim can claim that you've evinced,
you'd not have pierced the Venusberg as yet
of this Jungfrau." "Tannhauser might have winced,

if practice as a navvy was his net
for probing in the mount. I've heard no singing
about the joys of unrequited sweat,
and even Bonhomme Franklin couldn't make
a tasty moral out of months of swinging
a weighty tool, with blisters for the take."
Arbaces Brothers, long himself the wean
of mother toil, and minus lump or break

on tailored palms and fingers, bent to lean
his force behind the foot which shoved the shovel.
He searched the earth he turned, his glancing keen
above the nascent puffs which scantly marred

his Belvederë look. "What makes you grovel
in vain for what a timely playing card
bestows on you, *mon cher?*" She cocked a face
whose separate tender curves, in league, were hard

and hand-dismissed the claim with flippant grace.
"You start this way at every pimple city,
erupting like eczema out of space,
that we have plundered. Why do you begin
like any peasant that Susanna ditty
has set to digging dust for us to win?"
"I sang that song myself, my queen of tarts,
or I would not have spurred to live in sin

where grizzly bears and Digger Indian darts
surround the urban scantlings which you credit
to California's hives. From better parts
I came to these, a Midas with a spade,
to filch the golden eggs the geese here edit
and hide in creekside bar or forest glade
for Pennsylvania lads to carry home
and be admired for. There's the why I've stayed

a chronic menace to the peace of loam,
if not a constant one. If cards are trusty
where claims are mostly Barnum's, yet a gnome
can make a strike which dwarfs all monte banks.
And so I peck betimes." His movements rusty,
he shooed the charliehorses with his cranks
from side to side before he drew erect.
"But since my labor now has picked no thanks,

and since the clock won't let us now collect
from better friends of fortune, rest is ordered.
Or you can rest while I am upper decked;
there's still no end of work in sight for me."
She watched him leave the spit of sand which bordered
the racing creek, ascend the bank, and free

the reins which kept the dappled match of mares
from drifting with the carriage. Lissomely,

she swayed to join him, playing to the stares
of several passing men, their eyes proclaiming
the scarcity of women. French in airs,
Sabrina Danton hailed from Abbeville
in swamp Louisiana, where the flaming
flamingoes soared above the weird quadrille
of bearded cypress giants. At her birth
she'd not been earmarked for a gambler's shill;

but Cajun parents, thinking all of worth
that man had learned was France's special treasure,
had schooled her there—and then withdrew to earth,
their money frazzled, too, before the banns
which granted womanhood an honored measure
were read. The choice bequeathed had polar spans
without a mean: disbarred as dowerless,
she faced the world with meretricious plans

or fled from it to nunnery duress.
Not minded in that fashion to denature
a Gallic tooth for gaudy liveliness,
she'd learned the things Aspasia had to know:
the laws of neither priest nor legislature,
but honored more than both, which rule the flow
of Cockaigne's floods and neaps. And then to France
had come the word of gold, and women slow

to follow men who'd seized Cortez's chance.
The haeterae of Paris sent a legion
to cultivate the novel circumstance
of mateless men with wealth. Among this corps
of pioneer exploiters of a region
where providence presented to the whore
of brains and enterprise a sovereign booth
was she, Sabrina. Now she turned to pore

upon her consort's face, her gaze a sleuth
to track the matters that he never mentioned.
"You've lust to spare, *mon* Arb; so much is truth.
'I itch,' Descartes declared, 'therefore I am.'
And as a stag, you're thoroughly intentioned,
as whole of purpose as a battering ram;
nor do I file complaint. Yet when you delve
in *Mère la Terre,* your effort's but a bam;

you act as though you fear a fractured helve
when bringing down a pick. So here's the riddle:
if there's compulsion which you cannot shelve,
why does it fail to crack the whip of drive;
where are you when you're standing in the middle
between a daze and being full alive,
my king while you have cash?" He flicked the whip
to spoil a gadfly's sport. "As I contrive

to nab the currency which is the nip
of such a sultry cat, I'm Fortune's owner.
But still, as pecking could return a chip
to tickle Adam Smith, I'll pink the ground;
though gently, dove, as Lady Luck's a donor
and can't be forced, or bought."— He knew she frowned;
he did himself, while losing touch with her
and whisking where her query sent him, bound

for where he'd been the day the golden spur
had goaded him. "You've none but crumbled fences."
Urbane, the lawyer'd let him know the slur
of down-at-heels demeaned him. "Haverford
expects its gilded youth to keep its senses,
and pay discreet attention to the Lord
when not pursuing gentry's proper goal
of adding cents to pence; but you've not shored

your treasury, or shown an earnest soul,
and so are mortgaged out of sight of measures

to raise the wind. You're bankrupt on a shoal
of easy skirts, with other living hard;
had sterner women been among your pleasures
or gentler comrades, then your balance card
might show a kinder reading." So he'd lost
his heritage, an outcast from regard,

except for Cynthia's. He next had tossed
as offering to the gods and College Tavern,
his bottom eagle. "Rubicons are crossed
and empires won, but not at Mohacs Field,
where I've now fought and so can boast a cavern
for bank account: that yellow boy concealed
in Mammoth Cave's own monstrous emptiness,"
he told a crony. "Hit me while I'm heeled.

Beyond Omega there, as I confess,
I can't see—or the backside of Diana:
the lunar not the one of raw undress
that Actaeon gave his eyes for, lucky cove.
He's dead and doesn't have to claw for manna
in Bill Penn's wilderness." Sebastian Grove,
a master tight wire walker, never drunk
or sober any second, munched a clove

he'd sniggled from his punch. "Your final chunk
of bullion, Arb; your Uncas of mazuma?"
He brooded on this trouble like a monk
become aware that out beyond the walls
which calm his life—unless an idle rumor—
there's woe abroad. "They're making golden hauls
in pudding California, Arb, a duff
as rich in precious plums as stable stalls

are rife with less negotiable stuff;
but both are mined alike." He swung a shovel
in pantomime. "An hour should be enough
to scoop a compost heap to overjoy

the hungriest Croesus. That's not long to grovel
for royal opulence; or even, boy,
if you should have to scrabble for a day.
It seems enough, but luck is often coy;

we'll make it two, to give you margin, eh?
I'd go myself, if business wasn't pressing."
He sipped his punch and bravely shrugged away
the burdens which were shackling him. "But, Seb,"
Arbaces said, rejecting first the blessing
which might unloose his self-wove, fatal web
and let him fly again, "how many sheets
to windward of a Fundy's farthest ebb

from reason were you when you heard such feats
of sheer Scheherazade mental magic?"
"This wasn't coined by Coleridge, Poe or Keats,"
insisted Grove, his face becoming grave;
"nor any other mind that's mythophagic.
I read it in *The Ledger*." With a wave
he flashed that stone of Philadelphia fact,
extracted from a pocket. "You can crave

my pardon when I catch you in the act
of buying Brothers Hill again." "I'm going!"
Arbaces breathed. "My credit's not intact
with usury, but there are other banks
to which I have been true, and gamblers, knowing
as much of me, will surely show the thanks
they will invest at interest."—Someone yelled
and Dead Horse Hill—with diggings on its flanks

as well as stumps which marked the giants felled
for rearing Angel's Camp—was now his neighbor
in place of Grove. "Wait up!" His hailer held
a hand aloft and left the timber walk
that rimmed a street where canvas eased the labor
of walling half the stores. "I want to talk,"

the speaker certified, when Brothers jerked
to halt his trotting team, not gladly balked

of livery stall relief. "I think you worked
a Sammie Slick on me, when I was potted,"
the fellow said. "Before I mined, I clerked;
I know the odds of chance. I lost too much
and much too fast, by God!" Not now besotted,
the man was big enough, in socks, to touch
at all its points the doorway of the Doones:
a Viking of a Hoosier, talking Dutch

and meaning fight. "You've counted all your spoons,"
Arbaces asked, "and find that one's absconded?
I didn't pluck it from your pantaloons;
you brought it to me, friend." But while he spoke,
he felt Sabrina grasp the reins which bonded
the team to him, and he to them. "Like smoke
from snow I did!" The growl was deeper now.
"You cleaned me like I was a Sunday cloak

and munched my dust as though you was a cow
and it was middlings. I've a notion, mister,
you'll lose your laugh before I've cleaned your plough
and fed a gnat what's left; a pair'd starve."
They weren't alone, for hopes of blood or blister
had halted red-shirt miners. "Skin him, Marve,"
a grinning watcher urged, as Brothers then
descended. "If you mean to punch or carve,

you'll have to raise this hand, and tongue nor pen
will neither be enough." He cocked the pistol
he'd whipped from out his sleeve and barked again.
"Your bulk does not impress, as once it might,
before they made the equalizer, Bristol,
to bracket hulks with brats—allowed in sight
but never heard from till they are addressed
by men of brains, and bullets. Give the bite

you pledged your favorite gnat, or give your chest
a respite from gorilla drumming." Eyeing
the deadly hollow leveled at his breast,
the miner gulped. "I ain't a man of guns."
He bunched the thews unused to chains, so trying,
it seemed, to burst the ghost ballistic ones.
"And yet I could be. Green 'uns can be ripe;
and even Websters, Clays and Jeffersons

was taught before they knew." He turned to wipe
his forehead with a sleeve, not red but russet,
because of dust, and daubed a muddy stripe
athwart the sweat the derringer had drawn
with sun-ray force. "He needs a metal gusset,"
Arbaces said, "to brace his sagging brawn."
He palmed his toy destroyer with a laugh
Sabrina shared. "Sequoias can be sawn

as quick as cottonwoods, but he was calf
and not the fighting bull of private fancy."
They snuggled, driving on together, half
romantics as in all the ticklish times:
inebriates of life where it was chancy
and out of tune with all the proverb rhymes—
embalming the decorums of the pale,
where gain had peace and industry for chimes,

outside of which they prowled. "A sucker's wail
is music Bach and Mozart may have bettered,
but rarely; and not they, as I'll go bail,
have piped a note to top a popping cork."
He loosed the wires which kept the champagne fettered,
the redwood lair they shared in the New York
their shell a clocking later. "Let it shoot,"
Sabrina said, "and hope it kills the stork;

I do not like the nasty, foisting brute."
She sighed when she'd released her bodice laces

and laughed to see him look. "This Magic Flute
is one which even corks can scarcely match
for you, who have, methinks, an ace of aces
for which your sleeve is not the master hatch.
But now the wine, *mon cher ami*." Consumed,
the bubbles left the drink, to close and latch

the door behind which truth and knowledge gloomed,
and granted them the grace of briefly dwelling
where Psyche did when Eros, angel-plumed,
discovered her and joy. When Brothers woke
from finished Cupid's nap, he heard the belling
of memory's bloodhounds, though, from which no smoke
can screen a man. He tried to close his mind
against what they were rushing to evoke;

but Haverford contained him like a rind.
He eyed Sabrina, graceful in her sleeping,
and winced away, as if she were by kind
a rank untouchable, and sloughed the bed
as though he left a sewer. Dusk was steeping
the camp with cambric haze, and Venus led
the star parade alone.— But not for him;
he lived beneath a crescent moon, and sped

by fields whose frames of stone were mason-trim,
to meet one named for it. And she was waiting,
as clean of line as moons when young, and slim
as rarity itself, if something tall.
"You're Cynthia," he said, articulating
the name to show it symbolized the all
of loveliness. "I'd meant to take my leave
as lackland, shed of horses, Hill, and hall,

and go—" "You mustn't, Arb." She touched his sleeve,
and moonbeams, sifting through the vine-roofed arbor,
were agile on her ring. "You can retrieve
the Hill, or if you can't, why build anew;

but go from me you won't. On that I harbor
a wisdom fixture: one cannot be two
or occupy a brace of spots at once,
so willy-nilly I'll be off with you,

if you depart. A doubter is a dunce,
but you, I know, are clever; aren't you, darling?"
"And wise one time," he said. He thought of hunts
for snipe his wit had failed to save him from;
he thought of saddlings, casual as a starling,
with any Hiren hiring out her bum;
he thought of acres forfeit for a horse
he'd judged a lightning streak, and found it numb

as cooling lava. "No one could endorse
your find of wits; they've been in Bedlam's bondage
and left me what I wear and late remorse;
but yet one brilliant's glimmered in my brain—
a fern where lichen's been the general frondage:
I saw you, Cynthia, as the right domain
of all fair hope. But knowing that as truth,
and sure that losing you would be the bane

to acid-eat my links with sense and sooth,
I still did what—" He tuned his larynx deeper.
"But that was yesterday and in my youth;
and now I go—" "We go," she said. "No, I,
without the heart I tender you as keeper.
There's gold in California that will buy
the Hill and bring it back from down at heels—
with many added roods of wheat and rye,

alfalfa, orchards, oaks to draw the squeals
from happy porkers, hearing acorns falling,
and hay for Herefords, busy making meals
while eating theirs. Each field will be a square
of craftsman ashlars, hewn to fit the walling
our sons, at least the eldest one, the heir,

will never need to mend." "I knew you'd win,"
she pledged her word, "when you had learned to care

for—not for me—yourself. But have there been
conclusive proofs that Spaniards missed a metal
they elsewhere found as plenteously as tin,
though long in California? Are you sure
that treasure, wild and common as a nettle,
is not a myth?" "It's truth, and Simon pure:
a phrase that's from *A Bold Stroke for a Wife,*
which this is not. The gold's a sinecure

that cannot kick or bite or draw a knife
but merely waits my picking like a berry."
He kissed her tenderly. "As long as life
begins in California, I'm for it,
and presto is the pass word."—"Arb, *ma cherie,*"
Sabrina called, and made the arbor flit,
where he and trust had parleyed, "I've a mouth
a careless camel's filled with Gobi grit

while shuffling by." She pushed the sheeting south
and sat to give her lips a mimic fanning.
"I've either tried to counterbuff my drouth
with flaming Phlegethon or drunk champagne,
so water I must have, or you'll be scanning
the ashes of a Phoenix not in train
to hatch a squab, though sure to scorch a sheet."
A mermaid, bare above the linen main,

she smiled at him, but lust was out of heat;
so though he brought the water, he was sullen.
"Erupt, Vesuvius." "Why?" "It's time to eat
and act as rat-trap cheese; you can't collapse
from having drunk your tongue as furred as mullein,
or even hairy as a yak. The yaps
are waiting to be cleaned, so fill the tub;
and I will be along to soap the saps

when you have got them ready for a scrub.
I'm off to tank a bit." She didn't answer,
for, knowing him, she knew some galling rub
that ached apart from her was gnawing Arb.
Intent himself to take his chronic cancer
to where it would not have to bear the barb
of comprehending eyes, he hid his dirk
and derringers in the funereal garb

in which tradition made a joker work
and left, to wash away with trenchant liquor
the thought of what a troth-betraying shirk
he'd been since he had split from Terence Dade.
The fault had been his own, as not a sticker,
he brooded, as he passed the house he made
his faro tiger's den: the Buckhorn, owned
by one to meet Munchausen unafraid,

inspired Ross Coon. He found a bar and stoned
his stomach with a depth bomb, his companion
until replaced where barks of laughter toned
the talk of stags converged to drink their fill.
Their picks and cradles side-tossed with a wanion
which taught the echoes found on Dead Horse Hill
laconic Anglo-Saxon, there was glee
for men to halve like cake, who shared the thrill

of hardy comradeship in exile. He
had known its taste: the smack of good adventure
endured by all alike, and jauntily,
when he'd belonged. He'd sold his franchise, though.
They might not view a gamboleer with censure,
and some might brief a smile with their "hello";
but yet they didn't talk to one removed
by kind from them as far apart as crow

from turkey, each a gang bird it behooved
to flock with peers. His own weren't represented,

as he had guessed when choosing what had proved
Stylites solitude amidst a crowd.
The liquor doctored him till he assented
to actuality, and sewed the shroud
again about a haunter he'd released
to wreak its will. "All right," he said aloud,

"erase the writing at Belshazzar's Feast,
Eumenides; it's lost its power of daunting.
For if I've failed, I'm living high at least,
and am not more abortive than a herd
of sturdy, constant lads that labor's gaunting
to no avail. If Terence has preferred
a ditcher's role, he's close to Joyous Garde
no more than I. I wonder where the bird

is pecking while I conjure with a card
which gives me what his brand of spades is chary
of handing him. And while I heal with nard—
Sabrina's that—my misachievement's wound,
he wears a shirt a palmer'd think too hairy
and lives in dormitory, unsalooned,
with Noah's whole run of nature's saved mistakes."
He drained his glass, Pope's rightness pacan crooned,

and strolled to pluck his duck's attracted drakes.

4

A Once Told Tale

With cups of steaming coffee in their fists
the partners hugged the fire and harked the racket
of lupine mills, at work on human grists
both up and down the gulch. "He did cash in;
the one who thrust his hand where I could hack it,"
said Gordon. "Or I guess the grisly din
is half for him. God, what a threnody!"
"The wages—what's the patter, pard?—of sin

are death; and virtue, disappointingly,
is paid in equal coin. Though virtue's winner
tonight," said Dade, "and so morality
can say 'I told you so'—if I am good.
I know I'm famished, whether saint or sinner,
enough to join the wolves, and doubtless would
were I not weary as a—" "Soon we'll eat,
but meanwhile," Galloway implored him, "could

you moot some mellower topic than the meat
those varmints guzzle—even, say, narrating
your promised story of your previous feat
of turning sensate flesh to lifelessness?"

"I will," said Terence, "if it sweetens waiting,
though it's a memory I don't caress,
as I've apprised you. When the world was young
in Forty-nine, the Diggings could profess

the primal innocence of dreams that clung
to candid lads. At first, as you remember,
there was as fine a crowd to throng among
as decency that had a tongue for salt
could well demand. Though faith is now an ember
which singes dolts, the man was not at fault
who pressed its warmth. No property would bolt
from where your careless orders made it halt,

albeit neither Cerberus nor Colt
was vigilant to see it stayed at anchor.
An oriole of claims would never molt
its champion plumes, as now would happen, if
its owner napped." He paused and sipped. "The canker
of viciousness which nearly was the skiff
which crossed the Styx with us was then unknown
to most, as I believe. A boxer's biff

that bruised the flesh but never warped the bone
was what we knew of violence." Gordon nodded.
"And camp fire talk was lyric in its tone
as like as not. Its warp and woof were hope,
its shaping force romance. The visions wadded
within the brains of many had the scope
of Persian tales of wonder, and we talked
because the dreams were not content to mope

in silent anonymity. We hawked
for comets unabashed and told it frankly;
and no one laughed, because we all were chalked
with matching moonrays." "California then
was half Manannan's isle, in spite of rankly
concocted messes never meant for men—

like that," said Dade, "you serve. Time's altering hand
has spared the food; it's still as bad as when

I first exposed my liver to this land;
but that's the sailor's star. The pleasant fellows
who formed the vanguard didn't understand
that gold would be a means to drain the jakes
of every city human jaundice yellows
with septic, ruptured gall. The civic aches
of foreign lands have now a sovereign cure:
the felon packs his felony and takes

a clipper bound for California, lure
for every rogue who finds St. Johnstone's tippet
a menace to his throat." "And here he's sure,"
said Galloway, "of ground hog volunteers
to dig—" "I think you must have cooked a snippet
of Hercules; this looks like ass's ears;
or are they yours, now you've the Midas touch?"
asked Dade. "A miner's appetite pickeers

with what it finds, and shouldn't probe too much
in natural history's multiplex resources,"
responded Gordon. "Use a coffee crutch
to help it past your palate, and reflect
that you'll be cook again when light recourses.
What happened when the spate of hoodlums wrecked
the ship of kindly fools?" "As always, pard,
sophistication. I did not detect

the social shift till wisdom hit me hard,"
said Terence. "At the time I teamed with Brothers,
Arbaces B., an out of usual card
who knew of worlds first hand that I did not,
the underworld included in the others.
But yet he was John Harvard to the dot;
he'd made a votive pilgrimage to Greece
to be where Byron fired his lyric shot

for wine and war; he'd chant a Sapphic piece
or quote a Spanish league of Lucan's Latin.
He'd show you how the sharpers flam to fleece
the yeanlings such as I, or flirt in French
with any gambler's Gallic piece of satin
that might be nigh. He'd drink enough to quench
the thirst of Mose the Bowery Boy, and yet
the sun would find him standing by to drench

and dredge Long Tom. He'd sluice it with his sweat
but talked, perhaps, of Kant, and wouldn't mention
the wassail he worked off. I never met
diversity till Arb and I were yoked.
And, too, he had a wit of good invention;
he kept his powder dry, however soaked
he was himself—it always caught the spark.
But still there was some hashish that he smoked

which undercut the man. That corner's dark
to me, and for the nonce it doesn't matter,
as prior to my gest I didn't mark
his absent cog." As Terence cited this,
he clanged his cup upon his empty platter
and set them both aside. "As yet in bliss
of ignorance that Lucifer had sent
the Diggings reptiles pouched in the Abyss,

we left Slumgullion Gulch and pitched our tent
at Whiskey Slide in Forty-nine's October
and staked a claim which Brothers titled Lent,
for while we labored there we gave up gold.
But, covering the sore, and short of sober,
we lied aloud that Mother Lode had doled
a pile to make old Crassus smack his lips.
We didn't coin the jest, for it was old

when Leif the Lucky sailed with empty ships
from Norman's Woe, and bragged about the riches

he'd found among the Skraelings. Our eclipse
of sunny truth with fable's phantom moon
would not have fooled old probers of the ditches
and pits with which we've pocked the dirt cocoon
of sometimes latent gold. But where we aired
our Monte Cristo myth was a saloon

to which a pair of greenhorns had repaired,
though ripe in other ways. They held diplomas
from Botany Bay, perhaps; we never shared
their reminiscences, so that's a guess
distilled, post mortem, out of the aromas
of known ones, neatly paired as pawns in chess
with those who overheard the horns we blew
as fanfare for defeat." He paused to press

a smoldering brand upon his pipe, and drew
till fire was captured, and its vapor mounted
as straight as though its trainer was a flue,
so breezeless was the night. "Well, Arb and I,"
then Dade pursued, "while strolling home, accounted
for four men's share of shadows, two too shy
to show themselves. The careless boldly did,
for Mad Tom's mistress whitened all the sky

as we returned to Lent, which lay amid
some clumps of cedars luckily. Their sloughing
of lifeless lower branches killed the bid
of murder to be secret; for they shed
the bark which else would put a muffling stuffing
between a fracture and a furtive tread—
they snap like houses settling for the night."
"I know," said Galloway, and jerked his head

assentingly. "A secret stepper might
as well attempt to pass that master sentry,
a Guinea hen, unnoticed. Cedar's light
and scatters, so the ground about a grove

is brittle with it. Were these Sydney gentry
announced before you slept?" "Oh, Arb's a cove
who always says good night to Barleycorn,
and I'm polite myself at times. We drove

the peg from which to hang the hunting horn
of ended paper chase; if we'd not lingered
to shoot the bolt, I'd long ago have worn
a hemlock overcoat. But as we sipped,
a crack like river ice that's being fingered
by thawing winds resounded. Brothers nipped
inside the tent, rebounding with his gun,
though on the quiet. 'Bear or dog?' he lipped.

'I bet it's bear that drools for bacon.' 'Done,'
I took him up, for mice are clumsy slinkers
compared with bear, while canines find their fun
in making noise. 'We'll spot some miner's hound,
or else a skunk that's seeking other stinkers
and smells that claim of ours.' 'Let's stand our ground
within the tent, on second thought,' he breathed.
'Whatever's there won't near us, if we're found

in moon rays as revealing as were wreathed
for slept Endymion. Hound nor bruin neither,
nor even the rankest polecat ever seethed
in perfume's antipole, will press his raid
if we're in sight.' And so I primed my breather
of sudden death and stretched in ambuscade
beside him under canvas; but the booze
unstrung my vigilance, when nothing strayed

in view. I'd lost my grip on current news
when Brothers spoke, though not to me. 'You nearly
were shot as bears,' he chirruped. 'Did you lose
the trail to camp at monte? Have a drink,
and maybe it or we can steer you clearly
to where your digging lies.' 'We didn't think

you was awake and tried to tiptoe past,'
a voice explained why they were on the brink

of Lent so quietly they could be classed
with prowling beasts. But we were not suspicious
and thought that forty rod had laughing-gassed
their compass sense. Because but half awake,
I still was semi-consciously ambitious
to shoot whatever hydra, sphynx or drake
we'd thought we'd heard before I slipped asleep,
so I was gun in hand." "Did neither snake,"

asked Galloway, while getting up to heap
some fuel on the fire, "observe your rifle?
You'd think they would have shot." "They didn't creep
with trigger sticks for fangs," said Dade. "A stab
is silent, or its sound is such a trifle
it doesn't gossip, while a shot can blab
skulduggery's afoot; I've always thought
they reasoned thus. Though Arb and I could grab

our guns, and wouldn't care if firing brought
all Whiskey Slide to see what caused the shooting,
they knew for certain what we'd not been taught
and so had nerves that we had not. They planned
to leave the vampire's trail when through with looting
a camp which none had found them near, the brand
of Cain doffed like a hat. Now, more alert
than I was, Arb had grasped the lost demand

for his devise to render life inert,
when greeting guests, however unexpected.
He left it when he strode across the dirt
we'd sifted unavailingly for dust
(a California paradox connected
with mining, pard). Though then it seemed a crust
of gold was on the claim, so richly glowed
a barely gibbous moon, whose light nonplussed

the eye no more than dawning. What it showed
was what we were ourselves: a pair of hairy,
uncurried tramps, completely a la mode
for Ground Hog's Glory, say, or Hoodoo Bar,
or even Whiskey Slide, where there was nary
a valet nor a barber shop to mar
the shaggy dog misrules of bachelorhood
which guide us here." "We've carried it too far

and for too long," sighed Gordon. "God, I'm good
and sick of razorbacking it! What followed?"
"Well, Brothers brought them back to where I stood:
a lank one like myself, the other squat
as Midge the Miller. 'Guess we must have hollowed
a honey tree too many, lads, and got
our bearings tangled,' Limber Jim confessed.
He munched his words like mush he'd found too hot

and I supposed him foreign. Brothers guessed
exactly, though. 'How's Liverpool?' he queried,
while reaching for his flask. 'We haven't messed
on kippers lately,' Barrel Build replied;
'we're tars who tired of salt and jumped the ferry
that brought us to the better buttered side
of Mama Earth. Had luck?' 'Oh, lots of it,
but bad,' I told a man who thought I lied.

'This candle gleam of rye should help a bit
to light you to your camp,' said Arb, and handed
the chap a slice of quantum sufficit.
Now when he raised the cup, the hand that held—
the left one—showed its back, on which was branded
the letter B. The cat, you see, was belled;
oh, not with iron, but he'd been tattooed.
It told me nothing, but to Arb it spelled

the possibility our brags had brewed
a nasty malt. But meanwhile he was pouring

for Long and Slim, who groaned, 'I can't! I'm stewed
enough to cook an ostrich for the Queen,
and she'd as soon give queening up for whoring
as eat a toughish ostrich. I ain't mean
nor jealous, though, so give it to your chum;
and I will hold his gun, so he won't lean

so far to port he'll crumple like a thrum
while swigging with his right.' This run of fancy,
in keeping with a happy souse's sum
of winged but footless wits amused me, pard;
and though to give a drunk a gun is chancy,
I'd oiled my cortex, too, with spikenard
and meant to humor him. But as I made
a transfer move the voice of Brothers jarred

the peaceful scene to pieces. 'Keep it, Dade!'
he yelled, to yank me out of slack compliance
a jiffy short of death. There was a blade
in Quasimodo's hand, the lunagraph
of flashing beams announced; but my reliance
was Arb to cope with him. The lunar calf
of fuddlement had turned the Minotaur;
he leaped to seize my gun, and had it half

before my wits were mustered for a war
to end all wars for one of us. The pickle
of elks with tangled horns was then the score
for both of us. The rifle held us bound
as galley slaves, beneath the mortal sickle
that hovered like a condor, over ground
we ramped upon like wapiti, and snarled
as they cannot; it edged upon the sound

the wolves were making while their jaws were marled
with human clay. But in the end I stumbled,
for stepping on a nub of root, not gnarled
like many such but smooth as Yorick's pate.

I folded like a napkin, and he tumbled
atop of me, deflating with his weight
already gasping bellows." "Which one kept
the rifle?" Gordon asked. "On landing, fate

denied its use to both; the weapon leapt
in greased-pig style from shaken grips and slithered
apart from where I found myself inept
to throw the duckbill off. Or so I deemed,"
said Terence. "I was struggling, but I dithered,
the gun no longer threatening, till he schemed
to blind me and announced it. 'Pipe the world,'
he counseled me, 'as when a nail has reamed

your eye pits like an oyster is depearled,
you may be what you might call hard of seeing.'
His claw moved into view, its talons curled
like ospreys' when they plummet toward a prey;
but I had writhed at sight of Gloucester being
so maimed in what I knew to be a play;
I detonated, pard. The boiler burst,
and he was off me, spilled the other way

from where the rifle glimmered, half immersed
in shadows reaching from a cedar huddle.
He sprang for it, but fury put me first,
though not ahead enough for me to fire;
I grabbed the barrel from the molten puddle
or island in the murk, and with desire
to stamp him out, I bashed him like a bug.
I wreaked my will precisely with the ire

ophidians arouse, encountered snug
in tent or blanket. Door nails were no deader,
nor any bear whose monument's a rug,
than he when I had struck; my rifle's butt
was smeared as though with cheese, I found, the cheddar
of what had been his brains. And that's the what

and wherefore of the kill." When Dade had done,
he held a flambeau till its heat was cut

and lit his pipe anew. The lilting run
of water in the creek, the muted hissing
of wood that's spent the force to snap its gun,
and practice rustlings by a rising breeze
were all the sounds for minutes then. "The missing
exode now: the blade of Damocles
is pendant still," said Galloway. "What of
the dirk the goblin raised? It didn't freeze

aloft to wait your fire." "I stood above
the daunting miracle of life subtracted
until a rifle banged, to brace and shove
my sagging parts together." Terence smoked
before resuming. "Brothers, pard, had acted
against more odds than crowded me, though stroked
by Bowie's mortmain twice and badly slashed
before maneuvering to the tent which cloaked

the rabies antidote with which he flashed
the ape's percussion cap. So it was over.
So was the aureate age of trust, which crashed
throughout all Eldorado. Emperor Change
had upped the price of gold; replaced the rover
of Arden's wilds with hardened wights who range
a Limbus Patrum this side Paradise
so far that— Why, it didn't strike me strange

tonight that quiet solitudes could trice
from hat a demidemon." "You were liefer
to find sting-ray than tuna on the ice
of one you'd never met," said Gordon. "Still
your rod-divining couldn't have been briefer;
I don't see why it dipped to give the bill
of malice's particulars." "He held
himself so like the first I rendered nil;

perhaps all murder does," said Dade. "He spelled
his purpose by his stance to one the wiser
for what I now have told. An instinct smelled
the taint more rapidly than thought could move,
and memory erupted like a geyser
to warn me that I mustn't wait to prove
my hunch's theorem. Wherefore I'll keep
a second skull to ponder when the groove

unbidden recollection picks is deep
as Davy Jones's locker. For the present
let's slam the door on that, though." "I'm for sleep,"
said Galloway, "and do not fear to dream,
for I've a unicorn of thoughts, a pheasant
among the mud-hen others, sun supreme:
I'm leaving Backsidefirstland to the daws
who prize it; and in doze I'll glide that stream

in Avalon, as sleep has natural laws
that Nature flouts here. Breeze myself, and blowing,
I'll steer with sternson toward the flukes and flaws
of squall West weather." "Both the fire and I
have burned too low," said Dade. "I've lost the knowing
of where by preference the halcyons fly
and what the capital of the State of Grace."
He fed the flames. "Tomorrow I may try

believing elsewhere isn't misty space,
but now I'll smoke again before I slumber.
So choose the spot you will, to be the base
of visions, custom built, of Delaware,
and spread your blankets." "Needles in the number
that carpet Cibola's forest everywhere
you'd think a cushion, if you didn't know
they'll promptly scoot from under you, and bare

the rocks they tricked you on; no bonus, though,"
said Galloway, "of lovely siren singing."

He pierced the ground with sticks he'd cut—a blow
to forest rodents, passionate for salt,
the perspiration spice, so richly clinging,
that brined the boots he hung. He called a halt
to deshabille at modesty's frontier
and settled in his bedding, till a vault

of recollection livened him when near
the lapse of consciousness. "Another query,
so curiosity won't stake me here,"
he called to Dade, "an inch from Morpheusville.
Until you took the road to Canterbury
about this Chrichton, Brothers, and your kill,
you never mentioned him. Why is he blacked
from notice if, you say, he paid the bill

for scraping past the bar which nearly wracked
you both. Now why'd you split the span?" "I've hinted,"
said Terence, puffing, "that his structure cracked.
The secret drawer in which the key is hid
is one I never found, despite unstinted
exploring of the mystery. What he did,
I know, however. Jamshid's right-about
from white to black could not have been a skid

a whit more startling. Wounded, he was out
of action as a miner till he'd mended,
and boredom broke the wall of some redoubt
he'd had to patch before, I'd guess. It caved
when loafing with some blacklegs who'd befriended
a man who talked their Latin, when he craved
the liking that he scorned with half his brain.
In time he found some conies that he shaved,

for fun at first, and to display his grain
of knowing wood—I'm counting that a motive—
to those who watched, amused. He finished fain
of sorcery with cards—of lesser weight

than picks, and surer pay. I found him votive
to sharping; I was fool enough to prate,
because I liked the man, and earned, perhaps,
the mockery I drew. With that debate

our team was out of sorts and in collapse,
with neither," Terence shrugged, "no more than
     speaking
when parceling our common stock of traps
and fairly come-by gold. From Whiskey Slide
he went, no doubt, to richer fields for seeking
the Golden Fleece by means that crumble pride,
a flag he once had flown, as I'll endorse.
It's all I know; he may have left or died;

I never saw him after that divorce."

5

In and Out of the Woods

The careless man the firelight had preserved
from mastication waited, in the morning,
for two worked to see that he was served
with room enough for wickless human wax.
With care to keep a scouring rag adorning
reality, as rendered by an axe,
the partners lifted patience unperplexed
by fear or doubt. "A dreary pair of facts:

we hide him, making sure the wolves are vexed,
and cater to the worms," said Terence, shrugging.
"There are some words, but I've no tag of text
for one I've slain. Let others praise his worth
that did it while he lived," said Gordon, tugging
a stiffened arm, to make it fit the berth
they'd dug indifference. Noting then a nude,
a prodigy of hip and bosom girth

a rip along a sleeve revealed, he viewed
his friend with hoisted brows. "Our client, Terry,
reminds me, through the fact that he's tattooed,
of what you merely touched and hurried past:

why should the harmless B of bird or berry
inform this Brothers that a man was cast
in Girty's mold?" "He knew the British brand
repeater barracudas, which are classed,"

said Terence, as he fed the spade some land,
" 'Bad Characters', by army regulations,
and get the leper marks on either hand
of B and C, in needlework, cashiered."
He plumped the dirt on truce with inclinations,
for ill or good. "When he has disappeared
from every ken but ours, let's stake a claim
we'll file as 'Sightless Porkers Persevered

and Found an Acorn', or some kindred name,
in Angel's Camp. We must be certain owners."
"But needn't start a stampede by the fame
of what we've found; we'll mutter that we hope
we are about to leave the jinx bemoaners,"
said Galloway, "or some such casual trope.
Here, let me have the spade. I caused the grave,
and if you'll go for Hercules, I'll cope

with its demands. But what about the knave
you hurried to—can Bowdler hear?—the cellar;
and Haemophile, that fleeing couldn't save;
should we inter the bones?" "When ants have picked
and time has made them touchable. They're feller
than I can stomach, pard, and I predict
that yours will take delay in kindness." Dade
then strode to get the hinny, which was tricked

with gear it didn't wish; the hitch was made
which held the load secure; and they departed
the scene of violence, and wealth that played
the flying carpet, homing to desires,
as one was sure—and one, less single-hearted,
was wondering. And yet for all the lyres

that fancy strummed, or puzzlement which dimmed
the music of enchantment, there were wires

which telegraphed the news of where they trimmed
their sails for Angel's Camp. For cruisers, seasoned
in timber, they had eyes for all that skimmed
the air, or frisked on branches or the ground;
their ears were tuned to forest sounds and reasoned
about their causes; as they swiftly wound
among the soaring ponderosa trunks,
their nostrils filtered breezes, whether crowned

with blossom scents, degraded by a skunk's,
or sick with musk of snakeries. For hours
they held the silences of Trappist monks,
alive upon two levels—out of sight
of either's land in one, while tied by powers
of observation to the niche of light
that moved with them. Then Terence, in the lead,
espied a shape which warranted the fright

the hinny promptly showed. It nearly freed
itself from Galloway, the hybrid's warden,
it balked so furiously; and screamed, to plead
release to give to panic what it asked.
Half Hercules in fact, it rope-towed Gordon,
who found a single hand too greatly tasked
but could not drop his gun. For grizzly bear
were snarling in the thicket which had masked

the mother and a smaller brace, whose hair
was also ruffed in sign that they resented
the man who faced their summer nooning lair—
protecting Gordon's undesired retreat,
though slowly backing. Terence was contented
to honor truce, but frantic screaming beat
the war drum of the snarling parent beast
until its fury hemorrhaged and, fleet

though half a ton of toothy, vital yeast,
it charged. Beyond the sights that reflex hoisted
there yawned a maw whose size, for Dade, increased
until it seemed a Shenandoah Cave,
where stalactites and stalagmites were foisted
by rage's will to rend. He heard it rave
as typhoons do when roaring to destroy;
he seemed to taste the spume that welled to lave

a reef of lip to give a wrecker joy;
he smelled the curdling breath it belched in bounding
and felt the talons tear the breeches buoy
in which life makes the bid from ship to shore
it never wins—then felt in fact the pounding
the shoulder takes when bullets buck a bore
at powder's instigation. Black and thick,
the fumes next hid the surging carnivore

and Terence skittered sideward, cricket quick
but none too soon. He felt the rushing bruin
athwart his thigh; it spilled him, as a flick
of finger nail would sweep away a midge;
disarmed and prone, he saw the mighty ruin
his shot had made collapsing like a bridge
whose piers a flood has underswept. He rose
to watch the long, subsiding spinal ridge

and then the crimson bursting from the nose,
to tell him that he need not use the Bowie
he'd whisked from sheath. "In England, I suppose,"
he muttered, "Wordsworth, pacing in a wood
in quest of Nature's gifts at Nether Stowey,
discovered no such premium of the good
and bountiful dispenser of the stuff
that sonnets stem from. It's a shame; he could

have made a dazzler on a grizzly's ruff
of threatening hackles." Turning then, he shouted

to Galloway, in combat with the tough
determination of a minor mule
to go where bears were not. "The cubs are routed,
and ursa major's dead, so take the fool—
I take it back; so take sound common sense
to where he can be calmed. Meanwhile I'll cool

my nervous system at the small expense
of burned tobacco, since there's not a tavern."
Some minutes later fragrant smoke was dense
about the tree they leaned against. "I caught
some over-shoulder glimpses: what a cavern
of mouth—and Christ! the teeth with which it's fraught—
a grizzly has," said Gordon. "What a heap
of wrath for bits of lead to render nought!

And you had only one with which to keep
a hurricane at bay: in Boone's Kentucky
or Crockett's Tennessee they didn't reap
the lives of bear more deftly than you did;
but was it chance or skill?" "Oh, I was lucky,
but not today. My ball went where I bid
because I'd had the luck," said Dade, "to meet
a junior Dan or Davy here amid

the holes that hope has dug." "And found a cheat
so often," Gordon sighed. "But not for ever!
Ah, man, we've found a pot of gold as sweet
as any that's a rainbow's colophon!
What son of Hawkeye taught you how to sever
a grizzly's link with life?" "A paragon
of contrasts." Terence added to the mist
of hovering smoke. "For though he looked as wan

as Chaucer's starveling clerk, he was a cyst
of vigor. Graceful on the trail, he shambled
so awkwardly in town, he looked the gist
of all the bumbling hayseeds ever mocked

astage to please the townies, pard. He rambled
in speech so much you'd think his brain was crocked
and yet the man was clever at so much
that most are not, and had a noggin stocked

with subtle lore: antennae which could touch,
and coolly, marvels science still is learning."
"Relearning," Gordon puffed. "A shaman's hutch
I entered reeked with herbs my grandsire used,
but I'd forgot till then. Through urban spurning
of all things rustic, values are refused
when towns expand, and man a Hadrian Wall
against the rural—well or ill abused;

inevitable, I guess. How did they call
your homespun friend?" "His name," said Terence,
rising,
"was tripartite, like cock-a-hoop or Gaul."
He knocked the dottle from his pipe. "The first
was one of those, horrendous, brutalizing
ritual names which Gothic parents cursed
their children with more frequently than now:
a hyphened necklace of a Bible verse

which choked reciters. I've forgotten how
the syllables paraded; Doom was mentioned
with gusto, though, so maybe you'll allow
his right to drop it, using Olney Jones
except of Sundays; then the well intentioned
Gehenna pavement rattled as the bones
of Knox and company clicked on them." As Dade
so spoke, he picked from several handy hones

the rock which boded best to whet a blade
and spat to keep the temper safe from friction
while edging it. "I met him when I played
the wampum seeker first, as green as grass
would scorn to be—the snide newspaper fiction
conceived by Easterners without the brass,

or else with too much sense to hunt for gold,
n y only knowledge of the West. En masse

a baker's dozen of us left the fold
where lambs can thrive—in this case, pard, the schooner
which hauled us north from Panama—and trolled
for nuggets, not a hook upon our lines."
"I did it, too," said Gordon; "towed my spooner
in ocean space before I knew the signs
of what a bite was like." "Where Murderer's Bar
now stands—for there were neither crimes nor mines

to mark the gold so near, and yet so far
from ignorance," said Dade, "we camped on treasure
we didn't find. But that is where my star
and that of Olney for an April while
were binary. To let you have his measure,
he'd wheeled—get this—a barrow every mile
from Illinois on west. It held his tools
and gun; that's all; he traveled camel-style

and drank mirages; no canteen. His spools
of thread, and cloth, were deer, afoot till wanted;
his Bowie was his kitchen ware, his rules
for sleeping well, forget that ground is hard
and nights not always warm. He was undaunted
atavism, freed of trammels, pard."
"But why should such a moth conceive the need
of gold?" asked Galloway. "His wings were charred

against the Paphian's lamp, the lot decreed
for all except that suicide of passion,
the self-igniting bird," said Dade. "His need
for powder once enticed him to the town
of Cairo, where the clerk that wrapped his ration
was what he judged a halo in a gown,
and yearned for it as children do for cake
behind a bakery window. He was down

and took the count from love with speed to make
Kit Marlowe satisfied. It was consumption,
because he had no other want to take
the edge from craving; but his lacks were pence,
a job, a home—and even, pard, the gumption
to tell the corposant what was immense
within him." Terence tossed the stone away
but didn't sheathe his knife. "I mean to flense

this forest whale, since I am chef today,
and broil us grizzly porter house for luncheon."
"I'll get the grill," said Gordon. "Did he lay
his callowness so bare?" "A confidant
was what he'd never known; he drained the puncheon
and let me have it all, when sure I'd slant
no supercilious eye. But I was paid
for tact today; you didn't have to plant

my mortal hulk because of him," said Dade,
"my sylvan cicerone, intent and thorough
in shoeing tender feet. For once he flayed
a silver tip, to show how lead can glide,
unstopped by sinew that it else must burrow,
and strike the heart. The skull is fortified,
and shots at it can leave a kill in doubt;
but there's a thorax clue to ursicide,

a spiggot, hit, that turns the spirit out;
and so today my sighting didn't waver
or weathercock anent the spot to clout;
I knew." With this he forced his Bowie's nib
along a loin: a silver-tip engraver,
he peeled the pelt from hip to floating rib,
and from that half a baron of a bear
he carved a carnal plenty—chewed ad lib.

while Hercules was browsing, free of care,
at hand a trifle later. "Why'd you sunder,"

asked Gordon, using handy, brindle hair
for napkin, "ties with Johnny Appleseed?"
"Oh, I'd met Arb. We got along like thunder
and lightning then," said Terence, "and agreed
to leave the herd and weld a partnership.
Well, due to Arb's suspicion that the breed

of Ananias bred the limber lip
which warbled of a pond with bullion lining
its basin, we eschewed the sleeveless trip.
But Olney Jones stampeded with the ruck
who hoped to dodge the drudgery of mining;
they rushed to plunge for gold, as divers pluck
the oyster-fathered pearls—without the sharks
to mar the fun of playing chuck-a-luck

and always winning." "Count me with the marks
who bought the Gold Lake myth. I'd not have doubted,"
said Gordon, "tales of trees whose twigs or barks
were aureate, I suppose. In school I laughed
when history swore that old De Leon scouted
the Everglades for water with the craft
to hoist again the royals of his youth;
yet, given turn, I proved a dupe as daft

and bought my facts at any Gypsy's booth
in this New World that faces the Pacific."
"You'd never think a monster as uncouth
as Ursula could be so toothsome, cooked
by even one as far from scientific
as I," said Dade. He flung a bone that hooked
in whizzing flight and missed the aimed-for fir.
"Do you recall that any in the rooked

of wooden swords in search of Magi myrrh
resembled Nimrod?" "Half the Forty-niners
were diddled by the dimwit cockle-bur,
Stot—Stoddard," Gordon said, "who coined the pond;

but one who hoped to net its finless shiners
could dress in your description. If the bond
between the sketch and man was perfect, now
that I'm reminded, chance has waved its wand

and wafted him to Angel's Camp. The how
and what of such a waif are memory fixtures:
I recognized his stern before his prow
was turned my way, the night before we left."
"A week ago, when we and gold weren't mixtures,"
reminded Dade. "I guess he hasn't cleft
the mustard, any more than we had done,
or Mother Lode were long agone bereft

of that, her oddest, ill-adopted son."
He rose to kick the grate aside for cooling,
and kill the coals with dirt. "That flintlock gun
is one I'd share our secret finding with,
so he can give the star for whom he's drooling
a pile to twinkle at that makes him kith
to men of honored stature at a jump;
as gold's the stuff that is a Wayland Smith

for making mightiness of any lump
it cottons to."— But as he made a muddle
of dying fire and earth, and reached to dump
the coffee grounds as poultice for the boil
that scarred the humus,—matted by a huddle
of never counted centuries, a coil
of shadows thence away was deft to foal
another silence. Forest for his foil,

a buckskin-covered, hirsute figure stole
along the bank of frondage-shaded water
to where, below a falls, there boiled a hole
where canny trout would fin, awaiting prey.
"Oh, there's the son of a bitch, or else the daughter,
I'll chomp tonight," he breathed. He stopped to lay

his rifle gently on a fallen branch,
a nearby ponderosa's castaway;

he had no rod, or hook with which to ganch
the idling fish; his purpose was to tickle
the darter lurking near the natural stanch
which made the pool. He softly laid his poke—
a treasury like an outsize, deerskin pickle—
beside his gun, and doffed the shirt he'd soak
if wearing it while angling with his hand.
Then, quietly, as so much drifting smoke,

he stretched upon the needle-peppered sand.
The fingers he insinuated slowly
became seductive water, opiate bland
along the scaleless, rainbow-mottled skin;
but well before he'd charmed the creek fox wholly,
the woods disgorged another dextrous djinn
of sleight of hand, who coursed the water's shore
unheard by feral ears, because the din

of tumbling liquid was a covering roar.
The night had not been good to Vance, a weary
and disenchanted murderer, who wore
the signs of shivering sleeplessness, till dawn
had granted to a foodless man a dreary
retreat to Angel's Camp. A beaten faun,
but still an active one, and quick of eye
for all who might be relished, or be drawn

to feast on him, he saw the pool-side lie
of gun and poke and water-conning fisher.
The falls as his accomplice, he was spry
to filch the gold salami, and the arm
which made him equal to an angry wisher
of ill to him, and flitted. No alarm
was meanwhile felt by master angler Jones,
whose touch increased the power of its charm

until the fish's senses lost their tones
of wariness, and gave for sensual revel
the instant-action, wireless signal phones
it commonly maintained. It let the fist
of hostile hunger close before its level
of Mercury movement—helpless to resist
but striving frantically—returned to it.
"A beauty; six or over!" Olney hissed,

denying this appeal to manumit.
A second later, though, the trout was dropping
from hands which fluttered wildly. "Where's m' kit?"
He felt the ground, not trusting now the eyes
which failed him here. His supper fish, by flopping,
at length attained return to where the prize
of hedonism nearly was its doom;
but Olney didn't see. He searched the skies

for eagles or some bird of equal plume,
that might have thought his buckskin-guarded jewel
a morsel ravenous fledglings could entomb,
but soon would drop, apprised of wasted swoop.
He plunged into the stream, suspected cruel
enough to reach somehow and slyly scoop
his all in all: his future's aliment,
his golden noodles filtered from the soup

of years of painful panning. Solely bent
on garnering what he must before addressing
his prayers to loveliness, he hadn't spent
his dust for much but shot. The drinks and cards,
which kept his mateless fellows from assessing
their plight too painfully, weren't St. Bernards
that brought relief to him. He had a goal
he'd eyed so fervently, he needed guards

against ennui as little as the soul
of sainthood, forging eastward as a palmer.

But now where hope had been there was a hole
he didn't fill by floundering in the creek;
and so he snatched a notion as a calmer
of shrieking nerves. "My noggin's sprung a leak,"
he told himself. "I didn't tote my poke
but left it in m' cache with Lightnin' Streak"—

the love-name of his rifle. "What a moke
to rile myself for greens, and let my supper
absquatulate!" Contented with the joke
he'd played himself, he sought another pool,
seduced another trout into the upper
and deadly zone of air, and sped this fool
of fancied paradise to where he camped.
Now in the interim the miching ghoul

who'd ravished hope was whistling as he tramped.
He threw the rifle in the water stretching
to where his mind was now: the fleshpots vamped
to feed so men could drink. Among saloons
that bunched to make a subject for an etching
by Toby Belch, his goal was that of Coon's:
the Buckhorn, quill of firewater holes
because of Ross, a Boniface blue moons

discover only seldom. Later shoals
of dry esophagi would follow yearning
to this Sargasso Sea; but now the moles
of Calaveras County turned the earth
they kept their noses in. A few were burning
the midday candle, though, and had a berth
along the bar—or at the table where
Arbaces Brothers watched his bankroll's girth

expand, with eyes that steadily were spare
to mirror feelings. His were those of gloating
and high excitement, held in check with care,
despite a weariness that nagged at nerves

and seared his throbbing cerebrum—denoting
he hadn't slept since sidling from the curves
which made Sabrina luscious, at the thought
of other, untouched beauty. Next the swerves

and eddies of the tides of chance had brought
in sequence three, for sex or cards impassioned
and rife with gold they'd bet. Sabrina'd wrought
the miracle of forming from desire
the pillars of a faro bank, refashioned
as one for poker, once she'd found the fire
and opulence she wished. By stakes to kill
the faint of purse, she'd sorted from the mire

of piker ruck the trio with the will
and wherewithal to plunge. They hadn't faltered
when he at length replaced the sparkling shill—
a discard of the deal no longer eyed
with fervor which the Tristrams held unaltered
for any two Iseults of pasteboard, dyed
unskillfully and specked with Mosca dung.
The latter blurred the pricks which were a guide

to fingers trained for sensuousness among
the nuances of what would pass for level
to all but scholarship. He hadn't stung
with hornet fierceness, likely to repel;
he made a slope, with caution for a bevel,
on which their fortunes climbed betimes, or fell,
but in the main the latter. Night had waned,
and boarding houses clanged the luncheon bell

which tolled the birth of noon; but Arb had gained
as much from each to make it sacrificial
to cash and quit, so each perforce remained
for further bleeding. And another bled
from wells where missing treasure, though initial
to agony, was not the cause of sped

and maddened eyes impinged upon a pit
that normally was covered by a spread

of earth, so artfully concealing it,
a dog would not have dug investigation.
But now the cache was open to the wit
of any dull, myopic passerby—
who'd find, perhaps, the side by each relation
of jerky and of silk of brilliant dye
an oddness; yet he might not ask the man
whose gasps of pain forbade him a reply

the sense of velvet next to pemmican.

6

A Number of Preludes

As Brothers dealt the cards he chose to hold
and meted, like a god, the sweet or hapless
express from fate to those to whom he sold
the scoring chips, the partners yet were on
the spot where Dade had left a giant sapless,
albeit tasty. Readying to be gone,
though leisurely, to give the carnal lump
that each had wolfed a start to join his brawn,

they smoked to help digestion past the hump
and chatted till— "To arms!" said Gordon, reaching
to where his leaned against the grizzly's rump.
"We're not alone in Inglewood." "That pair
are clearly also graduates of the teaching
that made us Bachelors of Taking Care,"
said Terence, checking then his rifle's cap.
"To rob Sir Trite, they're skittish as a hare

or mincing reynard, fearful of a trap."
The bearded twosome and their burdened sorrel
approached, but halted short of camp. "The sap
been running right for you?" the leader called,

his voice as straight New England as a moral
emblazoned on a sampler. "Oh, we've hauled
some mites of dust to light beyond a ways;
but chicken feed's for chickens," Terence stalled.

"We're heading now for better grass to graze,
but where I wouldn't know." Forlornly shrugging,
he wried his mouth. "Well, there's no trail they blaze
to lead to gold, and that's a granite fact,"
the twang declared. "The only plough is plugging
to turn the furrow; that's what Bunyan backed,
and it'll do for Zebulon and me."
They wandered off, the while the partners packed

their gear on Hercules. "Duplicity:
your name is that," said Gordon, "or Mendacious;
the truth's not in you." "Nor can untruth be;
I let it out," said Terence, as they worked,
"to screen our trove. A lie so fine and spacious
must drain mendacity." With this he jerked
the diamond hitch to tautness, so its web
contained the hinny's load. "Your fancy firked

the hopes we'd made a strike for him and Zeb,"
said Galloway, "but what of the assassin
that got away? What's flotsam with the ebb
can float the flow." "It can. I think he won't,
nor will he tell of where his mate spadassin
is buried. Not," said Dade, "from *mauvaise honte*
but out of fear that dead men can confute
an axiom, and spin a yarn." "I don't

agree," said Gordon, "that we've lost the brute."
He freed the hinny's rope and started leading.
"He'll not return alone; I'll bid your suit
so far, and likewise think he'll linger mum
about the claim where jumping led to bleeding.
But though we left his mob forever dumb,

malfaisance wasn't childless when they died,
so he can get replacement rascals, chum,

and try again. I vote we don't abide
in Angel's Camp—bedamned to celebrating—
but long enough to register our nide
of aureate fledglings and restock with stores."
"Your vote is mine," said Dade, gesticulating
for emphasis. "For wine and song are chores
we can defer until the claim is cleaned.
Tonight perforce we'll slumber back of doors;

but next the word is 'slave' till we've demeaned
a mine to nothing but a worthless hollow."
In silence then they strode to reach the gleaned
and shovel-pitted banks of Angel's Creek,
their guide to a saloon, the Golden Swallow:
a gate to Angel's Camp, they used, to seek
the solace of transmuted rye and corn
while planning their advance. "Because you're Greek

for glibly leaving outraged fact forlorn,
you'd better see the camp alcalde, Terry,
and blow a modest, melancholy horn
about a claim which seems to show a trace
of likely color. I could never bury
the pride-of-Croesus truth within my face;
my joy would stage a prison break of hives
and toss the game." "I'll wangle legal grace

for what we claim, in language which deprives
the strike of any promissory glamor,
but—" As the barkeep, swapping liquid knives
for mineral ones, approached, he loosed the latch
and held his poke so it could speak the grammar
of California trade. The gleaming batch
of particles the crow-eyed tapster pinched
was proof that whiskey's price was treasure's match,

but Terence neither looked surprise nor flinched.
"As I was saying, pard, I'll smoke their optics,
if you will have our hippo-ass uncinched
and find a spot to lodge. I'll meet you, where?"
"The Buckhorn." "Right. Ross Coon's among the
    Coptics
of Angel's Camp I'll warrant debonair,"
responded Dade. "I'll scout for Olney Jones
while on my mission, too." They shot their pair

of throats. "My sails need several other stones
like that to ballast them," said Gordon, gripping
the bar with hands unsteady as his tones
had suddenly become. "We've made it here
to where the cleats of law will outlaw slipping;
I feared we wouldn't make it to the clear;
I thought the bear would balk us, or the men
whom you bedaffed. I watched the trees for fear

a stationed one, adroit at toppling when
it saw the chance, call no warning 'timber!'
in falling to destroy us, Terry. Then
I didn't trust the earth, which had the feel
of ambushed treachery, that might unlimber
a quake the like of Tennessee's, the Reel—
the Reelfoot Lake creator. Yawning wide
beneath our feet, it next would snap to seal

the momentary chasm, us inside.
But we're in port, and slackening of the tension,
induced by doubts we would be, has untied
my bowlines, and I'm yawing; so I'll use
the jury rig of Barleycorn's invention
to get me on my course again." The news
of Galloway's unstringing, now that all
was pie—when he'd been gallant while the hues

of past horizons spelled the gloom of pall—
amazed but tickled Dade. "*You* voiced the tenet

that we should keep our truck with Bacchus small,
the better thus to hasten to our claim
come rooster crow; but Cicero in the Senate
and Cicero in mufti aren't the same
it would appear." He slapped his partner's back.
"Enjoy your cups and stand absolved from blame;

but I must file our claim, a temperate jack
and not a jack o' lantern, with a candle
of happy fortune showing when I crack
my phiz to gab. And I must crack it now
for Camp Alcalde Andrew Malcolm Crandall
or wait until Apollo wakes to plough
a new diurnal furrow. Don't forget
the Buckhorn's where you'll find my shaggy pow."

He grasped his gun, removed its capsule threat
of deadliness and left, while Gordon bolted
a rescue syndicate which cornered fret
between them and the waiting former shot.
His dragging feathers thus completely molted,
he stabled Hercules, secured a cot
for Dade and for himself, and strolled to make
the cited rendez-vous. Another, not

as friendly with content, and minus cake
of holiday, as gaming was official
and not a careless tilt for chance's sake,
was first, however. Mindful of the leech
for whom her artful luring was initial
to skilled phlebotomy—the lot of each
she held for him, Sabrina had returned
to watch the come and go of overreach

with eyes that didn't show they looked or learned.
A restful sleep abetting her cosmetics,
and groomed like polished scarabs, she discerned
the progress of the play above a drink

that might have been the whey of schooled ascetics,
so sober and remote from grog and chink
her attitude proclaimed her. Yet she saw
the hefty poke the barkeep reached to sink

his fingers in, when Vance advanced to claw
the buckskin mouth ajar and call for whiskey.
"Monongahela's all that fits my craw
today," he said. "The common slop's for blokes
that don't know how to pan." He ran a frisky
glance along the bar, in hope to coax
a grin from some applauder of his wit,
and saw what he at first appraised a hoax

a trickster mind had played on matter, hit
by hot desire the instant. "What a bundle!"
he muttered, ogling clothes and body—knit
to form the paradox that what was hid
was doubly on display. "I'd like to trundle
my hoop atop that countess katydid,
but hell—" And then she briskly walked his way,
not seeing him, it seemed, until she slid

on something latent, setting her asway;
and were it not for him, she might have tumbled.
"Excuse my clumsiness," he heard her say,
but couldn't translate, stunned by her perfume
and touch of hand on his. "I surely bumbled
that exit," she went on, "but you can plume
yourself upon your readiness." She flashed
a smile that might have lightning-ripped the gloom

of Erebus; and he, at first abashed
by airs and clothes which marked her class exalted
beyond his reach for womanhood that cashed
its perquisites, became a customer
instead of window shopper who'd defaulted
to goods beyond his means. "Oh, I can stir,"

he preened himself, "and you're too sweet a plum
to drop and not be caught." "You're gallant, sir,"

she praised him. "For I've been informed of some
who make no try to keep a woman standing,
but much prefer her on her halidom
to on her feet." He blinked but gulped the hook.
"I'll pull the rug and rig a happy landing
for yours tonight," he promised. "Caesar's spook,
but this day's my day, mort! I make a strike
to buy the Bank of England with, and book

a glide for swans in which to swim my pike.
Hey, barkeep, bring my apple cake a jorum
of punch with bubble wine. By God! I'd like,"
he told his captor then, "to shuffle off
this farthing of a town—" "And walk the forum
of 'Frisco?" she enquired; and heard him cough
with fierce amusement, knowing why he flinched.
"Arh, that's for hogs, and not our kind of trough,"

he said, when he had cleared the throat she'd pinched
by indirect reminder of the gallows
where many another Sydney Duck was lynched,
and recently at that. "Let's buy New York—
or Paris. We could make it by All Hallows
by cutting through the Isthmus." "Or an orc
could carry us," she said, and ground the thought
of being salad on this gibbon's fork—

especially in Paris, which was wrought
of what was left of dreams—amongst the whiteness
her smiling bared. "Your second notion's caught
my fancy: Lafayette, we will return
your courtesy with more than cold politeness,
for where you helped the torch of freedom burn
we'll plunk for license, not mere liberty,
and leave the slow-poke French a length astern

when running out the Derby of our spree,
eh? What's your name, my willing and my able?"
He thought a moment. "Duke will fetch me, see?"
He swigged his drink. "I'm writing back to Burke
to tell him I'm a peer and that my label
is Duke of Angel Diggings." With a smirk
he gave the golden liverwurst a whang.
"I guess I know what peers are made of." "Turk,

untouchable or sheer orangutang,"
Sabrina sipped her punch, "can be a noble
with what you gave so cavalier a bang,
if there's enough to suit the heralds, lamb;
but Paris shrinks a guinea to an obol
or groat, we'll say. To make Montmartre your jam
you'll have to graduate from duke to prince,
and I can point a way." "You wouldn't flam

a country cove?" She saw the warring glints
of hopeful greed and Cockney-cock suspicion
within his scanning eyes; and downed the wince
her gorge experienced at getting close
to such a cayman. But to clinch submission
from watchful cleverness, however gross,
she beckoned him to pair his head with hers—
and in so doing breathe a Nimuë dose,

no more the bane of Merlin than of curs,
of ambergris's brain-enthralling attar.
She watched his glance glide down the bannisters
which wound from winsome shoulders to a breast
whose foothills cleared the mists of lacy matter
from granted vantage point. At her behest—
a cobra hypnotized without a flute,
he quivered at the warmth of breath that pressed

an ear and fired his cockle. "There's a newt
(without the lively style that makes me eager

to go your way), I used to try to suit
but couldn't, so I ditched the skitterflit."
"No split for you?" he asked. "The pay was meagre,
and so was he. He never wanted it."
"He *didn't*!" Vance was startled. "Why the guy
that let you pass him wouldn't sink his bit

in Cleopatra served in Christmas pie.
What was he—gelding?" "No, I prize the notion
he buggered double eagles on the sly."
Sabrina giggled, giving Vance a pat
of gay camraderie, a potent potion
because it showed that all she snickered at
was what she held his verso. "What's your call?"
he asked her. "Arb's a finger acrobat;

and good," she answered. "Jesus, ain't they all?"
he interrupted. "Gambling ain't for sisters
of charity. He makes the tickets fall
to suit himself, of course, the which I can't;
so what's my play?" "He palms so fast it blisters
the eye that tries to catch him at the plant;
he never has to mark a card," she said.
"He's *really* good, but guts is where he's scant;

he'd have a fortune, if his ick was red
instead of yellow as a caterpillar's;
but any time he's called with steel or lead—
have you a rod?" "I had one," he replied,
remembering where he'd dropped it when the killers
he'd captained met a man who hadn't died,
as scheduled. "But I gave it to a friend,"
he finished, feeling once again the slide

of Gordon's speeding, barely missing blend
of blood and metal. "I can buy me others,
and he was shirtless poor," said Vance, to end
his fiction on an altruistic note.

"This neutral's name is Arb?" "Arbaces Brothers:
a college boy who somehow missed the boat
to Easyton, he'll tell you. It's a lie,
like everything he says except his vote

of confidence in cash; but let it by."
Sabrina touched him, gesturing. "Get a shooter;
it's just to wave, you needn't mash the fly;
and— Are you listening or looking, Duke?"
She laughed to show an optical freebooter
was what she liked. He grinned at the rebuke
but raised his eyes. "I see and hear you, too.
I buy a rod and gamble with the fluke,

and—?" "Wait until he's cleaned the dummy crew
he's plucking now. Go easy on your betting
till showdown is a case of him and you;
and never bare your teeth, of course, till then,
so he'll believe you're, too, a fish for netting
the boot-top way." "I'll act like Bumble Ben,"
said Vance, "and let him guess me goose for sure
until I plunge and show this Jennie Wren

my joker on the call." "I can't endure
to wait until he finds who's organ grinder
and who's the vervet working to secure,"
Sabrina whispered, "what his master needs
to take—when having richly wined and dined her
and something-elsed her, if the future reads
as I expect—a certain girl to France.
So get the gun, my knight, and do the deeds

to tack a Paris sequel to romance,
begun tonight in Angel's Camp." But pausing
to wrap her in an appetizing glance,
a glutton lifting up a viand's lid,
he patted her in transit doorward, causing
a quaver which her brilliant smiling hid.

Alone, she shook her head. "Great living God!
It felt as though the suckers of a squid

were sliming me. This punch is not the rod
to chase away that glimpse of prostitution's
Gehenna of gone looks—when any clod
that has a sou to buy her food can tread,
including vile abstainers from ablutions
like him. I hope Arb shoots him. Brandy, Ned,"
she raised her voice to call. But though it burned,
the liquor didn't cauterize her dread

of what the future banked, when she was spurned
by prosperous lechery, for ever questing
the youth that passed for freshness, overturned
although all knew it was. "The scot's too steep,
the take too low," she bit the words, "for besting
an urge to shrink away from dirt and deep,
unlighted sludge. A whore must pay the shot
but shouldn't have to charm a midden heap

to please a man who wants her and does not,
or not for long." She looked about her, noting
a husky tossing whiskey down the slot
and putting gusto in the show case of
a happy grin: a miner who was floating
on inner clouds of which he was the glove,
a taut balloon. Alert to understand,
by skill of her starvation, that the dove

had found him in the flood and showed him land,
she studied Gordon. In a minute learning
his alphabet from A to ampersand,
she shrugged. "A waste of time to coo to him;
besides, my pigeon, Duke, should be returning
and mustn't guess, anterior to the trim
his wings will get, that I am not his true,
devoted turtle, for— Oh, there's the skim

of Dismal Swamp, en route to get his due."
She met the wink of Vance with one combining
delight in him and in the charted coup,
then turned to follow progress in the glass
that made the tavern twins. Intent on mining
the placer claims at hand for loot en masse,
Arbaces was astounded when he found
a fourth beseeching him to lift the brass

of which he had a buckskin covered mound,
and planked it on the table, plainly willing
to go the road with it. The sight unwound
the wraps of limitations from his hopes
and let him see the prizes that the killing
of four such banks—presented by the dopes
he milked like cows—could bring. He could regain
the Hill's ancestral, venerated slopes:

recoup the standing which he had in vain
applied to mining for its restoration.
He built the vision with a buzzing brain
that yet retained its constant watchfulness,
and curtained off his cyclone of elation
from eyes that conned his own. His glance no less
aware of what was current in the room,
he noticed Bristol, whom he'd made confess

that powder was his better, pause to gloom
at sight of him, before resuming motion.
It took him toward a now more busy loom,
where several tapsters wove the soothing spell
of bawdy wit, and news, and bracing potion
which banned the homesick dumps. The brogans fell
with regularity, but Brothers watched
their path across the sawdust asphodel

to brass-enrailed Elysium. "He's been scotched,
I think, but still I like to map a rattler,

in case his courage—when his belt is notched
with belts enough—achieves a second wind."
His learned fingers read the tiny tattler
that told he palped an ace; wherefore he skinned
the ducat from the bottom of the deck
and dealt it to a man who won a thinned

but yet a cheering pot with it. The neck
of Galloway had meanwhile long been craning;
he searched the door for Dade, a steady check
which netted nothing; so he toyed with time
by adding to the drinks he was containing
with conscious effort now. As yet sublime
of mood, and though he bubbled with his charge
of ecstasy, his motions didn't rhyme

with purpose—never clumsy in the large
but near enough to lose the name precision.
His tongue was now a state occasion barge,
preserving dignity but tardigrade;
and objects might be multiplied in vision;
mock-solemnly, he stared them down and made
the feigning duos fall in ranks as one,
a process that amused him till a blade

as big as he arrived amongst the run
of work-completed miners. As a neighbor,
he drew from Galloway an idle pun:
the froth of his content and muzzy wit.
"The Buckhorn's stag as Priapus's sabre,
but so's all California." "There's a skit
a rod away; the harlot," Bristol growled,
"who works as capper for the cheating nit

who's dealing there." His heavy features scowled
at Arb and his involuntary payers;
and Gordon, gazing where resentment prowled,
beheld the murderous ranger of the murk—

the lone survivor of the hopeful slayers
he else had slain. "Why, it's the Devil's clerk,"
he roared, "who tried to short me of the fare
to Delaware again!" Bare-hand berserk,

he lurched to reach a panic-straddled chair.

7

Of Sundry Departures

The man beheld the point which neared his throat
and could not keep the peril from approaching
although his hand might seem the antidote,
as he himself was wielder of the knife
that reached and pierced. Pursuant to the broaching,
a carotid discharged in spurts the life
of one who'd built a temple out of shreds,
to house enchantment on a planet rife

with storms to stand Gibraltars on their heads.
He'd watched collapse and had no second forces
for resurrection; knowing snapped the threads
which keep a man in breath, except the last.
And then he'd used the zed of man's resources
to finish what he felt was overpassed—
while one who meant to knit his clay with straws
was drawing near to make that friendly cast.

The claim affirmed as legal by the laws
the Forty-niners had perforce invented
(as caught-short government had seen no cause
for statutes covering tracts of public land

where freehold was the boon of him who dented
the surface with a mattock), Dade, as planned,
enquired for Jones. "I know the gangrel Pict,"
said Andrew Malcolm Crandall. With a hand

whose fur was red as Reynard's own, he nicked
a compass point. "The Ishmael has a burrow
or hollow tree, or form that he has slicked
by thrice-abouting, wolf-wise, in the grass
on yonder rise. Or else he's at his furrow;
he's panning color. What he wants with brass
would puzzle Doctor Subtilis, though. The loon
can live on burnside thistles like an ass

and mumps from passing deer for breeks and shoon."
The camp alcalde grimaced as he pondered
a paradox. "He never sees Ross Coon—
I knew the kittle chiel at Texas Bar,
and whiskey's not a way he ever wandered.
So might you tell me what could ever gar
a lad who looks to ravens for a meal
and roebucks for his duds, and doesn't star

his nights with twinkling usquebae, to feel
the need to swink for treasure?" "Cosmic wonders,
if Sophocles will pardon me the steal,
abound," said Terence, scooping up his gun,
"but man's the most amazing—in his blunders
no less than in his arts, of which the bun
he's learned to win from grains is not the least,
I'll add. But there are some to whom the sun

is not our star at all; I'll find this priest
of no neccssities, and thank you, Crandall."
Yet what he found was difference deceased:
a shape whose blood was exiled from its veins—
while several hapless viewers of the scandal
of life that fled from life appraised the grains

of causatory evidence. "He did
the Dutch for sure." A finger showed the stains,

which blackened steel, to Dade. "He made the skid
on purpose for himself, and then unloaded—
ghk! The knife's his own." "He popped the lid
and dumped himself," a wagging beard agreed,
"but why? How come his powder all exploded
today? He was as queer as loco weed
but never seemed to mind his lack of sense."
"You can't know what could get such cousins treed

in Usher's house, so I won't make pretense
to say." An ear was scratched in punctuation
of that disclaimer. "Wait a minute, gents,
what's happened to the mile of blunderbus
his grandpa used the day he took his station
at Lexington?" "You mean at Fort Ti, Russ,
with Jeffrey Amherst; 'twasn't new enough
for Bunker Hill and all; but still the cuss

and it were always close as sneeze and snuff.
I always thought it was a kind of gristle,
attached to him." "And his potosi, Duff;
that *was* attached, like Crockett and raccoons
or Paul and a Corinthians epistle:
nobody ever wrote the poor gossoons
but him. Yet never mind the thoughtful saint;
it's strange the Adam of all musketoons—"
"But those were hand guns." "Well, the term is quaint
and should apply," said Russell. "It is puzzling
that both the things he kept as close as paint
to hussies aren't about. Who's got 'em now?"
"I've met some cormorants adept at guzzling
what isn't watched, but— Well, and anyhow
I heard him say a measure more of dust
was all he'd need," said Duffield, "to endow

whatever men from Borneo find a must."
He viewed the open cache. "His pack rat addings
have not appealed to any reaver's lust;
what did he want with bolts of colored silk?"
"It's simple as the primal mental gaddings
of any other savage of his ilk;
a brightness snares the darkness of their minds."
But Terence turned from skin like curdled milk,

that had been acorn brown, and swept the kinds
and colors of the cloth with painful vision,
reviving Jones—enamored of the finds
of finery he thought would win him smiles
and so must buy, for all his fixed decision
to corner troy weight. "For such textile styles
he must have shopped in 'Frisco," Terence thought;
and then addressed the rest. "Above are files

of buzzards I'd deny; and he is nought
that we will take delight in, if he's steeping
in August's sultry one and double ought
another day. Will any help me beat
a box together for his instant keeping,
and bear him to the ultimate retreat
and origin of man?" As all concurred
that death was something that they must delete

they set about the task that none preferred—
while Gordon, not yet marking Vance, was trysting
with drinks instead of Dade; and Brothers purred
in silence as he dealt and gained and schemed.
"The tetrad of donators here assisting,
I'll have the bullion for a plunge," he dreamed,
while filling out a flush, magician-wise.
"The beacon flare of fortune having gleamed

to point the way to where Golconda lies,
I'll let who wants to pick the rustic punters

and march the cits across the Bridge of Sighs
in San Francisco. There's the lode of lodes,
the true Pactolus of mazuma hunters;
but any one who stalks in the abode
of ivory must arm with elephant guns
or end as game himself. Till now the nodes

of Pluto and my star have not been ones
that greatly overlapped; I lacked the candy
to ride me past the riffles—and the runs
of Arnold luck that will betimes beset
the cream of cheats. But now the rhino's handy
to make a Barbary Coast Plantagenet,
and see me through to coronation, if
I have the skill on which I plump my bet,

because I know it's mine. Adieu, then, Sif,
my Thursday girl, who labors for her living;
for I'll be through with all that has the whiff
of gaminess. The doxie's button of
the rattle chain of demi-reptile giving
of quos pro quids; I'm done with smutted love,
or will be when I board the ship I want.
And cards will go; when I am fist in glove

with Haverford again, I'll sneer 'avaunt'
to every foible savoring of the sterile
and apt to cause miscrop. The bloods may taunt
my homely, chastened way; but I'll not care,
with Cynthia—" A roar bespeaking peril,
and from a point his mind had marked "Beware
of liquor-nurtured storm," transplanted him
from dreamt proprieties, and faithful care

of what in his charge, to where his trim
was sharking rogue. Too long awake for coping
with suddenness, he saw a pouncing vim—
from Bristol's stand, a man of Bristol's thews,

who howled he'd square accounts. The telescoping
of half expected fact and pressing news
developed in his brain a photograph
of Bristol's threatening self—although the clues

to truth were near, unnoticed. No such daff
of preconception, Vance was Mercury-certain
a man, whose axe was all the cenotaph
which had been raised to two whom he had known,
was rushing at him, spotted through the curtain
of smoky air. In panic to the bone
and full forgetful of his purchased arm,
he fled the table with a muted moan,

his goal a hyphen spacing him and harm.
But Brothers, tangled still in his confusion,
envisaged loss of wife, baronial farm
and hope, if he allowed the charging man
to scatter winnings by his wild intrusion,
and dislocate the game on which his plan
for life-salvation rested. Twinkling swift,
he snatched from Erewhon a lethal ban

on further lunging toward the crooked thrift
he saw as menaced, triggered home the hammer,
and drilled the trifling hole that made a rift
the width of the ecliptic. Severed thus
from middle earth events—a frantic yammer
his message of farewell to all the plus
of newly found dominion, Gordon fell,
the while his slayer watched the crashing truss

supporting aspirations, as the spell
of his illusion left, to show him murder
instead of self defense. His anguished yell,
"There goes it all for what I didn't mean!"
restored him, though, from shock, and was the girder
of efforts to preserve the carnal glean,

the soul however fully harvested.
Reacting first, he put the door between

himself and soon pursuit; but though he led
he followed, too.—For Vance, alike the leader
of hounds and hare, was first to near the tread
of boots that beat the tuneless funeral march
of graveyard yeomen. "Man, this work's a breeder,"
said Russ, who walked with Dade, "of thirst. I parch
and pass the Buckhorn for a sorry job,
and one, I will confess, that wets my starch,

for all my desic— What's the hustle, slob?"
The doorway of the tavern they were passing
had spat a man, who had no astrolabe
for bearings in his haste, and took a fall
in braking to avoid collision. Classing
the runner's rigging, Terence found him small
but toucan as to beak, a pitted ridge
dividing eyes that bulged. "In holt or hall

I've seen that pelican combined with midge,"
decided Dade. And then aroused reflection
informed him Galloway had been the bridge
between him and the oddly feathered bird
he'd thought he'd met. "Why, it's the rank infection
I—" There he lost his trend, because he heard
a shot, a gasping cry, perdition's hue,
and feet that pounded with its final word

to bring another speedster into view
that followed Vance, who instantly had scrambled
erect and off again. But Terence knew
the second desperation which emerged
and so forgot the first he would have gambled
he could have tagged. "Let's hold it," Duffield urged.
"There's been a killing." "Enter Justice Lynch."
The man beside him brightened, as there surged,

as rapidly as each could fight the pinch
an exit meant for two enforced on fifty,
a crowd of lungs which clamored for a winch
to loft a man the law of Abingdon
would execute imprimis—being thrifty
of time—and then affix the benison
of trial on the act. "Let's join 'em, gents,"
said Duffield's partner biersman. "Putting one

that's croaked ahead of six alive is sense
that I can't see; and just because this biscuit
resigned his interest in the present tense
is not a bind on us, who've kept our salt
and hate to miss excitement. I will risk it
that he will still be here, nor won't find fault
with us for the delay." "You got me sold,"
said Russ. "You must've studied logic, Walt."

They lowered Jones, and five released their hold,
to sprint and join the chase. The sixth was laggard;
for Dade, though slouching forward, felt the cold
of Niflheim then. His rifle mightn't aid
the man whose haunting face had been so haggard,
while he remembered it as grace-arrayed
with lights few others had; but he could not
desert the past they shared, while Brothers paid

for what it was he'd done. "He'll soon have shot
what bolt a man preserves who exercises
by shifting cards from spot to handy spot;
he hasn't got a worm-in-hen-yard chance
of taking any long Olympian prizes
from men who've kept their timber seasoned."—Vance
had meanwhile found a menace in the speed
of Brothers, whom a rapid backward glance

from time to time revealed as in the lead
of what he deemed pursuit. "She says he's lily;

but with a pack for brace, he'll have me treed
unless I shake him. He's a wallaroo
for covering ground—if laying off the filly
that nearly was the dumpling in my stew.
Why even dingos out of Scotland Yard
should never get the Friday luck I drew:

I catch the queen of diamonds off her guard
by being there with dust, when she was steaming
at being passed for bradburies the card
would hug instead of her, and wouldn't split.
A peach I wouldn't snap at, even dreaming,
because I'd think she'd pay me back in spit,
stampedes at sight of me like cats for fish;
she goes for me like saints for Holy Writ;

I'm half a foot from home; she's in my dish;
and then Jack Ketch's big and tougher brother,
who'd like to snap my bones to make a wish,
arrives and pipes me." Marking then a break
between the buildings, narrow for another
of greater brawn, the felon spun to take
the path it proffered. Darting in the hole
with all the finish of a racer snake,

he wriggled like an eel that fords a shoal
until he'd left the Lilliputian alley
and so could give his bitterness its goal:
a place to lose his luck at Angel's Camp.
Because to him the shadow's doleful valley
and that of Angel's Creek were of a stamp;
though he could leave the last, he lingered in
the darkened hollow, hopeless of a lamp

he thought it hank for hank. "I sneak a skin
as full of gold as London fog of lifters—
and leave it lying like a rusty pin
before I'd more than bought a mite of grub,

a gun I chucked to lighten load, and snifters:
a half for her; and never got to club.
You'd think I wore a ring of light for hat
and flapped my wings and gave a harp a rub

in Angel's Camp upstairs; one mousy pat
for buying champagne punch! I bet she's sorry
she steered me as she did, and lost the fat
she could have helped me spread around, but hell,
her sniffles ain't what loads my funeral lorry.
I'll freeze and starve a second starlight spell
while getting God knows where, but out of here
where luck's a shyster."— Tear drops for the knell

of Vance's plans for her were never near
the eyes Sabrina leveled at disaster,
a thing she knew too well to let a veer
of fortune cloud her eyes; it sharpened them
as chasing does a fox's. Ticking faster,
(the moment Brothers drew and fired, to stem
the tipsy rush which Gordon couldn't check,
though Vance had scuttled thence), her mind was
   phlegm

personified. She knew there was a wreck
before Arbaces cried his resignation.
She knew the rest would hound him, at the beck
of instincts older than the rise of man,
before the first barbaric ululation
replaced the harmony of cup and can
and brought a band of killers to their feet.
She knew that though her quasi-lover ran

and had the gift of muscle to be fleet,
he'd lost the bottom of his sticking power
in ways that put no blubber on the meat
of those that Cibola as yet entranced.
She knew some more. "When mobhood is in flower,

its pistils might remember that I chanced
to cozen two or three, at the behest
of one for whom their hate is now enhanced

by sharing it like germs—which can't arrest
a life except in swarms." A secret scorner
and motionless, she furthermore assessed
the bank that Arb had left, and then the poke
deserted by its now regretful mourner,
and waited, as the peace restorers broke
the hinges in their haste to clear the door,
while out beyond the loudening shouts bespoke

the sympathetic wrath of many more.
They hadn't seen or learned about the killing
except to hear it named, but jumped to pour
along the street and swell the yelling throng,
and bay announcement they were likewise willing
to drink the blood of one who'd done the wrong
that Jeddart justice told them to requite.
She waited for the landlord to belong

to what his customers had led, by right
of ringside knowledge; but the Buckhorn's owner,
alone of all but her, bestrode the site
of what had happened but a minute since.
Alone—herself apart—he was the donor
of moments spared to test for any hints
of life that might remain in Galloway.
Then, sure the heart had nothing to evince,

Ross Coon arose and turned to hushed dismay.
A man in middle life with crow-foot crinkles
about his eyes that told he could be gay,
he wasn't now. "The bullet snuffed the light,"
he said, Virginia-voiced. "At times the wrinkles
will smooth away, but this one keeps its bite.
I'll rig you what ain't wine and isn't red
with bitters in it." "No." Her tone was tight.

"I haven't time for shock; and bitters fed
to bitter dose is adding nothing needed.
A whore must do her moping for the dead
when sure she's safe from those who are alive."
He frowned. "The crime of Brothers can't be deeded
to you, because you had to shill to thrive,
and you're—" "They didn't dangle death in pants
from Yuba bridge," she cut him short. "A hive

of heated stranglers hasn't got a lance
to break for chivalry, if that's the chatter
you mean to soothe me with; I'd take a chance
on vipers first. They might not wish to hang,
or whip, or make a tar and feather batter
for fritter case, or kick about and bang;
but all those things have been the lot of whores
in this my native land, done by a gang

that loathe it when a fiction bully scores
an act of cruelty on strength that's puny.
Tell those who've never fought Ephesian wars
that manhood pampers women." "Guess I need
a drink myself." He took one. "Guess I'm moony
and don't know some about the human breed
I used to, ma'am. All right, we neither want
a Yuba tassel here; we're fast agreed.

Now what's your asking?" "Money for my jaunt
to otherwheres." She pointed at the table.
"I think I have as good a claim to vaunt,
or better than the fools that stocked the bank,
to what it holds. I've got to cut my cable
but also have to eat, and do not rank
as one that Heaven protects." He eyed the crust
of gold that rose above the copper tank

beside the scales which gauged the worth of dust,
and whistled. "That'd feed a whale battalion

and make 'em loosen belts for fear they'd bust;
but on my books you're goner's next of kin.
And on the self-same pages any stallion
that dumps his oats in any gambler's bin
is fined, it says, for angeling a crook.
Now how're you going to get to where the tin

will buy the elephants you aim to cook
and scare the doorstep wolf to death?" "The wagon
and team that I inherit. Help me hook
the second to the first; and with my clothes,
a pistol, water, food, a brandy flagon,
and this to carry me—" She held the pose
of lifting weightiness and viewed the bulk
of Vance's theft. "Imagination stows

restraints that make the soul an oafish hulk;
I want but couldn't touch that, out of feeling
that I'd be bound to him. Gold isn't sulk,
so I suppose that it will find a home."
"It might," he said. "And I don't find I'm stealing;
that heap of sweepings from a hippodrome
won't call for it. He seemed to want away
in spite of how you made him cook his comb."

He hid the poke. "But still it ought to pay
for Hennessy for you. And now, ma'am, amble.
I'll tote the dust and sock it in the shay
and harness up, if you will fetch your duds,
and borrow needings for your exit ramble
from stores whose keepers all have orphaned spuds
and bullet pipes. Unless my guess is bad,
the camp's the kind that poets chew their cuds

about; a town's desertion makes 'em sad
and full of rhymes, you know." "I'm off to pillage."
She darted in a shop and out. "The shad
have run the river, all except for you."

She waved the pistol she'd purloined. "The village
is empty now as any Goldsmith knew.
Why aren't you with the flies that scent a wound?"
"I'm lynching-sated; when you've watched a few,

you've seen 'em all; but don't you tell I crooned
that boredom dirge. In spite of it, moreover,
I've got to go to this one (since you spooned
the carats here), and make sure I'm beheld
by pigs—who might expect return to clover
through helping scrag the man to whom they'd shelled
their bullion, being twenty-one, and sound
of mind as they will likely be till felled

by Grim, the reaper. Soon as you are bound
for burgs I've never heard about, I'll borrow
a livery steed and whiz it over ground
to catch up with the tribe. You got some lead
to make that steel devise a cause of sorrow
to thugs and such?" "The calibre," she said,
"is that of Arb's, and there's a fair supply
of shot and powder in this cattle shed

that's labeled a hotel. It will be shy
of me and certain groceries in a jiffy;
could you—?" He nodded. He was waiting by
the chaise when she decamped from the New York.
"The team's in shape," he said; "the weather's spiffy;
you look O. K. yourself; you're in the pork;
and there's the road." He flicked his hat. "Good luck."
"Good bye, Ross Coon," she said. And then the cork

was drawn from her emotions, so the cluck
which moved the team was muffled by her sobbing.
"I—" What she might have said were words that stuck
in her convulsive throat. She used the whip
and sped from Angel's Camp. "By now they're mobbing
my living for a while. The bedroomship

was good as such things go, and we could laugh;
but now I'm heeled, I'll give the sticks the slip

and strut in such a style the golden calf
will bawl to pal with mine. 'Frisco's the city
for those who can afford to give the staff
of moneyed life its way. I'll own the town;
and this catharsis—one of transient pity
to two of vanished terror—will not drown
my eyes with future tears. But all the same,
if I had not his mistress's renown

and consequential dread, I'd stay and claim,
among the nonsense of his known possessions,
the locket which a woman of ill fame
was cautioned not to spring. I'd see the grace
which lured that Harlequin to make professions
he never did to me; and gain a case
of laughing fits, I'd hope. But he'll be gone;
and she. Her shadow won't again deface

my flesh, when they have stretched her straying faun."

8

A Bleak Reunion

He had a derringer he had not fired,
and tossed aside on finding that perdition
had swallowed him; but when he was enmired
in weariness that turned his legs to stone,
he dropped it, too. "I've even no ambition
to fight the flies with which I will be blown;
I'm finished, and it doesn't matter who
survives to boast he forced me to atone

for folly's deuce of clubs. I'm glad they flew
to sting me; if they only knew, they're saving
a shipless Flying Dutchman from the screw
of his suspended state of death in life.
I shivered, hearing Wagner's strains engraving
a sketch of perpetuity for wife;
they were not dour enough; he wasn't taught
the truth of what it means to toot the fife

and know there'll be no music ever—or ought
that's not an ass-praised rope of Ocnus labor;
poor Ancient Mariner!" The words were wrought
without the aid of lips, which couldn't form

a murmur then, as neither one could neighbor
the other, for they fluttered in the storm
his lungs had launched to ease his thudding heart.
Nor could the leader of the vengeful swarm

attest his triumph when he seized a part
of what the moment had renamed as treasure
for instant spending. Neither with the art
of man's definer, next they traded looks
of which the calmer showed Arbaces' measure
of fate accepted, noteless when the hooks
of other clutching talons closed on him.
The speechless captors stood about like spooks

detailed to haunt a house, in spirit grim
but all without the power to harm, till bellows
were drawing wind to spare again. The slim
Phidippides who'd tagged him pattered first.
"I nabbed the louse!" he crowed. "I caught him, fellows,
though he was antelope. I—" he rehearsed
his feat again to men who didn't heed,
because their ears and minds were mainly versed

in what they said themselves. "He blazed more speed
than what I thought a goat that trains by sitting
could spring at Epsom Downs." "Some hemp to feed
is what we got to have." "Where's Crandall at?
We've got to do this right, and can't be fitting
a noose and neck together till it's pat
that he's been sentenced." "Where in hell's a tree?
The Hindu rope trick never hung a rat;

we need a branch to swing Arbaces B.—
for bastard—Brothers." "Say, the flume is handy
and high enough to make a Christmas tree
to string this cranberry on." "That's thinking, friend!
Let's get this over quick. I left a dandy
deposit in his bank I think he'll lend,

and give me interest." "All you get's a third
of what he had before he fired, to end

a game I thought would cost me." Brothers heard
the comments—hot, detached, self-centered, cheerful—
and did not act as though he knew they chirred
or snarled about himself. He didn't balk
when rushed beneath a strut, so far from fearful,
it angered some, who ached for him to talk:
a plea for life which they could bellow down.
They wanted instant payment of his chalk

but had to wait while some one loped to town
to fetch the jute; they fretted in a fury
which grew, when Crandall's figurative gown
of magisterial dignity was donned,
and Brothers wouldn't notice judge or jury—
or any one until a broken bond
of amity was partially restored.
He straightened up as Dade appeared, and conned

his troubled face. "Now why among a horde
of Myrmidons before transfiguration
is lone-shoe Jason found? I wish the Lord
had sent a hungry aardvark in your stead;
but you're a salve for eyes whose occupation
will soon be recessed." "Close your clacker!" said
a man of two who held him. "You're in court."
"The kangaroos are breaking Priscian's head

and furnishing the shade of Coke with sport,"
Arbaces then remarked. "The prosecutor
and judge at least have noises they export
from vacuum empires. Though he's not at roost,
I more admire defending counsel's bruter
but painless gift of wordlessness; I used
to own more tolerance but had more time
to waste on fools." At that a captor loosed

a blow that rocked him. "Damn it, I've a rhyme
for that you'll get next time you hit him, mister!"
said Dade, and whirled on Crandall. "Granting crime,
and peers to pass on it have been convened,
there's got to be defense; and any blister
who holds to the contrary hasn't cleaned
the sties in Hell he should. If you're a judge,
conduct your—" "In a jiffy you'll be beaned,"

an interrupter warned. "Nobody'd budge
to help the murdering son of three cur bitches,
because we ain't his kind, and wouldn't fudge
excuses for a cutthroat. Lock your jaw
or beat it." "We're not burning Salem witches
but passing on a man—invoking law
to do it, too," said Terence, feeling glad
he'd kept his rifle. "Crandall, this is raw,

and you're alcalde." But he bent the brad
instead of piercing skin which had been hardened
by dipping in the Styx that flows from mad,
one-minded crowds. "I'm baillie of the camp
and warn you, birkie, that you won't be pardoned
a second cheep of court contempt." "My stamp
is not Calhoun's or Webster's," Dade returned,
"but if you'll grant permission, I will vamp

an obbligato of defense." He churned
a general wrath by that unhostile proffer
so torrid that the jury half adjourned
to join the rest who menaced Terence then.
For he had dared enact the arrant scoffer
at decencies as understood by men
who'd donned the cross to battle for the right—
so they appraised themselves—and brave the fen

to slay envenomed creatures of the night.
This concept as their basis of reaction,

they saw in opposition but the blight
of rank Satanity. They'd been denied
the armed crusader's fullest satisfaction
by Arb's passivity; they'd yearned to side
with martial holiness and prove their will
to conquer Lucifer, despite his pride,

with muscle crush and yells to cheer the kill;
and they'd been cheated by the lack of struggle
in Beelzebub. But now they sensed the thrill
that Richard knew, and Tancred: here were threats
to aid Azazel by a man who'd smuggle
the worst of Hell's brigade of evil gets,
they never doubted. Savoring their heat,
they built it up. "He wants to cancel debts

a murderer hasn't paid!" "He wants to bleat
excuses for the crime of wanton killing!"
"We ought to flog the would-be gallows cheat;
he's jawed the judge!" "A flogging ain't enough;
we'd ought to have a double necktie billing!
Let's get another rope." The first to snuff
the loosened lust for slaughter, Terence leapt
to find a flume-supporting pillar, bluff

enough for backing. He was thus adept,
and with his rifle rising to his shoulder,
before the others climbed their wrath and stepped
at last upon its ultimate of zones.
And he, too, raged, although his eyes were colder
than those that glared in nearing, while his tones
might roof an igloo. "One'll come along
to heel me, if the After This has bones

for mongrels to exhume, when taint is strong
and whets their taste for all that stinks. Who's Fido?"
They stopped to search each other, when the gong
of deadly danger boomed; they meant to rush

but, lacking the contempt for life of Dido
or Joan suttee has doomed, they hoped to flush
a Nathan Hale in some one else's glance.
Their hate, though, gathered voltage in the hush

which followed Dade's announcement that advance
would lose the charge its leader; heat was rising
and bringing on the boiling point, where chance
would call to some one—maddened by delay—
the gods were prone to speed the enterprising
and foil the pale-horse rider. Dade was fey;
he watched the mercury climb, and knew the herd
would surge the moment one among them's clay

was fired enough to take a step. The bird
of time, for him, he saw, had ceased to winnow;
and then a rider came. The horse he spurred
was not, however, spectral; it was black,
and frisky as a rain-roused pickerel minnow
for shaking stall confinement. From its back
the landlord of the Buckhorn grasped the scene
and shouted to distract the hovering pack:

"That ain't the Puritan on Fiddler's Green!
Besides, I can't hold Nugget here; he's ramping,
so move your heads and heels—or what's between
may learn a horse shoe isn't always luck."
They gave before the restless pony's stamping
and lost decision when they had to duck,
though lowering at a man who looked, bemused,
from Dade to them. "Unless I've gone amok,

this ain't the warrior that my eyes accused
of shooting—" Here he glanced at Dade a second
and changed the sentence that his thoughts had fused.
"He's not the pistoleer that sunk my trade;
he wasn't even there when Bedlam beckoned
and everybody answered. There's the blade

you left your drinks to blunt; and one's the count;
a solitaire's concerned with having played

the devil with my income. Damn it, Fount,
you're knocking off my freest, steadiest spender;
I've lost a second, which they'll have to mount
for every man's museum; now you want
to rob me of another elbow bender;
and that's a tinhorn deal." The gangling, gaunt
but square-faced man he'd picked as sagamore
among the lynchers glowered. "He can haunt

your doggery and pay a ghostly score,"
he growled. "The copperhead's for freeing Brothers,
and as they're in cahoots, we aim to bore
a graveyard hole for him." "They call it court,"
said Terence then. "They give the name that mothers
legality, and then they whelp the tort
of banning a defense. My felony
was offering to speak—" They roared him short.

"To save a murderer!" "He admits it; see?"
"J. Fountain Mitchell," Coon retorted slowly,
"I used to have a hound that had a flea
that killed another dead as Kelsey's stones;
and all the rest—all decent fleas, and holy—
were fast afoot to pulverize the bones
of him who'd slain the image and the spit
of Pulex—god of vengeance for the groans

that earthly antics cause the fleas that flit
with tablets, listing low, terrestrial morals.
They nabbed the malefactor in a bit
and found a Tyburn tree about in fruit,
and looped a noose. All right; nobody quarrels
with Lynch, if he's the judge. But these here cute
but ticklish varmints still weren't satisfied;
they didn't only want to rift a lute

but wanted to be virtuous when they tied
the knot with thirteen rungs around a throttle
they meant to close—if Flea Almighty tried
to intervene. They held a court, they claimed,
but couldn't stick the label to the bottle
because a thing ain't changed, if wrongly named;
a flea of Avon taught me that. A mob
is wild against defense; a court is tamed

and listens to it. It's a simple job
to sort the two; and killing Dade for trying
to popularize the meerschaum, not the cob,
could not convince a stranger that you're nice.
So lynch, or try—but let's abjure the lying;
Ross Coon has spoken. Wah!" The fractured ice
might yet have formed again, but he'd observed
what those afoot could not. He threw the dice

a second time. "A mob's not granite-nerved,"
he said to Dade, as though he marked the weather,
"but still there are precautions to be served
when bilking one. For Christ's sake! Dade, old sock,
get over fighting tigers with a feather;
the next time that you hold a slavering flock
of lions off, remember to insert
the cap that blows the powder loose, to knock

the bullet on its way." The malapert
descent of burlesque on the situation,
as in all cauterizing, burned and hurt
but quelled the poison. Soothing to the wound,
moreover, was the knowledge that deflation
from drama down to comedy had pruned
the plumes upon the bonnet Dade had worn.
The grins were sheepish first, but they ballooned.

"I didn't have virginity to mourn,
as I've been had before," a man admitted.

"He'd pulled the cap, in camp; and I'd've sworn
I saw a bullet with my name engraved."
"He stood like brave Horatius when he spitted
the big Etruscan boob, and Rome was saved,"
another pointed out, "but didn't know
he'd left his sword at home." The laughter caved

the rabies of the lynchers, to bestow
the minds of men again. And Dade was grinning,
though shakily, and not all sure the bow
of Heracles no longer threatened him;
he leaned upon his grounded weapon, winning
repose of faculties—upon the rim
of chaos from reaction—while the rest
returned to present business. With the vim

rechanneling hadn't lessened much, they pressed
a try to build in border land the fences
against the will indiscipline's addressed
Justinian reared upon the Golden Horn.
So Crandall, now anew with proper senses
of what a wig demands, when it is worn
to keep the Pandects honored, called to Dade.
His tone was no confession of the scorn

for corpus juris dignities he'd bayed,
nor did it beg excuse for threats he'd spouted
at one who'd volunteered as legal aid;
it more suggested Dade had slackly plied
a role the court had blessed: "It's time you clouted
a proper speech thegither, counsel; side
your client now and trim the caddie's suit
as best you can. And gin he can provide

a prief in mitigation, why we'll loot
the lad escape the woodie." Terence plodded
to where his former partner waited, mute
until the hands which fixed him loosed their gripe,

and bailiffs walked aside, as Terence nodded
to signify to ears the time was ripe
for them to leave the eaves. He'd left his gun,
and now he fiddled vaguely with the pipe

he hadn't tried to fill. "My Blackstone's one
with dining out with Barmecide; it's missing.
I'm sorry that the name's not Littleton—"
"Of course, it's not," said Brothers. "Nor St. Joan.
You're Kempion, who won a bride by kissing
a dragon thrice, or else the Blarney Stone.
You're Henry, patient of a woman's will—
the king who pumped a beauty from a crone;

I wish I'd learned the trick. You're Tuck or Tyl—
a man to talk to; I don't need attorneys.
Body of Caesar (credit Bobadill),
I'm done!" "Or not," said Dade, and used a hand
to argue with. "There may be legal byrnies
to shield you, Arb." "There aren't. For what I planned
was not what happened, which but makes it worse:
I downed a waif of John Doe's faceless band."

"But what derailed you?" "Theseus, I'll rehearse
the prelude, not to scramble from the corner
I plunged in, but to help you scan the verse
I'll say to you at last. It will not save
my clerkly neck, but I would die forlorner
if it were bottled still. To be the knave,
while knowledged as the king of hearts—to grasp
the blessing of the island Venus gave

but always find Doll Common in your clasp,
instead of lullabying Amoretta,
denotes a man and horse without a hasp
to unify the centaur." Terence stuck
the briar in his mouth. "I knew vendetta
had broken out and dumped you in the muck

somehow." He slid the words along the stem
his teeth had nicked. "You had the stuff to pluck

a jewel from the northern diadem,
it always seemed to me." "I had profusion
and not enough. I *yearned* to have a gem
the sky had set; I yearned for everything
and, not Fitz Philip, had his great illusion.
But yet not quite, because Aladdin's ring,
confounding evil, never was among
the gifts I asked St. Nicholas to bring;

I overlooked it, Faust." "I'll start the bung
of delicacy," said Terence, "thereby letting
the swipes of curiosity flow. What flung
your ardors in the Limbo of the Moon,
where headlessness is regnant in a setting
that ghosts would shrink from?" "That is coming soon."
Arbaces found a last cigar to smoke.
"To have a lute and can't be taught a tune,"

he said, when it was lit. "I've cracked that joke
but not its mate. To be a wild-horse rider—
which all are here, for there would be no folk
in Eldorado else—and have no road
to run the mustang on, and be the guider
of mettle to some Glatisant's abode,
is having a petard without a fort
to use it on. Petards must yet explode,

because they're that; and finally the sport
of detonation is the great consoler
for hunts unundertaken." With a snort
that shrugged his sholders, Brothers shook his head.
"The pathless rider thinks he is controller
of powder with no talisman of lead
to bring the red swan down. It's all the pride
that's left to him; but reins become a shred,

and then they snap." He tossed his smoke aside.
"My own did that today. I lost all rudder
and shot with Hoder's shaft." "The rope's here!" cried
a youthful quidnunc. "Quiet, staumrel wean!
A cauf whose gab should still be at the udder,"
admonished Crandall, "shouldn't cause us teen
by using it to clatter in my court.
There'll mayhap be no need of ropes this e'en

except to bang a bellowing stirk that's short
of reverence for his boortrees. Counsel's reding
the prisoner, and blellums won't abort
his efforts any mair!" "A grieved mistake
perhaps will prove a solid ground for pleading;
I'll try," said Dade. "It will not help, Du Lake.
As Talleyrand (when d'Enghien was slain
by Elba's guest, without a franc at stake),

remarked, to give the act its due disdain:
'It overpassed a crime—it was a blunder.' "
Arbaces stiffened lips against a pain.
"You'll lie tonight to one you'll know unnamed;
you'll scribble fiction I won't pause to wonder
the nature of; and I'll remain acclaimed
a martyr to a faith I mightn't spurn
and couldn't keep. My memory will be framed

in hers, the stalwart on the Grecian urn;
and that's her meed: Diana can't be sullied
by knowing that Silenus was the turn
of one she's ray-wrapped, Ossian. Thanks to chance,
you've joined the Arimaspians who've gullied
the hides of Dead Horse Hill; so I can prance
on air without the fear she'll have no news,
so might investigate and learn the trance

which had befooled her." "I'll perform the ruse
you wish, of course," said Dade, "if necessary;

you're not at Ravenstone as yet." "The clews
of honest evidence will guide me there.
Like Takeley Street," said Brothers, "or a cherry
that's half consumed, it hasn't got a pair
of sides, Orestes." Reaching briskly out,
he seized his once friend's arm. "Yet I will wear

the scarf of Pantagruelion weave, and flout
the law of gravity so much the gladder
because I have this chance to quash a doubt,
Leontes. No, I'll batter down the fence
I raised myself—and left myself the sadder
for handicraft contrived by impotence.
Hell, Terry Dade, I threw the partnership
because I couldn't dodge my rut of bents

when we gave death at Whiskey Slide the slip;
but I was wounded. California's calling
had been my chance to break Alcina's grip;
and for a while I aped the Argonaut
and didn't know myself that my enthralling
was signed and sealed in blood. For months I thought
to take a crown from Cibola home; but forced
to halt my drive, I once again was caught

by my reality and swiftly coursed
to where I'd been. Tolosa's gold was stolen,
and when you taxed me for it, though remorsed,
I'd not admit to you I'd shown my mold
the King of Yvetot's: a trifle, swollen
about a nothingness. But what I sold
was what I craved. That's all. And now it's said,
have on and be my Suckfist." "Now you've told

what brings the swallows back, I hope my head
can muster anagrams to lure the jury
to whiteball you," said Dade. "We'll drink—" "The dead
prefer a wake to personal carouse;

attend to it," said Brothers, "when the Fury—
Tisiphone's the jade, I think, that ploughs
the backs of spirits scourged to Muspelheim—
performs her office. Voice what legal vows

you will, but watch how handlessly I'll climb."

9

A Talk with Caput Mortuum

A man of those who'd heard the hullabaloo
which left the town instanter desolated
(except for Coon, Sabrina and a few
malaise had lagged, or else were early drunk),
was moved to laughter by the mob elated
with mortuary hopes. From on the bunk
where'd he'd been sanding down a timber peg,
replacing one that splintered into junk

when it had been the sword of Scanderbeg
which cleared a joint of some he'd found annoying,
the single-footed grinner made a leg—
this time by bowing briefly in salute
to those who pounded by his window, joying
to howl their fury. "Most'll follow suit;
they got to flock the same as whooping cranes.
They all got tomahawks for a galoot

because the war cry's yelled, and, like the Janes,
they got to trail with fashion." Quickly strapping,
in place below the stump, the shank his brains
no longer centered on, he reached the door,

to chuckle north and south. "The crows're flapping
to peck the sick one, sure enough." He tore
Virginia with his teeth and mouthed the quid.
"Imagine quitting whiskey just to gore

a crippled bull; but what I wouldn't bid
to do, I'm glad they done. I'm dry, and busted
as last night's leg; and here they've took the lid
from off saloons. It ain't no fault of mine
if no one's home to see the bar is dusted."
He watched and chewed for minutes. "Mighty fine!"
said Peg-leg Smith at last. He stepped and tapped
to where "The Gold Oasis" was a sign

he found inviting. But the liquor lapped
in neither of the barrels which he sampled—
though flavored with the sugar run he sapped,
tobacco in his jaws the while—could meet
Sir Hubert's standards. When he'd spat, and trampled
a mouthful of the second to delete,
symbolically, its taste, he swung away.
"The chinch who sells that rotgut is the cheat

they'd mobrify, if I could have the say.
I've guzzled liquor that you had to hurry
and down before it ate the cup, but— Hey,
there's Coon, and mousing for the gambler's frill.
It's graveside spooning, wah, but ain't my worry;
I'll see if whozis taps a better still
than whatzisname." The second barrel house,
though closer to Petronius's will,

yet left a hole for elegance to grouse
at quality below the salt. "It's better
than what Jim Kirker scalped alive a louse
for selling us at Taos once, but hell,
I got to have the best today." A setter
that sought a peacock, he made exit. "Well,

Ross Coon is quick, or else I done him wrong,"
he said, observing matters to dispell

or water his suspicions. "Go it strong!"
he said beneath his breath, as Ross was nearing.
"You won't be missed. Good whiskey was my song,
and now you're off to join the sparrow hawks,
I know where I can get it." Blithely steering
for Coon's dispensary, he eyed the chalks
which pointed up a box's gloomy cast
and rapped it with his wooden leg. "The gawks

who'd leave a dive to watch a spook go past
a circle in a rope can't be expected
to know what's decent," he explained at last
to unreproachful Jones. But next he clucked
reproach himself, as roving eyes connected
with blood that led them to a well-spring sucked
by rimming flies. "A drunk! I'll fine the coon,
I hope; the chances is he ain't been plucked.

The dead don't shine for any lynch baboon;
they want 'em warm, so they can start the cooling."
He bent. "By God, I belched a silver spoon!"—
But while he celebrated opulence,
the sober court of Lynch's overruling
received and weighed the argument defense
adduced and lost. As Brothers broke the grip
which had no words for footnote, Ross's sense

of what was needed led him now to slip
to earth and intervene as Dade, unseeing,
was slouching by. "Get on," he said, "and nip
for camp; the Buckhorn's staking you to rye.
I'll bring your gun." A moment later fleeing
the sight and sound of struggles hoisted high
and left to give the coming moon a man
who had no fear of falling, Dade was nigh

the town before his clearing mind began
recalling that he had agreed to rally
with Gordon where, by Coon's galenic plan,
he'd doctor addled nerves. "The Blue Hen's cock
is sound," he thought. "Of course, he didn't sally
to join the howler monkeys. What a rock
to plant my elbow by upon the bar!"
And then remembrance lashed him with a shock

instead of proffering balm; he viewed the scar
which wanly blemished relaxation's entry.
"There'll be a door in earth to thrust ajar
for Jones," he sighed, while at the hitching post
where Nugget joined the horizontal sentry.
"I'd like to drink a Lethe highball toast
to that, for one's—" Across the sill he stopped
and followed blood upstream to meet a ghost

which braved the waning day. The fist he chopped
the air with bruised a thigh. "The silent liars!
They could have told me that the cause I propped
was— No, they couldn't." He relaxed his hand.
"No more a mob, but jurisprudence pliers,
they saw defense's bastions must be manned,
and I had volunteered." His shoulders stooped,
and voicing what he didn't understand

that other ears could catch, he trudged, and drooped
above his fallen partner. "Maybe many
were truly unaware that we had trouped
in harness. You were rarely at the drink;
though tapsters knew me as the doubtful penny
whose homing they could count upon, the ink
of loving missives was the fluid which
you rather favored. Coon was sure, I think,

that you and I had earned the Dunmow flitch,
but he's the Odin's eye of Bonifaces."

"He went out drunker than a fiddler's bitch,"
said Smith, from where he leaned beside the flask
he'd commandeered. "If he had temperance paces
by usual, he didn't muff the task
of changing clothes the last chance at the booze;
I'd say he'd wrapped himself around a cask

before the bullet found him." Seeking clues
to what had happened, Terence lifted features
which hid annoyance, planted by the news
so jocularly given. "Were you here?"
"Not me," said Peg-leg, "but I know the creature's
whiff and sign, alive or dead; and beer
nor watered milk is neither the perfume
that you can nose yourself by squatting near.

I done it—er—to take the pulse the tomb
had took already. Gone as beaver trapping,
he told me how he'd won an eagle plume
for downing forty rod with just one throat.
He might have knowed that skull and bones was tapping
his shoulder, Dade, and hurried here to float
a final jamboree—and wasn't palmed
no trading musket. Man, he rode the goat

and, foxy, kicked the bucket, self-embalmed.
You need a peg yourself." He graced a tumbler
and stumped to proffer what, partaken, calmed
and organized a deeply brooding mind.
"A seldom drinker is an easy stumbler,"
he mused, as links of reason were aligned.
"I think he saw the man he owed a fist:
he must have done it; something speed inclined

the pock-faced ferret. Say that he was grist
for Arb's magician-powered mill. If guessing,
an even bet; Macheaths cannot resist
the chance to toss away the loot they put

their necks in chancery for. Suppose him pressing
his kale on Arb; and Pard, unsure of foot,
was making toward the table where they gamed
and threatening the chunk of Sydney soot,

though Arb, his conscience naturally maimed,
mistook the cause and target of the curses.
But why was Gordon soused?" Aloud, he aimed
pursuant words at Smith, a poet who
was pouring forth the mellow, liquid verses
a second quart of inspiration blew
from who cared where to him. "I knew them all,"
said Dade, as though the other also knew

the matters he found enigmatical.
Impelled to speak, and glad of any hearer
who might construe the rebus which the fall
of three by separate ways devised for him,
he drank again and slowly drifted nearer.
"I knew them all, and knew what was the swim
of each's thoughts, and where they traveled from,
and what they hoped to find in pristine trim

upon return. But neither was the chum
or even raw acquaintance of the others,
who now are linked by me." "That's kind of rum,"
said Peg-leg. "Who'd the coffin catch?" "It's Jones,
the buckskin longhair." "I knowed him and Brothers—
who's swinging now, I'd say—but Mister Bones
upon the floor I'd never met till now.
Why'd Brothers take," Smith asked, "to heaving stones

at strangers? Hell, the man who has to plough
a stranger under sure is short of feuding."
"His feud was with himself," said Terence, now
regarding Galloway anew. "The one
you asked about was rarely found including
the creature, as you call the bottled sun—

which lights and warms but likewise sometimes burns.
Though why it did today's a mental dun

I can't evade or meet. The mystic querns
the gods employ were this time fast in grinding.
I left the fellow dizzy at the turns
of happy luck for him and one allied;
a scant two hours later, next, the binding
of soul and—" Terence paused. "I know," he sighed,
"reaction hammock lashed. He had despaired
of ever doing more than buck the tide;

and then he made a strike." "He did?" Smith pared
a thumb nail with a Bowie. "That was lucky
and maybe worth a drunk." "He never cared
about the gold except for what it pledged,"
said Dade. He sipped the amber from Kentucky,
the native choice of Smith. "He would have kedged
the breadth of seven seas to reach his home
and have the few and decent things which hedged

the cosmos of desire for him. To roam
was never what he wished; he loved his county;
you'd think the place was Kubla's pleasure dome
to hear him talk of it. There was a girl
he longed to make a woman, with the bounty
of children in the offing. And the pearl
of jobs for him was one of service, Smith:
his urge was helping children's minds unfurl.

The glory of the Eldorado myth
meant only these to him. The tails of greedy,
he never would have come to mingle with
the seekers of the Diggings, if he could
have met his needs without it." Peg-leg's beady,
outdoorsman's eyes were gleaming in their hood
of bristling, greying eyebrows as he spat.
"He wanted out of here? Why, that's no good;

they shot him just in time." The dictum sat
uneasily with Dade, who yet was looking
for needles Hodge's mutilated prat
could never find. The sun set in his glass.
"We all arrived with but the thought of booking
rebound as promptly as we could amass
the fortune no one doubted he could snatch,
and be at once a sorcerer of the class

that own the wishing rods which let one match
attainment with desire. So what we wanted
the gold for was to conjure with, unlatch
the gates of Thebes and come into our own—
or somebody's. Our dreaming wasn't haunted
by non-essential quillets; any throne
would suit us. But its splendor wasn't here;
it beckoned from at home; the monotone

that Echo moaned was, 'When will fortune veer
and free us from a land of bootless striving?' "
"You want the venison but cuss the deer
because he makes you hunt him." Chuckles came
from Peg-leg's matted beard. "I know what's driving
the moose that hears the bugle just the same
as though I heard it still. I wasn't weaned
no more than any California's claimed

at reveille." The bottle then careened,
and whiskey found the plimsol line of glasses.
"So when I could I got my feathers preened
and skittered back to where I'd cracked the shell.
In memory all waffles and molasses,
the spot was mush, and cold. The girls I'd fell
in love with, which was most that was around
had married clodhops who had farmed a spell

instead of trapping for the pelts I found
across the Mississippi, Dade; for beaver

was all the gold we knowed of." Terence frowned
as though the bourbon, which was prime, was raw.
"I guess the man who's not a swift retriever
of treasure might not get the mother in law
he'd indirectly counted on. You know,
we'd hardly thought of that, though it's a flaw

in scheming I can glimpse. A half our woe
was suffered for suspended animation
inflicted on the women that we owe—
or thought we did—reclaim; it didn't pierce
our consciousness that their enamoration
could switch to those who had not thrust in tierce
to stagger Ladon." "Who the hell is he?"
Smith asked. "The monster, bruited as fierce,

who guards the golden McIntoshes we
had thought to pick like pippins—fill a barrel
and winnow back with, crow-line, like a bee,"
said Dade, who then resumed his pensive trend.
"Immutability was the apparel
we had to give the past, I think, to lend
some reason to the present; what we'd left
was what must wait unwavering at the end

of our anabasis." His fingers deft,
he filled the pipe he didn't see. "The changing
of Enid's heart is luckily a theft
of thought that Galloway did not endure."
He nodded at the face that flies were ranging
in confidence they had a sinecure.
"I don't know what's at home." "You're out of one
except for where you are," said Peg-leg. "Sure,

you don't know what's to east of you; and, son,
it wouldn't matter if it had been frozen
so every bit of frosting on the bun
was just as when you hit the trail—you ain't.

You've trapped the Yellowstone, or maybe chosen
a squaw you traded for the mustang paint
you rode to rendez-vous at Jackson's Hole.
You've turned a wicked Injun to a saint

without a scalp to itch. You've maybe stole
a thousand horses at a clip and herded
the lot behind the water that'd roll
for miles to pace you, fake but awful real.
I don't know what you've done." "You haven't worded
a likeness of my life, but yet I feel
the import of your picture," Dade replied.
"I've been to Colchis and must bear its seal."

He smoked upon the parallels which tied
his own career to Smith's. "And what's your calling
since you've retired from trapping; have you plied
the shovel and the cradle?" Peg-leg waved
and hit the bottle, saving it from falling,
however, with the quickness which had saved
his own and often hunted scalp. "I got
a better game than any Joe that's slaved

to find a chunk of metal you can tot
the value of. A mine that you've invented
can top all Montezuma's, and the lot
Pizarro borrowed from the Incas, Dade.
I got me one I've never quite consented
to map, you see." He stamped his peg and brayed
his joy at the deception. "But the drinks
they buy to get me jabbering-drunk have made

the mine a steady— Wup! I hear the finks
returning from the strangulation party."
He prodded Dade. "Drink up, before the ginks
who'd ask for pay're back behind the rail,
and let me fill your horn." "I'm not that hearty;
the Laurie whistle's yours. I'm turning tail

as soon as I have done the act of grace
I hate to. Farewell, Galloway, and hale!"

said Terence, when he'd covered up the face
he wouldn't see again. "Their fellow miners
will furnish him and Jones the resting place
of turned down glasses. No one but myself
would care, I doubt, to rob the flying diners
of one who shuffled cards to get the pelf
that did not buy him Tara." "Going back
to whistle Brothers from the airy shelf

they put him on? The buck has lost the knack
of caring where he's at," said Peg-leg, spitting.
"But dawn will bring the ravens or a pack
of buzzards," Terence said; "and though a husk,
he can't be thimble-pitted by the flitting
obscenity preferrers." In the dusk
that now was deep, he swung aboard the horse.
"So long," he called, "I'm grateful for the musk—

and wisdom for a chaser." Then his course
was counter to the crowd of thirsters striding
to reach the grog deserted to enforce
the law that hobbles Cain. Nobody asked
his errand, and, unhurried in his riding,
he called to none among the semi-masked
patrollers of the twilight. "I must write
a second letter to a woman asked

to wait, but will not know if it will blight
a hope—which may be blunted by the spacing
between departure and this separate night—
or cause a shrug of pity and relief.
For Jones there'll be no note; his peri chasing
was wholly in, I think the misty fief
of Cambinskan. He likely never knew
his Canacee's cognomen; but the grief

I may or may not cause the other two
is something I must cause or not on paper.
And there's another thing that I must do:
a tierce of missives, and the third the worst.
For death can be a handiness, escaper
of consequences as it is, and versed
in all the arts of getting credit for
the might have been. If Gordon perished, nursed

until the final instant by a corps
of tender hopes that never will be tested
in action's crucible, I'll have to score
an aria so different from the first
I hummed Penelope, before I wested,
the ring may snap which was to be the rune
reducing two to one." He found a shape,
impervious to temblor and typhoon,

which wore the evening star upon the nape
from which a rope ascended; and he halted.
"I'm for the Indies, rounding any cape,
and steering with your eyes, and his, and his—
which couldn't see the cosmos which has malted
my barley. But the change has happened, viz.,
I'm taken by the zone I came to loot.
I can't renege to London or Cadiz

and act as though I didn't cut my root,
when first I cradled gleams on Feather River,
a tiny strike but seeking's darling fruit;
I thought I'd shipped the zodiac, you know;
or knew, for you were there." He quelled the shiver
his words evoked and watched the body show
the wind's direction, as it slowly swung
and lost the star. "I'll bed you, Prospero,

in what is now my land." Aground, he strung
the reins about a shrub. "And then I'm sending

in what she may decide a foreign tongue
the message which will draw her or affright,
to broach a fresh betrothal or an ending—
if she is not already the delight
of some Melampos, now translating worm
endearments for her." Loosening the bight

about the anchoring pillar, he was firm
but gentle with the mannikin he handled,
although its antic twistings made him squirm,
yet not as much as when corporeal ice
descended and demanded to be dandled.
Though more than careful in his sawing, twice
his barlow nicked the winceless marionette
of which he held the string until a slice

relaxed the noose. "The letter she will get,"
said Terence, as the locket which, in strangling,
its owner had displayed, was quickly set
in place, "will pledge the switch of to and from
that brought me here—when I have finished wrangling
the treasure which unwed widowdom
will share with me to honor Gordon's bents.
But neither could the Nibelungen sum

of all the wampum Worth Street represents,
nor even can the woman made of flowers,
though every line of hers is eloquence
of searching forcefulness, persuade my stay."
Inanimate rebellion fought his powers,
but Dade at length contrived to win his way.
"Here in the land where flowers will spring from you
that failed while you lived, my hand of clay

and heart of golden hopes," he breathed, and threw
the hitch that held aloft the Cossack rider
disdainful of the reins, "is where we two,
if she'll be one, will face the wind and take—

if vinegar, when it supplants the cider,
or sourdough with ale in place of cake—
Hesperian sends." The homeless moon for lamp,
he led the silence thunder couldn't break

in weary plodding back to Angel's Camp.

EPILOGUE:
THE AMERICAN GAMUT

The American Gamut

In flesh apostate to the shaping bone;
a singleton with mercury for core:
America connotes a maverick zone
whose focal star had not been glimpsed before
it gleamed above this wayside point of halting
along a line of march whose reckoned lore
no Mandeville could hope to reimburse
with lies to match the stumbling and the vaulting

of Man—the variant of the universe:
its villain, zany and protagonist,
its engineer, its termite, triumph, curse,
its mystic and its cold anatomist,
its loving scholiast and false expounder,
its feckless ape and frenzied moralist,
its candle moth and gloom-enchanted owl,
its canny limner and its mad confounder

of forms, its paladin and pimp on prowl,
its mocker and its body-snatching mope,
its molder of fake bones for which to growl,
its never yielding duelist with hope,

its architect of laughter, arch explorer
of rainbow shreds and desperate misanthrope.
This legislator, ever in revolt
against restraining laws, has turned a soarer

in regions proper to the lightning bolt
and, pressing on, has ventured in the void
where asteroids, the scales that comets molt
and airless typhoons, monstrously deployed,
were long without companions.
                                        More extension,
as always, looms because the known has cloyed,
because the will to see what can be done
is stronger than the negative propension

to rest secure; and, too, because to run
each river to its source is balm for minds
which glean no easement else beneath the sun.
And some, disdaining doubts of what the finds
on solar near or star-patrolling planets
may bring to them, will toss aside like rinds
the ties they had on earth, to strike away
with all the confidence of migrant gannets

that profit lies in change. Yet they'll not say
they were the first who ever blindly stormed
the barricades of space, to take as pay
for an abandoned world another formed
of elements as hidden from their guessing
as any fused in spheres that may be warmed
by Betelgeuse or Vega.
                                  The renown
of dour Columbus, never once professing

the summit emerald flashing in his crown,
was bait for others, dazzled by his gift
of globe enlargements. Those who did not drown
or perish, parched, when windlessly adrift

on seas where rotting, jetsam horses floated,
or melt apart with scurvy, yet were swift
to close with fates which thrust them underground
in coasts they never knew could not be coated

with plating which would liken what they found
to what they'd left. But still the lemmings came:
a half as questers, half because the hound
of want or incubus of legal blame
were prompting forces.
                    Late among the parters
from realms where they had seldom such a name
that many mourned their going were the first
to risk America—and end as martyrs,

marooned in Europe mentally, immersed
in sinking sands of ignorance about
a warlock of a land which only nursed
the few it warped until they were devout
to ways they had not known where thinner covers
of smaller trees were bathed in air less stout
to foster driving foot and brain unrest.
In time from these and fellow bear-meat lovers

to north and south of those so put to test
thus cruelly at first emerged a breed
secessionist from shores on which there pressed
the water links between the plant and seed,
with pendulum insistence that in motion
from side to side there was no change to read
but that of passing time.
                    They broke the hold
of tentacles and tidal arms of ocean

which grappled what was new to what was old
and were as no men were before, for good
and evil both. Their fool's and valid gold
had valences not elsewhere understood;

they felled the great Yggdrasil of tradition
and grafted on its stump a different wood
for planks political, for legal arks
and social totem poles. They wrought a fission

between a man and all his earlier marks
of earth possession. Land was not to keep
but space to roam, as night for astral sparks,
and wilfully as dream's nomads of sleep.
They surged like salmon up the racing rivers
which silver-veined the nightshade forest, deep
as Alexander's empire. In this realm
of Gothic dusk and seldom sunlight slivers

they fought such fire-fly wars to overwhelm
the native sons of shadow as romance,
without the hand of history at the helm,
would never dare propound.
                              In this expanse
of primal paradise regained they flitted,
as fox-foot and acute of ear and glance
as lurking food and clothing sources, sly
as ghosts by day. But Archimedes-witted

as well as fauna-feral, they could fly
on those and all the levels in between,
so nothing needed was in short supply
to stud with farming steads the forest screen
about the nonesuch towns the rivers nourished
and maimed alike. Aspiring and unclean,
these were a meeting ground for hell and hope
where pestilence and April vigor flourished

and evil, coprological in scope,
was virtue's alter ego, as they built
in tanglewoods the steps by which to grope
away from buckskin savagery.
                              To jilt

the wilds of which they long had been the clients
for walls in which they felt their manhood spilt
was not, however, thinkable for some.
The chronic borderers could put reliance

in nothing but the lure of space to come;
for what they had not seen was what they prized,
and what they knew they left for those to plumb
whose minds and spirits were not hypnotized
by hugeness. They, the antitrades of shelter,
eschewed what beaver instincts energized
and pushed into a new untrammeled land
whose water-shorted rivers drained a welter

of cantons, open as a beggar's hand,
with woods but where the mountains reached for rains
which passed the snake dance deserts.
                                        As they fanned
along the trails they made the region's mains,
they marked its map with names which logged their
    courses:
the furs they took in peril of the pains
of death by ritual torture at the will
of feather-flaunting tribesmen, with whose forces

they traded scalps in headlong horseback kill
and badlands ambuscade; the buried gold
they squandered quick as filched, to taste the thrill
of prodigality; the manifold
and mighty hunts which swept away the bison
and cleared the range for blood-eyed cattle, bold
to use their outsize horns; the towns they reared
to roister in on every next horizon—

and left like empty flasks because they feared
the lock and key of order and routine.
Yet, eaten cake, the frontier disappeared
from wilderness and shifted to the scene

of drifting wharf-side cities on the seaboard
of pristine landing.
                    Misconstructed, mean
and bottom-fouled, these dingy merchant tramps
were hulls with little in the way of freeboard

or pumps for bilges, binnacles or lamps.
The cornered spaciousness no longer spent
on wilted wilds and ex-volcanic camps
was flumed, like steam which blows itself a vent
on this new sphere of frontier exploitation:
Metropolis. A stunted element
to which were added water, depth and light,
it flowered as a multiplex creation

in turn evoking master craftsman sleight
at hatching thought as action to fulfill
its logics. Far apart as sun and night
from prior ones, these prompted to distill,
from sheer mechanics, verities of being
in which the role of naturalness was nil,
and ground itself was out of bounds in parks,
museum pieces seldom for the seeing

of sons of pioneers who'd found their marks
in touchless things.
                    They waged a war on time
and tore at it like gore-attracted sharks,
to make begun and done an instant rhyme;
and distance was a saboteur they hated
out of all ho, as guilty of the crime
of sanding gears, where oiled efficiency
was all their love, so distance was abated

of most its dragging force by artistry
implacable of goal. Yet most they fought,
in endless, bitter strivings to be free,
the snare of drudgery, where man was caught

when first he found within his mind the power
to leave the beasts behind; for what was wrought
to win dominion frittered to a trap
in nature like the siren jungle flower

whose lovely, richly scented petals snap
on fondlers of its charms.
                                    This was the foe
whose might Europa's stepsons could not knap
though ceasely attempting overthrow,
as every tool they forged to flail at drudging
became a changeling chain of toil, to slow
the beaten, striking hand. But in their heat
to blast what sometimes inched away, for budging

with shoulder strength, they found such ways to cheat
inertia of its empery they smashed
normalities of force and freed their feet
to tread in new dimensions. Unabashed
by precedent and proverb, they were agile
in one-eyed Moby Dicks, the first that clashed
with sunken, sunless maelstroms; they were deft
to outmaneuver gravity in fragile

velocipedes with ailerons; and cleft
the atom so exquisitely they broke
the seal which held its power in check, and left
the cosmic gateways open.
                                    From the cloak
in which the speechless future is enshrouded
there's nothing to be learned about the folk
who here have stretched and widened out the road
which man has furthered since beginnings clouded

in umbrage where the only light that glowed
was his refusal to be reconciled
to any lot he had. But whence there flowed
the amperage of which the crackling child

became America, and what engendered
in isolation volts to rack a wild
but Stone-Age stifled land until the world
was shaken, too, are patent matters, tendered

in trust for eras yet to be unfurled
in still uncharted airts.
                The nation's tale
which dwarfs its wars is of a people hurled
by energies that would not grant them bail
across a waste, its marvel-haunted takers
when once they'd wrenched apart the barless jail
of canned conceptions. When this bastille burst,
the New World was in being. For its makers,

with modern man's endowments half dispersed
in leatherstocking exile, learned to draft
and fashion what they needed unrehearsed
by voices of the frozen rules of craft.
They hammered what would cut the mustard better,
if that entailed the switch of fore and aft,
and next in raw barbarity refined
a separation, loosing law from letter,

to make an open country of the mind—
which owed a debt to scamps and scalawags,
the founders of a sceptic school, inclined
to doubt the contents of all bricks and bags
before assessment. Through their raffish laughter,
as much as through their struggles with the hags
of want and peril, they of that frontier
evolved the gifts Americans hereafter

may take to some like plastic hemisphere.